# AAT

# WORKBOOK

Intermediate Units 7 & 8

# Reports and Returns

**August 1997 edition**

The fifth edition of this Workbook contains the following features.

- Details of the format of the Central Assessment
- Graded practice exercises
- Trial Run Devolved Assessments to attempt under timed conditions
- All AAT Central Assessments set so far up to and including June 1997
- Five trial Run Central Assessents to attempt under timed conditions

**FOR JUNE 1998 AND DECEMBER 1998 ASSESSMENTS**

BPP Publishing
*August 1997*

*First edition 1993*
*Fifth edition August 1997*

*ISBN 0 7517 6088 9 (previous edition 0 7517 6924 X)*

***British Library Cataloguing-in-Publication Data***

*A catalogue record for this book*
*is available from the British Library*

*Published by*

*BPP Publishing Limited*
*Aldine House, Aldine Place*
*London W12 8AW*

Printed by Ashford Colour Press, Gosport, Hants



*We are grateful to the Lead Body for Accounting for permission to reproduce extracts from the Standards of Competence for Accounting and to the Association of Accounting Technicians for permission to reproduce Central Assessment tasks. The suggested solutions have been prepared by BPP Publishing Limited.*

## HOW TO USE THIS WORKBOOK

This Workbook covers Unit 7: *Preparing reports and returns* and Unit 8: *Preparing VAT returns*. It is designed to be used alongside BPP's Units 7 & 8 *Reports and Returns* Tutorial Text. The Workbook provides Practice Exercises on the material covered in the Tutorial Text, together with Devolved Assessments and Central Assessments.

As you complete each chapter of the Tutorial Text, work through the *Practice Exercises* in the corresponding section of this Workbook. Once you have completed all of the Sessions of Practice Exercises, you will be in a position to attempt the Devolved and Central Assessments.

The tasks involved in a *Devolved Assessment* will vary in length and complexity, and there may be more than one 'scenario'. If you complete all of the Devolved Assessments in this Workbook, you will have gained practice in all parts of the elements of competence included in Units 7 and 8. You can then test your competence by attempting the Trial Run Devolved Assessment, which is modelled on the type of assessment actually set by the AAT.

Of course you will also want to practise the kinds of task which are set in the *Central Assessments* for Unit 7. The main Central Assessment section of this Workbook includes all the AAT Central Assessments set from December 1993 to December 1994, and by doing them you will get a good idea of what you will face in the assessment hall. When you feel you have mastered all relevant skills, you can attempt the five Trial Run Central Assessments. These consist of the June 1995, December 1995, June 1996, December 1996 and June 1997 Central Assessments. Provided you are competent, they should contain no unpleasant surprises, and you should feel confident of performing well in your actual Central Assessment.

### Class Exercises and Class Assessments

Each session of this Workbook includes a number of exercises without solutions to be attempted in the classroom. There is also a Class Devolved Assessment and a Central Assessment without solutions. The answers to these and to the Class Exercises will be found in the BPP Lecturers' Pack for this Unit.

### A note on pronouns

For reasons of style, it is sometimes necessary in our study material to use 'he' instead of 'he or she', 'him' instead of 'him or her' and so on. However, no prejudice or stereotyping according to sex is intended or assumed.

## STANDARDS OF COMPETENCE

The competence-based Education and Training Scheme of the Association of Accounting Technicians (AAT) is based on an analysis of the work of accounting staff in a wide range of industries and types of organisation. The Standards of Competence for Accounting which students are expected to meet are based on this analysis.

The Standards identify the *key purpose* of the accounting occupation, which is to operate, maintain and improve systems to record, plan, monitor and report on the financial activities of an organisation, and a number of *key roles* of the occupation. Each key role is subdivided into *units of competence*. By successfully completing assessments in specified units of competence, students can gain qualifications at NVQ/SVQ levels 2, 3 and 4, which correspond to the AAT Foundation, Intermediate and Technician stages of competence respectively.

### Foundation stage key roles and units of competence

The key roles and unit titles for the AAT Foundation stage (NVQ/SVQ level 2) are set out below.

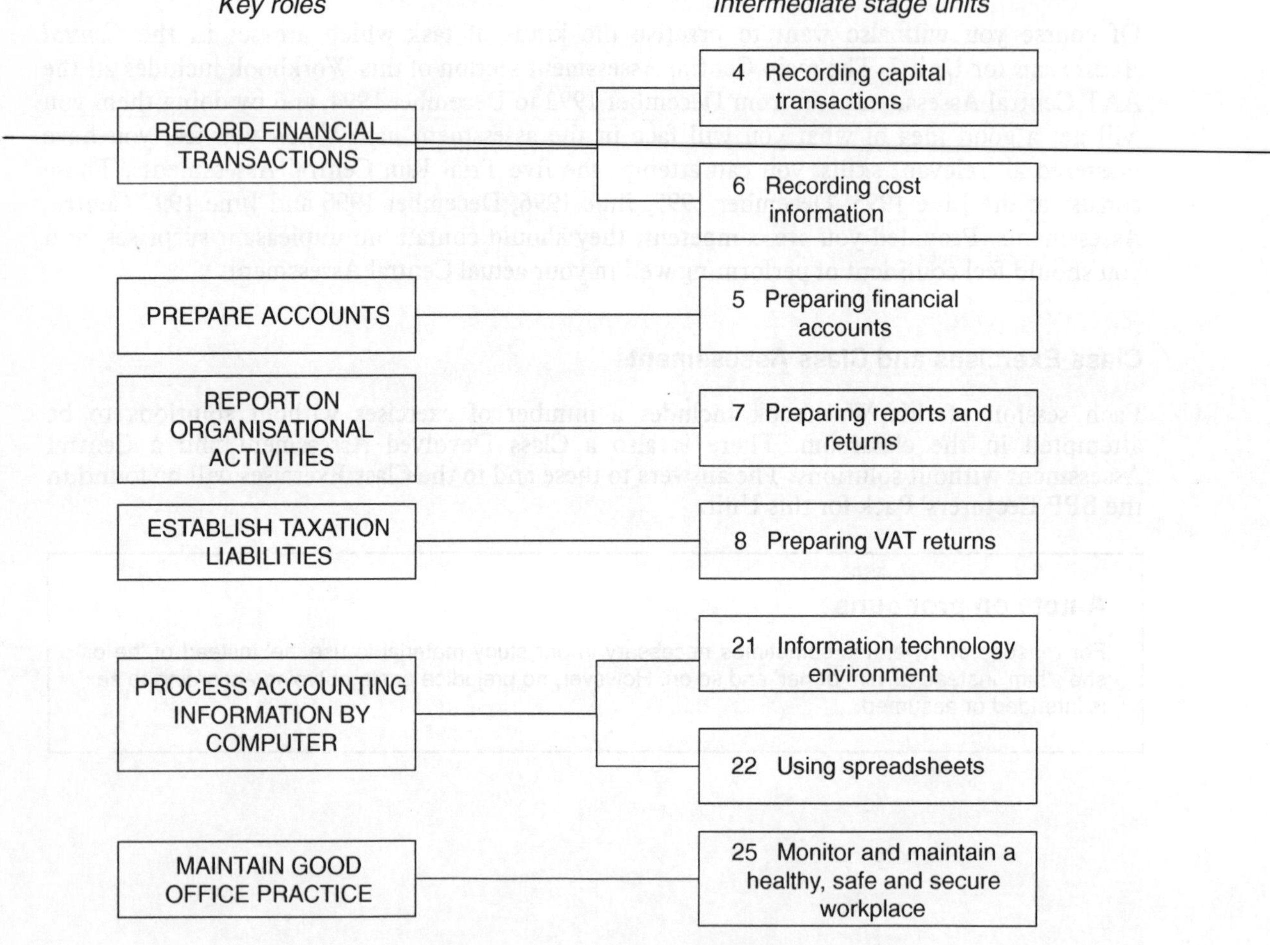


### Units and elements of competence

Units of competence are divided into *elements of competence* describing activities which the individual should be able to perform.

Each element includes a set of *performance criteria* which define what constitutes competent performance. Each element also includes a *range statement* which defines the situations, contexts, methods etc in which the competence should be displayed.

Supplementing the standards of competence are statements of *knowledge and understanding* which underpin competent performance of the standards.

The elements of competence for Unit 7: *Preparing reports and returns* and Unit 8: *Preparing VAT returns* are set out below. The performance criteria and range statements for each element are listed first, followed by the knowledge and understanding required for the Units as wholes. Performance criteria and areas of knowledge and understanding are cross-referenced below to sessions of Practice Exercises in this Workbook, which correspond with chapters in the BPP *Reports and Returns* Tutorial Text.

## Unit 7: Preparing reports and returns

### Element 7.1 Prepare periodic performance reports

| *Performance criteria* | | *Session(s)* |
|---|---|---|
| 1 | Reports are prepared in a clear and intelligible form and presented to management within defined timescales | 2-6, 8 |
| 2 | Information about costs and revenues derived from different units of the organisation is consolidated in standard form | 9, 10 |
| 3 | Cost and revenue data derived from different information systems within the organisation are correctly reconciled | 9, 10 |
| 4 | An appropriate method allowing for changing price levels when comparing results over time is agreed and used | 7 |
| 5 | Transactions between separate units of the organisation are accounted for in accordance with agreed procedures | 10 |
| 6 | Ratios and performance indicators are accurately calculated in accordance with the agreed methodology | 9, 11 |

*Range statement*

1 Analysis of results by different divisions, services, departments, products, processes or sales areas

2 Performance indicators of: productivity, cost per unit, resource utilisation, profitability

3 Methods of reporting: written reports, graphical presentation and diagrams (bar charts, pie diagrams), tables

| *Knowledge and understanding* | | *Session(s)* |
|---|---|---|
| *The business environment* | | |
| 1 | Main sources of government statistics | 2 |
| 2 | Awareness of relevant performance and quality measures | 9, 11 |
| *Accounting techniques* | | |
| 1 | Use of standard units of inputs and outputs | 9 |
| 2 | Time series analysis | 6 |
| 3 | Use of index numbers | 7 |
| 4 | Main types of performance indicators (see Range statement) | 9, 11 |
| 5 | Graphical and diagrammatic presentation (see Range statement) | 4, 5 |
| 6 | Tabulation of accounting and other quantitative information | 5 |
| *The organisation* | | |
| 1 | Background understanding that the accounting system of an organisation are affected by its organisational structure, its administrative systems and procedures and the nature of its business transactions | 1 |
| 2 | Background understanding that recording and accounting practices may vary in different parts of the organisation | 1 |

## Element 7.2 Prepare reports and returns for outside agencies

| | *Performance criteria* | *Session(s)* |
|---|---|---|
| 1 | The conventions and definitions used by the external agency are correctly used in preparing the report or return | 2 |
| 2 | Relevant information is identified, collated and presented in accordance with the external agency's requirement | 2, 8 |
| 3 | Calculations of ratios and performance indicators are accurate | 9, 11 |
| 4 | The report/return is presented in accordance with the external agency's deadline | 2, 8 |

(*Note*. This is a 'generic' competence for organisations in both the public and private sectors, eg returns to trade associations, reports to government grant awarding agencies, statutory returns to DOE by local authorities, returns to Department of Health by Health Authorities.)

*Range statement*

1. Returns on standard forms
2. Written reports on specific issues
3. Graphic and diagrammatic presentation of information
4. Tabulation of accounting and other quantitative information

| *Knowledge and understanding* | *Session(s)* |
|---|---|
| *The business environment* | |
| 1 Main types of external organisations requiring reports and returns: | |
| (a) regulatory | 2 |
| (b) grant awarding | 2 |
| (c) information collecting | 2 |
| 2 Main sources of government statistics | 2 |
| 3 Trade associations | 2 |
| *Accounting techniques* | |
| Methods of presenting information (see Range Statement) | 3-5, 8 |
| *The organisation* | |
| 1 Background understanding that the accounting system of an organisation are affected by its organisational structure, its administrative systems and procedures and the nature of its business transactions | 1 |
| 2 Background understanding that a variety of outside agencies may require reports and returns from organisations and that these requirements must be built into administrative and accounting systems and procedures | 1 |

## Unit 8 Preparing VAT returns

### Element 8.1 Prepare VAT returns

| | *Performance criteria* | *Session(s)* |
|---|---|---|
| 1 | VAT returns are correctly completed from the appropriate sources and submitted within the statutory time limits | 12 |
| 2 | Relevant inputs and outputs are correctly identified and calculated | 13 |
| 3 | VAT documentation is correctly filed | 13 |
| 4 | Submissions are made in accordance with currently operative VAT laws and regulations | 12 |
| 5 | Discussions with VAT inspectors are conducted openly and constructively to promote the efficiency of the VAT accounting system | 12, 13 |

*Session(s)*

*Range statement*

1 Exempt supplies, zero rated supplies, imports and exports

*Knowledge and understanding*

*The business environment*

| | | |
|---|---|---|
| 1 | Basic law and practice relating to all issues covered in the range statement and referred to in the performance criteria. Specific issues include: | |
| | (a) the classification of types of supply | 13 |
| | (b) registration requirements | 12 |
| | (c) the form of VAT invoices; tax points | 12 |
| 2 | Sources of information on VAT: Customs and Excise Guide | 13 |
| 3 | Administration of VAT; enforcement | 13 |

*The organisation*

| | | |
|---|---|---|
| 1 | Background understanding that the accounting system of an organisation are affected by its organisational structure, its administrative systems and procedures and the nature of its business transactions | 1 |
| 2 | Background understanding that recording and accounting practices may vary in different parts of the organisation | 1 |

## ASSESSMENT STRUCTURE

### Devolved and central assessment

The units of competence at the Intermediate statge are assessed by a combination of devolved assessment and central assessment.

*Devolved assessment* tests students' ability to apply the skills detailed in the relevant units of competence. At the Intermediate stage, evidence is collected in an Accounting Portfolio. Devolved assessment may be carried out by means of:

(a) simulations of workplace activities set by AAT-approved assessors; or
(b) observation in the workplace by AAT-approved assessors.

*Central assessments* are set and marked by the AAT, and concentrate on testing students' grasp of the knowledge and understanding which underpins units of competence.

### The Intermediate Stage

Units of competence at the AAT Intermediate Stage (NVQ/SVQ level 3) are tested by central assessment and devolved assessment as follows.

| *Unit number* | | *Central assessment* | *Devolved assessment* |
|---|---|---|---|
| 4 | Recording capital transactions | N/A | ✓ |
| 5 | Preparing financial accounts | ✓ | ✓ |
| 6 | Recording cost information | ✓ | ✓ |
| 7 | Preparing reports and returns | ✓ | ✓ |
| 8 | Preparing VAT returns | N/A | ✓ |
| 21 | Information technology environment | N/A | ✓ |
| 22 | Using spreadsheets | N/A | ✓ |
| 25 | Health and safety | N/A | ✓ |

#### Unit 7 Central Assessment (R & R)

The Unit 7 *Reports and returns* Central Assessment consists of one 2-hour paper requiring the consideration of case studies and the preparation of reports for management.

# *Practice exercises*

# 1 The organisation, accounting and reporting

## Objectives of this session

This session tests your knowledge and understanding of the following areas.

- **The effect of organisation structure on accounting systems**
- **Differences in recording and accounting in various parts of the organisation**
- **The variety of reports and returns required internally and externally**

### Exercise 1

Level: EASY

A report is prepared every month analysing the results of the business. It comes in four sections: a summary for the company as a whole, and then separate reports for Europe, America and the Far East.

(a) What does this imply about the organisation structure?

(b) What effect would the imposition of a functional structure have on the work of a junior accounts manager in Europe?

### Exercise 2

Level: EASY

Sara Jeeves works for Autobuttle Ltd, a company manufacturing a variety of products of domestic utility. She does work for two individuals. One day, she hears them in furious argument about her job for that day.

'I don't care what you say, I've got to get those figures for Robobutlers to the director of the Automated Domestic Service Division by Thursday. This is a vital need, as she's thinking of killing the product.'

'Give us a break, the UK director's coming on his monthly visit and I've got to put the best possible gloss on our performance.'

What might this tell you about the management structure of Autobuttle Ltd?

### Exercise 3

Level: EASY

'Non profit orientated organisations should not have to prepare accounts.' Briefly state whether or not you agree with this proposition, and why.

### Exercise 4

Level: EASY

(a) What, briefly, is the purpose of an accounting system?

(b) Why might an organisation's bankers be interested in the output of a firm's accounting system?

### Exercise 5

Level: EASY

Give one example of a periodic return which has to be made to an outside agency by any organisation with which you are familiar. What is the main purpose of this return?

### Class Exercise 1

Level: MODERATE

Which of the following business organisations has a legal personality separate from its owners?

(1) A partnership regulated by a partnership agreement
(2) A plc
(3) A private limited company
(4) A sole trader's business called 'Joe Bloggs and Company'

Select one option A, B, C, D or E.

A All of them
B (2), (3) and (4) only
C (2) and (3) only
D (1) and (4) only
E (3) and (4) only

# 2 Business and accounting information

### Objectives of this session

This session provides practice in the following skills and techniques.

- **Understanding the need for clear, correct and intelligible information for the preparation of reports and returns**
- **Being aware of the main types of external organisation requiring reports and returns**
- **Understanding the range of accounting reports**

### Exercise 1 Level: EASY

Identify the characteristics of good information.

### Exercise 2 Level: EASY

(a) Information of various kinds is required from within an organisation, and also from outside.

*Task*

Make a list of as many outside agencies requiring reports or returns from a typical limited company as you can.

(b) *Task*

In the case of a particular organisation, for example one which you work for or have worked for, identify any special kinds of reports and returns which it is required to present to outside agencies.

(c) In sections (a) and (b) of this exercise, we have considered the external demand for information from organisations.

*Task*

Now make a list of some of the 'external' information demands in the form of reports, forms and returns on you as an individual or your household. A list of five will be long enough.

### Exercise 3 Level: MODERATE

Outline as many different types of accounting report produced by your department (or any department with which you are familiar) as you can. To what extent do they display the qualities of good information, as identified in Exercise 1?

### Exercise 4 Level: MODERATE

An organisation has started to collect monthly information regarding employment and labour costs from its various departments. At the moment it only records average rates of pay in each department. Suggest three other items of management information that you believe should be collected relating to employment.

### Exercise 5 Level: ADVANCED

(a) Identify four stages in the processing of information.

(b) Demand for information within an organisation usually originates from two main sources, these being categorised as internal and external.

Specify three examples from each category.

### Class Exercise 1 Level: MODERATE

You are required to present a brief talk to a group of trainees in your organisation on the importance of information, in which you should cover the following points.

(a) What is information and why is it so important to an organisation?

(b) Illustrate what information needs to be supplied to the management of an organisation, with particular reference to financial information.

# 3 Statistical information

## *Objectives of this session*

This session provides practice in the following skills and techniques.

- **Understanding the uses of statistics**
- **Knowing the different types of statistical data**
- **Knowing the main sources of government statistics**

### Exercise 1

Level: EASY

Comment on the following statements.

(a) Sales of footwear are up on last year, but not as much as clothing.
(b) Turnover of company X has increased by 150% in the past two years.

### Exercise 2

Level: MODERATE

Look through the following list of surveys and decide whether each is collecting data on attributes, discrete variables or continuous variables.

(a) A survey of statistics text books, to determine how many diagrams they contain.

(b) A survey of cans on a supermarket shelf, to determine whether or not each has a price sticker on it.

(c) A survey of athletes, to find out how long they take to run a mile.

(d) A survey of the results of an examination, to determine what percentage marks the students obtained.

(e) A survey of the heights of telegraph poles in England, to find out if there is any variation across the country.

### Exercise 3

Level: MODERATE

Identify which of the following are secondary data sources.

(a) *Economic Trends* (published by the Office for National Statistics).

(b) The *Monthly Digest of Statistics* (published by the Office for National Statistics).

(c) Data collected for an attitude survey by means of personal interviews, using a non-random sampling method.

(d) Historical records of sales revenues to be used to prepare current forecasts.

### Exercise 4

Level: MODERATE

Name five important sources of statistical data published by the government in the UK and state briefly what each one contains.

### Exercise 5

Level: MODERATE

The *Annual Abstract of Statistics* includes long-term analyses of statistics for which more detailed analyses are available elsewhere.

In which publications would you find detailed short-term statistics covering the following? Identify the publisher in each case, and the frequency of publication.

(a) The level of unemployment.
(b) Trends in road transport.
(c) UK imports and exports.
(d) Geographical distribution of the resident population.
(e) The Retail Prices Index.

### Exercise 6

Level: MODERATE

A manufacturing company has a copy of the *Employment Gazette* which contains statistics relating to:

(a) employment and unemployment;
(b) earnings.

State for what practical purposes both (a) and (b) could be used by the company.

## Exercise 7

Level: MODERATE

An accountant is studying the *Employment Gazette* and is particularly interested in the Retail Price Index.

(a) How could the company use this information in practice?
(b) Explain whether this information is primary or secondary data.

## Class Exercise 1

Level: MODERATE

Comment on the following statements.

(a) In 19X7, 20% of the urban population of country Z spoke the national language as opposed to English. The corresponding proportion for the rural population was 45%. Obviously the majority of the national language speaking population lived in rural areas.

(b) 840 pupils of the ABC School of Motoring have passed their driving test. If you wish to pass the driving test, enrol with us.

(c) Consumer advertising was up by more than 300% in real terms between 19X2 and 19Y2.

## Class Exercise 2

Level:MODERATE

To which one of the following publications would you refer to find the Retail Prices Index?

(a) *Employment Gazette*
(b) The *Blue Book* on National Income and Expenditure
(c) *Business Briefing*
(d) *Bank of England Quarterly Bulletin*

(Choose one.)

# 4 Presenting data: graphs

## Objectives of this session

This session provides practice in the following skills and techniques.

- **Skills and techniques in presenting information graphically**
- **Drawing and interpreting different types of graphs**

## *Practice exercises*

### Exercise 1

Level: EASY

The figure below purports to show the profits of four divisions within a firm during the period from 19X0 to 19X5.

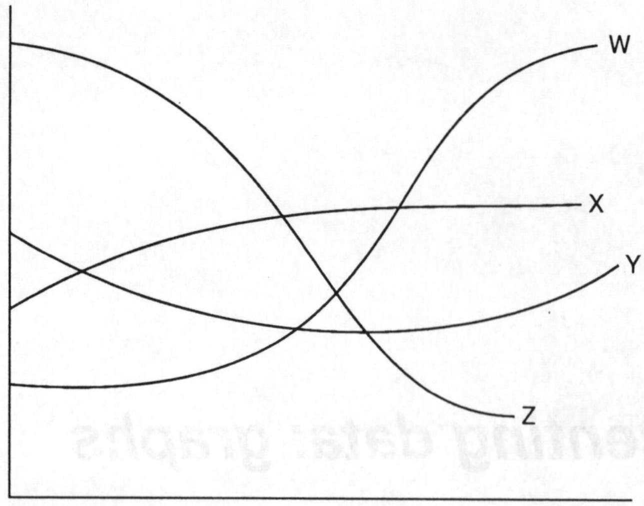


*Tasks*

(a) Criticise the graph by outlining a series of rules for correct graphical presentation.
(b) Suggest briefly some alternative methods of presenting these data.

### Exercise 2

Level: MODERATE

The quantities of spodgets produced by SPG Ltd during the year ended 31 October 19X9 and the related costs were as follows.

| *Month* | *Production* Thousands | *Factory cost* £'000 |
|---|---|---|
| *19X8* | | |
| November | 7 | 45 |
| December | 10 | 59 |
| *19X9* | | |
| January | 13 | 75 |
| February | 14 | 80 |
| March | 11 | 65 |
| April | 7 | 46 |
| May | 5 | 35 |
| June | 4 | 30 |
| July | 3 | 25 |
| August | 2 | 20 |
| September | 1 | 15 |
| October | 5 | 35 |

You may assume that the value of money remained stable throughout the year.

*Tasks*

You have been asked to carry out the following tasks.

(a) Draw a scatter diagram related to the data provided above, and plot on it the line of best fit.

(b) Now answer the following questions.

(i) What would you expect the factory cost to have been if 12,000 spodgets had been produced in a particular month?

(ii) What is your estimate of SPG's monthly fixed cost?

## Exercise 3

Level: MODERATE

A wholesaling business incurs three types of cost per product line carried in stock. Two of these costs, for product P only, are as follows.

| *Cost type* | *Annual cost (£)* |
|---|---|
| I | 2.5 x |
| II | $\frac{225,000}{x}$ |

where x units represents the maximum stock carried.

*Tasks*

(a) For values of x equal to 50, 100, 200, 250, 300, 350, 400, 500 and 600, calculate and tabulate the values of both costs, I and II, and the total costs I and II.

(b) Using one sheet of graph paper, plot cost I, cost II and the total of costs I and II, each against the values of x. Comment upon the features displayed in the three plots of your graph, and advise the business of the best value for x.

(c) (i) If cost type III is a constant £600 regardless of the size of x, superimpose a plot of this cost on your graph in (b).

(ii) If you were to plot the total of all three costs, I, II and III, describe and comment upon the form it would take. (Do not present this plot.)

## Exercise 4

Level: ADVANCED

Annual profit data from 50 similar construction companies in 19X8 are as follows.

| *Annual profit* £million | *Number of companies* |
|---|---|
| –10 to under –5 | 2 |
| –5 to under 0 | 0 |
| 0 to under 5 | 2 |
| 5 to under 10 | 3 |
| 10 to under 15 | 6 |
| 15 to under 20 | 11 |
| 20 to under 25 | 13 |
| 25 to under 30 | 9 |
| 30 to under 35 | 4 |

*Tasks*

(a) Construct a cumulative frequency distribution and draw the ogive (cumulative frequency curve) on graph paper.

(b) Use your ogive to estimate the three quartiles and explain their meaning.

(c) Deduce from your ogive the profit exceeded by the top 10% of companies.

(d) Deduce from your ogive the number of companies, out of 500 similar companies to those above, whose annual profit in 19X8 was between £8,000,000 and £18,000,000.

## Class Exercise 1

Level: EASY

Blunt Products Ltd has five factories, and output at each factory for the last five years has been as follows (in thousands of standard hours).

| | | | *Factories* | | |
|---|---|---|---|---|---|
| *Year* | *A* | *B* | *C* | *D* | *E* |
| 19X1 | 250 | 608 | 326 | 563 | 294 |
| 19X2 | 258 | 638 | 339 | 597 | 323 |
| 19X3 | 271 | 670 | 353 | 627 | 333 |
| 19X4 | 290 | 704 | 381 | 645 | 363 |
| 19X5 | 316 | 746 | 419 | 652 | 370 |

*Tasks*

(a) Convert these figures to a basis which enables the changes in output to be readily compared.

(b) Plot your findings on a graph.

### Class Exercise 2

Level: MODERATE

Three companies hire out portable telephones but offer different charging systems. Company A charges a fixed daily hire charge of £24 plus £0.25 for each minute of call length. Company B charges a fixed daily hire charge of £15 plus £0.30 for each minute of call length; Company C does not charge a fixed hire charge but charges £0.40 for each minute of call length. Portable telephone units from all three companies can record the lengths of calls made.

*Tasks*

(a) For each company A, B and C, calculate the total daily charge for a hired telephone used for 50, 100, 150 and 200 minutes, and present your results in a table.

(b) Graph, on a single pair of axes, all three sets of your results in (a), using axes labelled 'total daily hire charge' against 'daily call length in minutes'.

(c) For what range of daily call lengths would:

(i) company A be cheaper than company B;
(ii) company A be cheaper than company C; and
(iii) company B be cheaper than company C?

# 5 Presenting data: tables and charts

---

## *Objectives of this session*

This session provides practice in the following skills and techniques.

- **Tabulating accounting and other quantitative information**
- **Presenting information diagrammatically**
- **Using tables, bar charts and pie diagrams**

---

### Exercise 1

Level: EASY

Set out the main guidelines which should be followed when data is presented in tabular form.

### Information for Exercises 2 and 3

The number of telephones installed in a country in 1960 was 5,246,000. Ten years later in 1970 the number was 6,830,000, and by 1980 the total installed in that year was 12,654,000. Another ten years later the number for 1990 was 10,194,000. In 1960 B Co Ltd saw 2,114,000 of its telephones installed, more than any other kind; A Co Ltd was second with 1,810,000; C Co Ltd third with 448,000; and the 'all others' group accounted for 874,000. In 1970 A Co Ltd was in first position with 3,248,000; C Co Ltd was second with 1,618,000; B Co Ltd third with 1,288,000; and the 'all others' group installed fewer telephones than ten years earlier: 676,000. In 1980 A Co Ltd installations alone, 5,742,000, exceeded total installations of just 20 years earlier. B Co Ltd was in second position with 3,038,000; C Co Ltd third with 2,228,000; and the 'all others' group installed just 1,646,000. 1990 data indicated that relative positions remained the same since 1980 with A Co Ltd at 4,932,000, B Co Ltd at 3,138,000, C Co Ltd at 1,506,000 and 'all others' at 618,000.

### Exercise 2

Level: EASY

Convert the information given above into tabular form.

### Exercise 3

Level: EASY

(a) Interpret the same data by calculating and further tabulating appropriate percentages to show comparisons of the telephone installations by the producers in the four years given.

(b) Comment on the percentage trends in (a).

### Exercise 4

Level: MODERATE

By 19X9, the Soyuz Insurance Company had been in business for nine years. It now employs 20,770 people, of whom the largest group (36%) were sales staff, the next largest group (21%) were actuaries and the third largest group (18%) were accountants. Other groups of employees made up the rest of the staff.

Things had been very different when the company first began operations in 19X0. Then, it had just 4,200 employees, of whom the 1,260 actuaries were the biggest group; there were 1,176 sales staff and just 840 accountants.

By 19X3, the company had nearly doubled in size, employing 7,650 people, of whom 2,448 were actuaries, 2,372 were sales staff and 1,607 were accountants.

By 19X6, the company employed 12,740 people, and the growth in numbers had been most noticeable amongst sales staff, of whom there were 4,840. There were 3,185 actuaries. Accountants had increased substantially in number to 2,550.

The company's managing director has been very pleased with the growth in business over the past nine years, but has tried to limit the growth in the numbers of staff who are not sales staff, actuaries or accountants.

*Task*

Present the data above in tabular form.

Are there any comments you would make about what the information in the table should tell the managing director of the company?

## Exercise 5

Level: MODERATE

Records of the patients suffering from either minor or major ailments seen by doctors at a local clinic over the last few years show the following.

In 1990, a total of 2,550 patients were seen: of these 650 were adult men, 800 were adult women, and the remainder were children. Of the men, 234 were suffering from a minor ailment; of the women and children, 360 and 616, respectively, were suffering from minor ailments.

In 1995, a total of 2,900 patients were seen by the doctors, 750 being men, 1,060 women, and the remainder children. Of the men, 320 were suffering a minor ailment, whereas 550 women and 720 children had this type of ailment.

*Tasks*

(a) What is the purpose of representing this type of data in tabular form?

(b) Draw up a table showing all the data by class of patient, ailment type and year. Insert in your table both actual numbers and percentages, calculating the latter on a base of the total number of patients seen in each year, correct to one decimal place.

(c) Give three appropriate interpretations of the information your table provides.

## Exercise 6

Level: MODERATE

The commission earnings for May 19X3 of the assistants in a department store were as follows (in pounds).

| | | | | | | | | | |
|---|---|---|---|---|---|---|---|---|---|
| 60 | 35 | 53 | 47 | 25 | 44 | 55 | 58 | 47 | 71 |
| 63 | 67 | 57 | 44 | 61 | 48 | 50 | 56 | 61 | 42 |
| 43 | 38 | 41 | 39 | 61 | 51 | 27 | 56 | 57 | 50 |
| 55 | 68 | 55 | 50 | 25 | 48 | 44 | 43 | 49 | 73 |
| 53 | 35 | 36 | 41 | 45 | 71 | 56 | 40 | 69 | 52 |
| 36 | 47 | 66 | 52 | 32 | 46 | 44 | 32 | 52 | 58 |
| 49 | 41 | 45 | 45 | 48 | 36 | 46 | 42 | 52 | 33 |
| 31 | 36 | 40 | 66 | 53 | 58 | 60 | 52 | 66 | 51 |
| 51 | 44 | 59 | 53 | 51 | 57 | 35 | 45 | 46 | 54 |
| 46 | 54 | 51 | 39 | 64 | 43 | 54 | 47 | 60 | 45 |

*Task*

Prepare a grouped frequency distribution classifying the commission earnings into categories of £5 commencing with '£25 and less than £30'.

## Information for Exercises 7 and 8

*Tutorial note.* Exercises 7 and 8 can be completed using a computer, if you have access to software for drawing pie charts.

During his review of the year's trading to 31 October 19X0, the chairman of Superexports plc said 'our sales to countries within the European Union amounted to £786,675 and to the rest of Europe £218,825, whilst sales to North America amounted to £285,400, to other developed countries £92,200 and to developing countries £188,750. Our exports to the oil exporting countries amounted to £145,150 and to countries with centrally planned economies £33,750.'

## Exercise 7

Level: EASY

Prepare a table setting out Superexports plc's sales to the different markets, rounding figures to the nearest thousand pounds.

## Exercise 8

Level: MODERATE

Using the figures from your table (Exercise 7), present the data in the form of a pie chart.

## Information for Exercises 9 and 10

TAA is a trading company. The sales of its four products P, Q, R and S over the period 19X0-19X2 were as follows.

| | *Units sold* | | | |
|---|---|---|---|---|
| | *P* | *Q* | *R* | *S* |
| 19X0 | 560 | 330 | 810 | 400 |
| 19X1 | 620 | 300 | 760 | 520 |
| 19X2 | 650 | 270 | 710 | 670 |

## Exercise 9

Level: MODERATE

You have been asked to carry out the following tasks.

(a) Represent the data given above in the form of a percentage component bar chart.
(b) Comment on the trends in sales of the products.

## Exercise 10

Level: MODERATE

This exercise follows on from Exercise 9.

Given that selling prices were £3.50, £5.00, £3.00 and £6.50 for products P, Q, R and S respectively throughout 19X0-19X2, calculate the percentage change in TAA's total sales revenue between 19X0 and 19X2, and provide a comment upon your result.

## Exercise 11

Level: MODERATE

Your company is preparing its published accounts and the chairman has requested that the assets of the company be compared in a component bar chart for the last five years. The data are contained in the following table.

| *Asset* | *19X3* | *19X4* | *19X5* | *19X6* | *19X7* |
|---|---|---|---|---|---|
| | £'000 | £'000 | £'000 | £'000 | £'000 |
| Property | 59 | 59 | 65 | 70 | 74 |
| Plant and machinery | 176 | 179 | 195 | 210 | 200 |
| Stock and work in progress | 409 | 409 | 448 | 516 | 479 |
| Debtors | 330 | 313 | 384 | 374 | 479 |
| Cash | 7 | 60 | 29 | 74 | 74 |

*Tasks*

(a) Construct the necessary component bar chart.
(b) Comment on the movements in the assets over the five year period.

## Exercise 12

Level: MODERATE

*Real unit cost performance: public utilities*

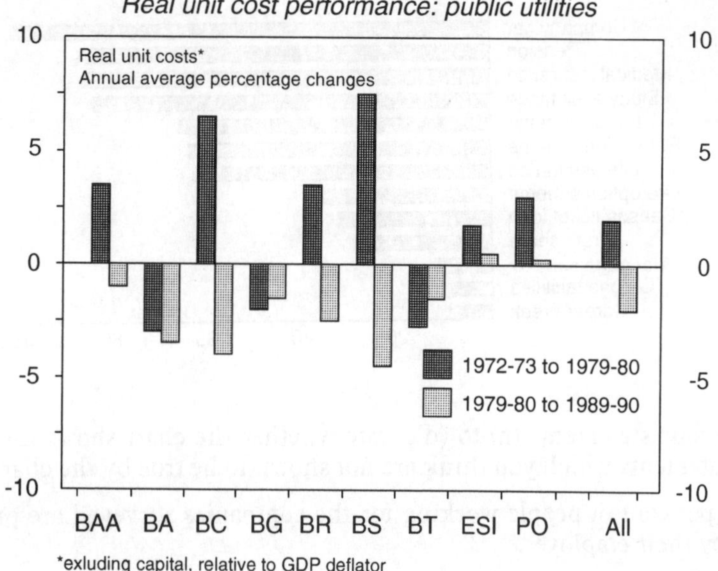


*exluding capital, relative to GDP deflator

*(Source: Treasury Bulletin)*

The chart above is one of the following.

Component bar chart/Multiple bar chart/Histogram.

(Circle your choice.)

## Class Exercise 1

Level: EASY

The trend in total annual sales of a company over a ten year period could be shown appropriately using which one or more of the following?

Table/Pie diagram/Percentage component bar chart

(Circle your choice(s).)

## Class Exercise 2

Level: MODERATE

Present the following information in the form of a table, including in your table the percentage changes in the volume of UK car sales of different origins of manufacture and overall between the first quarter of 1992 and the first quarter of 1993.

453,000 cars were sold in the United Kingdom during the first three months of 1993: this is an increase of 46,000 on the same period one year earlier. Of these 453,000 vehicles, 205,000 were made in Britain, with 188,000 coming from the rest of the European Union (EU). Cars built in Japan made up 41,000 of the 453,000 total. Imports from countries other than EU members and Japan comprised 19,000 cars in the first quarter of 1993. This compares with a figure of 18,000 cars originating in these other countries for the same period one year earlier. In the first quarter of 1992, 184,000 of cars built in Britain were sold in the UK. In this period, UK car sales included 166,000 vehicles imported from the rest of the EU and 39,000 vehicles imported from Japan.

## Class Exercise 3

Level: MODERATE

The chart below shows findings from an annual survey of UK companies employing financial staff from a firm of recruitment consultants, as published in *The Independent*.

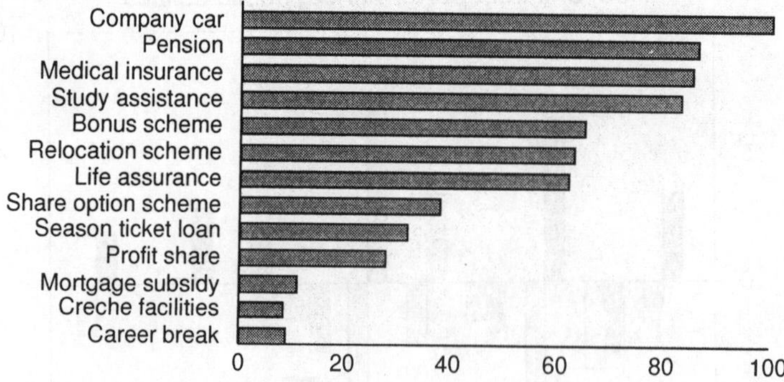


*Task*

For each of the four statements (a) to (d), state whether the chart shows the statement to be true. For any statements which you think are not shown to be true by the chart, give reasons.

(a) Over sixty per cent of people working for the companies surveyed are provided with life assurance by their employer.

(b) A greater number of the companies surveyed offer medical insurance compared with those offering study assistance.

(c) A company car is offered as a benefit by an increasingly large number of the companies surveyed.

(d) The benefit offered to fewest employees of the companies surveyed is career break.

## Class Exercise 4

Level: MODERATE

The management of Chawley Plastics Ltd wish to present some information about results to employees. It has been decided that a visual form of display would be the best way to communicate the information.

The relevant data are as follows.

| | *19X5* | *19X4* | *19X3* | *19X2* | *19X1* |
|---|---|---|---|---|---|
| | £'000 | £'000 | £'000 | £'000 | £'000 |
| Sales | 5.2 | 5.1 | 4.8 | 4.0 | 3.5 |
| Costs | | | | | |
| Direct materials | 1.5 | 1.4 | 1.2 | 1.0 | 0.8 |
| Direct wages | 2.3 | 1.8 | 1.6 | 1.3 | 1.0 |
| Production overhead | 0.7 | 0.7 | 0.6 | 0.5 | 0.4 |
| Other overhead | 0.6 | 0.5 | 0.4 | 0.3 | 0.2 |
| Taxation | 0.0 | 0.3 | 0.4 | 0.3 | 0.3 |
| Profit | 0.1 | 0.4 | 0.6 | 0.6 | 0.8 |

*Product groups, as a percentage of total sales*

| | *19X5* | *19X4* | *19X3* | *19X2* | *19X1* |
|---|---|---|---|---|---|
| Product group | % | % | % | % | % |
| W | 33 | 36 | 38 | 30 | 25 |
| X | 5 | 10 | 12 | 18 | 25 |
| Y | 46 | 36 | 30 | 30 | 25 |
| Z | 16 | 18 | 20 | 22 | 25 |
| | 100 | 100 | 100 | 100 | 100 |

*Tasks*

Prepare two different visual displays to show:

(a) sales by product group;

(b) a comparison of 19X4 with 19X5, analysing total sales into costs, taxation and profit, with particular emphasis on direct wages.

# 6 Averages and time series

### Objectives of this session

This session provides practice in the following skills and techniques.

- **Analysing time series**
- **Finding the trend and seasonal variations**
- **Forecasting**

## Exercise 1

Level: EASY

Write brief notes explaining the following terms to a colleague.

(a) The mean
(b) The median
(c) Time series.

## Exercise 2

Level: EASY

For the week ended 29 May, the wages earned by the 69 operators employed in the machine shop of Mechaids Ltd were as follows.

| *Wages* | *Number of operatives* |
|---|---|
| under £ 60 | 3 |
| £60 and under £ 70 | 11 |
| £70 and under £ 80 | 16 |
| £80 and under £ 90 | 15 |
| £90 and under £100 | 10 |
| £100 and under £110 | 8 |
| £110 and under £120 | 6 |
| | 69 |

*Task*

Calculate the arithmetic mean wage of the machine operators of Mechaids Ltd for the week ended 29 May.

## Exercise 3

Level: MODERATE

The following grouped frequency distribution gives the annual wages of 200 employees in an engineering firm.

| *Wages* £ | *Number of employees* |
|---|---|
| 5,000 and less than 5,500 | 4 |
| 5,500 and less than 6,000 | 26 |
| 6,000 and less than 6,500 | 133 |
| 6,500 and less than 7,000 | 35 |
| 7,000 and less than 7,500 | 2 |

*Task*

Calculate the mean, the median and the mode of annual wages.

## Information for Exercises 4 and 5

The cost accountant of Ware Howser Ltd has calculated standard costs for handling items of stock in a warehouse. The costs are based on the labour time required to deal with stock movements, and are as follows.

| *Time required for job of handling stock* Minutes | | *Standard cost* £ |
|---|---|---|
| Less than | 10 | 9 |
| ≥ 10 and up to | 20 | 11 |
| ≥ 20 and up to | 40 | 13 |
| ≥ 40 and up to | 60 | 15 |
| ≥ 60 and up to | 90 | 23 |
| ≥ 90 and up to | 120 | 29 |
| ≥ 120 and up to | 180 | 38 |

The warehouse operates a working day of seven hours per man, and a five-day week. There are 12 men employed. Only one man works on each stock movement.

An examination of the time sheets for a typical week showed that the following costs had been incurred.

| *Standard cost* | *Frequency* |
|---|---|
| £ | |
| 9 | 240 |
| 11 | 340 |
| 13 | 150 |
| 15 | 120 |
| 23 | 20 |
| 29 | 20 |
| 38 | 10 |

### Exercise 4

Level: EASY

Using the information above, estimate the mean handling time for a stock movement.

### Exercise 5

Level: EASY

(a) Using the information above, estimate the total number of hours in the week spent actively moving items of stock.

(b) What is the percentage capacity utilisation of the labour force in the warehouse?

### Exercise 6

Level: EASY

What is a moving average? For what purpose are such averages used?

### Exercise 7

Level: EASY

Sales in pounds of a particular product for the last five years have been: 100, 110, 108, 112, 106.

Calculate a 3-year moving average to the nearest pound.

### Exercise 8

Level: MODERATE

What is meant by the 'underlying trend' in a time series?

### Exercise 9

Level: MODERATE

The following figures relate to the sales (in tens of thousands) of flanges during the period 1980 to 1995.

| *Year* | *Sales* |
|---|---|
| 1980 | 55 |
| 1981 | 52 |
| 1982 | 45 |
| 1983 | 48 |
| 1984 | 65 |
| 1985 | 70 |
| 1986 | 62 |
| 1987 | 55 |
| 1988 | 58 |
| 1989 | 75 |
| 1990 | 80 |
| 1991 | 77 |
| 1992 | 55 |
| 1993 | 73 |
| 1994 | 85 |
| 1995 | 90 |

*Task*

Draw a graph showing the sales year by year for the period and superimpose on it the five year moving average line.

### Exercise 10

Level: ADVANCED

Profit figures for the Revolving Disc Company for the two years 19X7 and 19X8 turn out to be as follows.

| | *Profit (£'000)* | |
|---|---|---|
| | *19X7* | *19X8* |
| January | 8.6 | 8.7 |
| February | 7.0 | 7.2 |
| March | 6.3 | 5.3 |
| April | 5.0 | 4.8 |
| May | 5.2 | 4.6 |
| June | 11.9 | 10.7 |
| July | 12.6 | 13.2 |
| August | 10.4 | 12.9 |
| September | 6.2 | 7.5 |
| October | 5.0 | 7.2 |
| November | 10.3 | 13.6 |
| December | 14.9 | 18.0 |
| | 103.4 | 113.7 |

These figures appear to reflect the fact that sales increase during the school summer holidays and in the run up to Christmas.

*Task*

On a graph drawn to a reasonable scale, plot:

(a) the monthly profit figures;
(b) the annual moving average;
(c) the three-monthly moving average.

Comment on the difference in the two moving average lines.

### Class Exercise 1

Level: EASY

Which of the following is not one of the four components of a time series?

The historical data/The trend/Cyclical variations/Random variations

(Circle your choice.)

### Class Exercise 2

Level: MODERATE

M, N, O, P, Q and R are operatives employed in the sheet metal work department of AT Engineering Ltd, whose records for the week ended 9 June 19X0 show their attendance, in hours, as follows.

| | *Mon* | *Tue* | *Wed* | *Thu* | *Fri* | *Sat* |
|---|---|---|---|---|---|---|
| M | 8 | 8 | 9 | 9 | 8 | 4 |
| N | 9 | 8 | 10 | 8 | 4 | |
| O | 8 | 8 | 8 | 8 | 8 | |
| P | 9 | 10 | 9 | 10 | 9 | 4 |
| Q | 10 | 9 | 10 | 9 | 10 | 4 |
| R | 8 | 4 | 6 | 8 | 8 | |

Hours worked in excess of eight on Mondays to Fridays are paid at basic hourly rate plus one third, and all hours worked on Saturdays are paid at double the basic rate.

The basic hourly rates for each operative are as follows.

| | |
|---|---|
| M, O and R | £3.60 |
| N and P | £3.75 |
| Q | £4.20 |

*Tasks*

(a) Prepare a statement showing the wages of each of the six operatives and the total wages for the week ended 9 June 19X0.

(b) Using the total wages of all six operatives, calculate the weighted average wages cost, to the nearest penny, per operative hour.

## Class Exercise 3

Level: MODERATE

The following is a time series of an organisation's quarterly profits.

*Time series: Quarterly profits of an organisation*

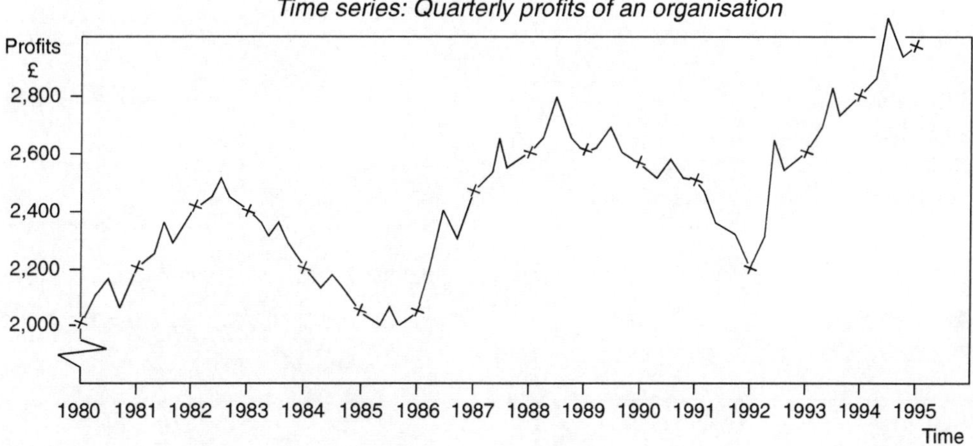


*Task*

Explain, and comment on the limitations of:

(a) the long-term trend;
(b) the cyclical movement;
(c) seasonal variations.

# 7 Allowing for changing price levels

## Objectives of this session

This session provides practice in the following skills and techniques.

- **Index numbers**
- **Using an appropriate method to allow for changing price levels when comparing results over time**

## Exercise 1

Level: EASY

Fill in the words missing from the following.

The period for which the value of an index is taken to be 100 (or 1,000 or 1.00) is called the __________ period. Changes in the prices faced by UK manufacturers are tracked by the __________ indices published by the Office for National Statistics.

## Exercise 2

Level: EASY

The price index of a company's major raw material is:

| *1989* | *1990* | *1991* | *1992* | *1993* |
|---|---|---|---|---|
| 100 | 110 | 112 | 106 | 120 |

Recalculate the index for the years 1992 and 1993 using 1991 as the base year. (Answers to the nearest whole number.)

## Exercise 3

Level: EASY

The MN Company's sales over the last four years, together with the Retail Prices Index for each of the years is as follows.

| | *Year 1* | *Year 2* | *Year 3* | *Year 4* |
|---|---|---|---|---|
| Sales £'000 | 27,500 | 29,680 | 32,535 | 34,455 |
| Retail Prices Index | 217 | 228 | 246 | 268 |

*Tasks*

Remove the effect of increased prices from the annual sales figures (ie deflate the sales figures) and comment on the result.

## Exercise 4

Level: EASY

Sales for a company over a five year period were as follows.

| *Year* | *Sales* £,000 |
|---|---|
| 19X5 | 35 |
| 19X6 | 42 |
| 19X7 | 40 |
| 19X8 | 45 |
| 19X9 | 50 |

*Task*

Work out a sales index based on the sales for 19X6 (19X6 sales = 100).

## Exercise 5

Level: EASY

A price index measuring the cost of shoes over the period 19X0-19X3 is as follows.

| *Year* | *Index* |
|---|---|
| 19X0 | 96 |
| 19X1 | 98 |
| 19X2 | 100 |
| 19X3 | 113 |

*Tasks*

(a) What year has been chosen for the base year of this index, as far as you can tell from the table above?

(b) By how many points has the index risen between 19X0 and 19X2?

(c) By what percentage has the index risen between 19X0 and 19X2?

(d) If a typical pair of shoes cost £7.50 in 19X1, how much did they cost in 19X3?

## Exercise 6

Level: EASY

A chart like that below was published to show sales per employee of the supermarket chain Tesco, which rose from £77,200 in 1986 to £99,400 in 1990.

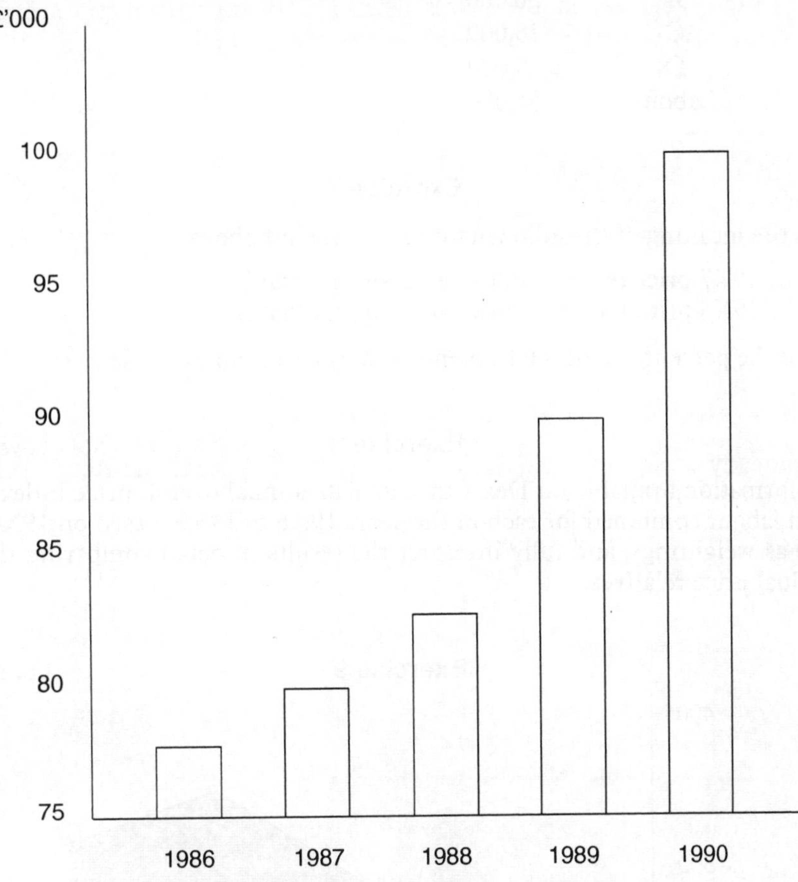


*Tesco: sales per employee*

The average Retail Prices Index in the years 1986 to 1990 was as follows (January 1987 = 100).

| | *RPI* |
|---|---|
| 1986 | 97.8 |
| 1987 | 101.9 |
| 1988 | 106.9 |
| 1989 | 115.2 |
| 1990 | 126.2 |

*Task*

Comment on the significance of the data and on the way in which it has been presented.

## Information for Exercises 7 and 8

Dex Ltd produces a range of products from four materials A, B, C and D. A cost accountant has calculated the following price relative indices for the years 19X6 to 19X9 based on prices in 19X5.

| *Table 1* | *Item* | *19X6* | *19X7* | *19X8* | *19X9* |
|---|---|---|---|---|---|
| | A | 112 | 115 | 116 | 120 |
| | B | 98 | 96 | 95 | 90 |
| | C | 103 | 105 | 109 | 110 |
| | D | 117 | 120 | 120 | 120 |
| | Labour | 110 | 115 | 121 | 125 |

Total annual expenditure in 19X9 on these items was as follows.

*Table 2*

| *Item* | £ |
|---|---|
| A | 20,000 |
| B | 30,000 |
| C | 15,000 |
| D | 5,000 |
| Labour | 55,000 |

### Exercise 7

Level: EASY

(a) Explain the meaning of the following items in Table 1 above.

(i) The 19X7 price relative index value for material D.
(ii) The 19X9 price relative index value for material B.

(b) Calculate the percentages of total expenditure by cost item in Table 2.

### Exercise 8

Level: MODERATE

Using the information available on Dex Ltd, calculate annual overall price index numbers for materials and labour combined for each of the years 19X6 to 19X9, based on 19X5, using your results of (b) as weightings, and fully interpret the results in detail comparing them with the 19X9 individual price relatives.

### Exercise 9

Level: MODERATE

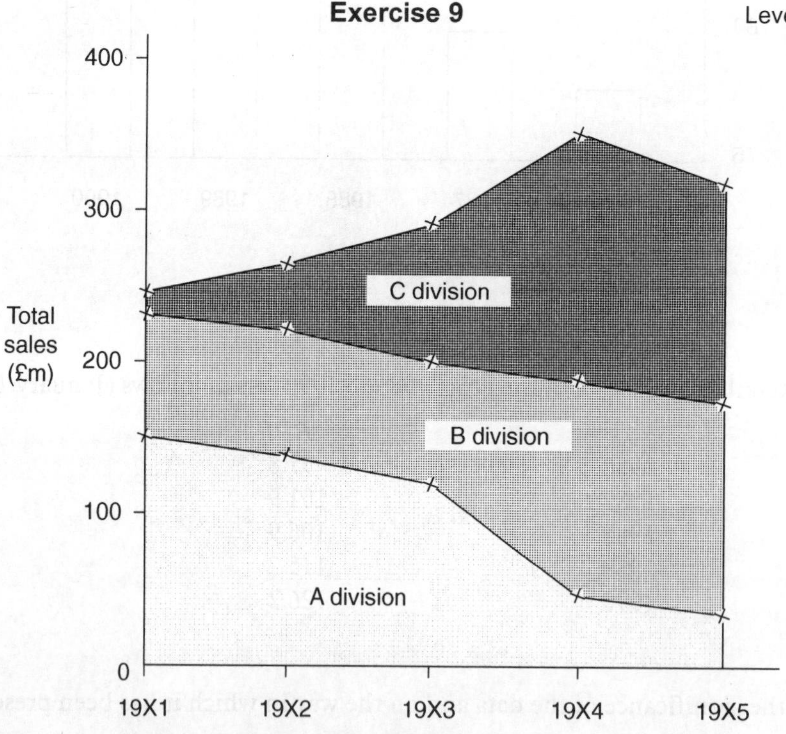


The chart above shows total sales of Retailer plc, a retailer of a wide range of consumer goods, which has three divisions, A, B and C. Total sales were £249 million in 19X1 and £322 million in 19X5. The consumer price index has had the following average values: 19X1 - 221.7; 19X2 - 234.2; 19X3 - 239.4; 19X4 - 250.1; 19X5 - 259.2.

(a) 'The growth in total sales between 19X1 and 19X5 is attributable to sales growth in C Division. Both A and B divisions experienced declining sales over the period.' True or false?

(b) The real value of total sales increased over the period 19X1 to 19X5. True or false?

### Exercise 10

Level: MODERATE

Your company wishes to construct a price index for three commodities, A, B and C. The prices in 19X0 were £2, £3 and £5 respectively and quantities consumed in the same period were

5,000, 6,000 and 3,000 respectively. The prices for 19X1 and 19X2 are given as percentages of 19X0 prices.

| | *19X1* | *19X2* |
|---|---|---|
| A | 100 | 110 |
| B | 108 | 115 |
| C | 90 | 100 |

*Task*

You are required to construct a price index using 19X0 as a base point.

## Exercise 11

Level: MODERATE

AMP plc is a growing printing company that specialises in producing accounting manuals for several accountancy training companies. The manuals are written by the training companies and passed to AMP. The company uses three main stages in producing the manuals:

(a) the preparation of the plates;
(b) the printing of the text;
(c) the assembly and binding of the manuals.

The cost of the materials used in the manufacture of one manual, 'WBA', is:

| | | *19X3* | | | *19X4* | |
|---|---|---|---|---|---|---|
| | *Quantity* | *Price* | *Pence* | *Quantity* | *Price* | *Pence* |
| Cover board | 1 | 10.8p | 10.8 | 1 | 10.6 | 10.6 |
| Paper | 230 | 30p/100 | 69 | 250 | 31p/100 | 77.5 |
| Ink | 5 | 1p | 5 | 6 | 1p | 6 |
| Bindings | 1 | 2p | 2 | 1 | 3p | 3 |
| | | | 86.8 | | | 97.1 |

Calculate an index number which indicates the overall change in prices in 19X4 (19X3 = 100). Use 19X3 quantities as the basis for the calculation.

## Exercise 12

Level: MODERATE

A factory manager wishes to establish a productivity index by which to measure changes in productivity from month to month. Three products are manufactured: hocks, nocks and socks. Each product has a different work content, and is therefore given a weighting. The weightings to be used are as follows.

| | |
|---|---|
| Hocks | 9 |
| Nocks | 4 |
| Socks | 5 |

In addition, some months contain more working days than others, and the index must be designed so as to offset the effects of this.

Data for October, November and December 19X3 were as follows.

| | *October* | *November* | *December* |
|---|---|---|---|
| Working days | 22 | 20 | 16 |
| Output (units) | | | |
| Hocks | 30 | 25 | 24 |
| Nocks | 24 | 28 | 20 |
| Socks | 18 | 20 | 16 |

October 19X3 has been selected as the base period, with a productivity index of 100.

*Task*

Calculate a productivity index value for November and December 19X3.

## Exercise 13

Level: ADVANCED

*General index of retail prices 13 December 19X9*
*(15 January 19X1 = 100)*

| *Group* | | *Group weight* | *Group index number* |
|---|---|---|---|
| 1 | Food | 203 | 318.5 |
| 2 | Alcoholic drink | 78 | 373.2 |
| 3 | Tobacco | 39 | 450.0 |
| 4 | Housing | 137 | 381.6 |
| 5 | Fuel and light | 69 | 469.0 |
| 6 | Durable household goods | 64 | 253.0 |
| 7 | Clothing and footwear | 74 | 217.1 |
| 8 | Transport and vehicles | 159 | 371.7 |
| 9 | Miscellaneous goods | 75 | 353.4 |
| 10 | Services | 63 | 350.0 |
| 11 | Meals out | 39 | 375.7 |

*Task*

Using the information in the above table, calculate the following.

(a) The 'all groups combined' index number.
(b) An index number for all groups combined excluding housing.

## Exercise 14

Level: ADVANCED

'Glow' is a polishing compound used in the metal finishing trades. It is produced by mixing the four ingredients G, L, O and W, in the proportions 6, 5, 4 and 3 respectively.

Indices of the cost prices of the four ingredients for the years 19X5 to 19X8, using 19X4 as the base year are as follows.

| | *19X5* | *19X6* | *19X7* | *19X8* |
|---|---|---|---|---|
| G | 103 | 107 | 115 | 120 |
| L | 104 | 111 | 118 | 123 |
| O | 107 | 113 | 117 | 121 |
| W | 102 | 106 | 110 | 118 |

*Tasks*

(a) For each of the years 19X5 to 19X8, calculate the material cost index of Glow.
(b) For 19X8, calculate the material cost index using 19X7 as the base year.

## Exercise 15

Level: ADVANCED

The mean weekly take-home pay of the employees of Staples Ltd and a price index for the 11 years from 19X0 to 19Y0 are as follows.

| *Year* | *Weekly wage* | *Price index (19X0 = 100)* |
|---|---|---|
| | £ | |
| 19X0 | 150 | 100 |
| 19X1 | 161 | 103 |
| 19X2 | 168 | 106 |
| 19X3 | 179 | 108 |
| 19X4 | 185 | 109 |
| 19X5 | 191 | 112 |
| 19X6 | 197 | 114 |
| 19X7 | 203 | 116 |
| 19X8 | 207 | 118 |
| 19X9 | 213 | 121 |
| 19Y0 | 231 | 123 |

*Task*

Construct a time series of real wages for 19X0 to 19Y0 using a price index with 19X6 as the base year.

**Class Exercise 1** Level: MODERATE

(a) Fabro plc uses four raw materials, A, B, C and D in its production. Twice as much B as A is used, three times as much C as B is used, and the usage of D is half as much as A. The prices of the materials in the years 19X6-X8 are as follows.

| *Raw material* | | *Price per kg (£)* | |
|---|---|---|---|
| | *19X6* | *19X7* | *19X8* |
| A | 2.50 | 2.50 | 3.00 |
| B | 1.00 | 1.20 | 1.50 |
| C | 4.00 | 4.50 | 4.50 |
| D | 5.00 | 5.00 | 6.00 |

*Tasks*

(i) Taking raw material usage as a good indicator of relative weight, what is the set of weights to apply to A, B, C and D?

(ii) Calculate weighted aggregate price of raw materials indices for 19X7 and 19X8, based upon 19X6.

(b) An index of Fabro's labour costs is as follows.

| | *19X6* | *19X7* | *19X8* |
|---|---|---|---|
| Labour cost index | 120 | 130 | 160 |

*Tasks*

Explain how each of the following conclusions may be deduced and briefly discuss whether each is valid.

(i) 'Labour costs have risen by 40 points since 19X6'.
(ii) 'Since 19X6 labour costs have risen by 33 per cent'.
(iii) 'The average increase in labour costs since 19X6 has been 20 per cent'.

**Class Exercise 2** Level: MODERATE

An index of machine prices has year 1 as the base year, with an index number of 100. By the end of year 9 the index had risen to 180 and by the end of year 14 it had risen by another 18 points.

(a) What was the percentage increase in machine prices between years 9 and 14?

(b) What was the average annual percentage price increase between years 9 and 14 (to one decimal place)?

**Class Exercise 3** Level: MODERATE

A company is engaged in the business of assembling toys and consumer durables which it then sells direct to major UK retail chains. Management wishes to present a series of data showing sales in real terms over recent years.

*Task*

Giving reasons, explain which of the following indices would be most appropriate for adjusting the monetary sales figures of the company into 'real' terms.

(a) General index of retail prices (RPI)
(b) Producer prices index: materials and fuels
(c) Producer prices: manufactured goods

# 8 Writing reports and completing forms

## *Objectives of this session*

This session provides practice in the following skills and techniques.

- **How to write material for reports in a clear and intelligible form**
- **Completing standard forms**

Report writing and form completion skills are also required in tasks included later in this Workbook.

## Exercise 1

Level: EASY

(a) Where in a report might its conclusions be set out?
(b) What is meant by 'the terms of reference' of a written report?
(c) For what reasons might parts of a report be contained in appendices?

## Exercise 2

Level: EASY

(a) List the headings you might use as a framework for a:

(i) short formal report;
(ii) short informal report.

(b) List ten words you might use instead of 'said' to report someone's speech ('He said that...')

(c) How would you rephrase the following so that they were suitable for a formal report, and why?

(i) I investigated the matter.

(ii) 'I will investigate further', Mr Harris told me.

(iii) 'There must be a problem in Accounts,' he said, 'since it obviously isn't our fault'.

(iv) Accounts pretended not to have received the complaint.

(v) 'It is outrageous, what those layabouts in Accounts are getting away with!' fumed Mr Harris.

(vi) I said I'd give it a go myself, if they weren't sufficiently on the ball.

## Exercise 3

Level: EASY

Your company is considering the possibility of exporting its products to Russia, and a report is to be prepared for management.

*Task*

Write out the information given in the table below in narrative form, using approximately 100 words, for inclusion in the report as a subsection entitled 'Russia: country data'. (The information given is considered to be sufficiently recent for this purpose.)

| ***Russia*** | |
|---|---|
| Area (1,000 sq km) | 17,075 |
| % of former Soviet Union (FSU) territory | 76 |
| Population 1990 mid-yr (millions) | 148.3 |
| % of total population of FSU | 51 |
| Growth rate 1980-90 (percent) | 0.4 |
| Density 1990 (per sq km) | 8.7 |
| GDP, at current market prices, 1989 (bn roubles) | 573.1 |
| Industry as % of total GDP | 46.6 |
| Services as % of total GDP | 37.8 |
| Agriculture as % of total GDP | 15.6 |
| Exports in 1989 (bn roubles) | 140.9 |
| Oil and gas exports as % of total | 31.2 |

*Source: World Bank*

(GDP = Gross Domestic Product)

## Exercise 4

Level: MODERATE

You have been asked to contribute to a section of a report on the effects of regulations on the activities of public enterprises in the period before privatisation. (You do not need to have worked in the public sector to complete this Exercise.)

The table below identifies the main changes to the competitive environment faced by the largest enterprises in the nationalised industry sector from the late 1970s to 1990.

| *Enterprise* | *Main changes to competitive environment* |
|---|---|
| British Airways | Routes liberalised: North Atlantic (1977); UK (1982); Europe (1984 onwards). |
| British Coal | Better defined contracts for supply to electricity generators (1989); reduced protection from imports of coal and from gas. |
| British Gas | Gas Act (1985); partial competition in supply to industrial customers. |
| British Rail | Increased competition from deregulated buses (1986), coaches (1980) and domestic aviation (1982). |
| British Steel | Unwinding of EC steel quotas (1980 onwards). |
| British Telecom | Liberalisation of apparatus (1981); value added services (1981) and second terrestrial carrier (1982). |
| Electricity supply | Energy Act (1983): partial competition in supply. Electricity Act (1986); competition in supply (1990). |
| Post Office | Courier services deregulated (1981). Restructured into separate businesses. |

*Source: Treasury Bulletin*

*Task*

Present the information given in the table in narrative (non-tabular) form.

## Exercise 5

Level: MODERATE

(a) How many forms do you handle or have to fill in at work, at school or college, or in connection with other matters? List as many sorts of forms as you can think of.

(b) Get hold of any copies of forms that you might have filled and kept: you might also be able to get samples of forms you use regularly at work, or bank or Post Office forms (eg opening an account, insurance, redirection of mail, application for driving test). If you really cannot find any, there may be subscription or order forms in a newspaper or magazine that you could cut out.

Study them.

Are they easy to fill in? Are all the items to be input clearly identified and explained?

What features do they have in common? Are they good forms, do you think?

Try drafting your own version, if you think you could 'iron out the bugs'. Improvement?

## Exercise 6

Level: MODERATE

Try using the 'task time log' work measurement form on the next page to 'measure' a week's study or work. Pick two or three 'projects' (eg an assignment, or piece of work, your 'spring cleaning' at home - or whatever).

Break them down into component tasks (eg read a chapter of a text, draft an answer plan, complete the answer). You can now enter the project name and task names on the form.

Also add as 'tasks' (with 'Project:' left blank): 'telephone' and 'recreation'.

*TASK TIME LOG*

NAME ______________________ WEEK BEGINNING | | | 19 |

DEPARTMENT ______________________

| TASK \ DAY | | | Mon | Tue | Wed | Thu | Fri | TOTAL |
|---|---|---|---|---|---|---|---|---|
| 1 | Project: | P | | | | | | |
| | Task: | A | | | | | | |
| 2 | Project: | P | | | | | | |
| | Task: | A | | | | | | |
| 3 | Project: | P | | | | | | |
| | Task: | A | | | | | | |
| 4 | Project: | P | | | | | | |
| | Task: | A | | | | | | |
| 6 | Project: | P | | | | | | |
| | Task: | A | | | | | | |
| 7 | Project: | P | | | | | | |
| | Task: | A | | | | | | |
| 8 | Project: | P | | | | | | |
| | Task: | A | | | | | | |
| 9 | Project: | P | | | | | | |
| | Task: | A | | | | | | |
| 10 | Project: | P | | | | | | |
| | Task: | A | | | | | | |
| 11 | Project: | P | | | | | | |
| | Task: | A | | | | | | |
| 12 | Project: | P | | | | | | |
| | Task: | A | | | | | | |
| TOTAL | | P | | | | | | |
| | | A | | | | | | |

P= Planned time taken

A= Actual time taken

For each task you've identified, enter the amount of time you expect the task to take you (P) each day. When you've completed the task, or day, enter the time it actually took (A).

Fill in your weekly totals for each task (in the right hand column) and your daily totals for all the tasks of each day (in the bottom row).

### Class Exercise 1

Level: MODERATE

A report is to be prepared on the utilisation and remuneration of accounting staff in your organisation. The organisation has divisions in all regions of England. One section of the report is to discuss comparability with national trends and is to include a subsection headed 'Accountants' regional salary trends 1993 to 1995'. This subsection is to discuss the percentage levels of salary increases awarded in different regions from 1993 to 1994 and from 1994 to 1995.

*Task*

Write the subsection entitled 'Accountants' regional salary trends 1993 to 1995' for inclusion in the report.

The subsection should contain 100 - 150 words of narrative. The chart below, derived from survey results published in *The Independent,* is available to you. The information shown in this chart should be used as the basis of your subsection, although no chart can be used in the report itself.

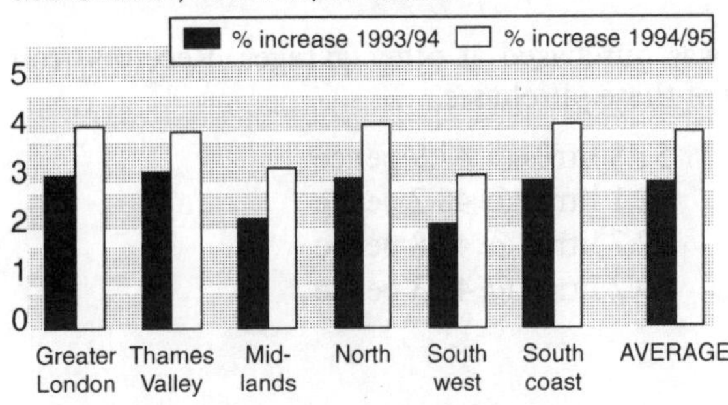


## Class Exercise 2

Level: MODERATE

Identify the company or individual to which the following reports, returns or forms must be sent on completion. (Be as specific as possible.)

(a) An application for change of use of a building

(b) Notification of a change of keeper of a commercial vehicle

(c) Application for support under the Loan Guarantee Scheme for businesses

(d) A report of a fatal accident at work

## Class Exercise 3

Level: ADVANCED

You are working for the Certifying Auditor of the Larkmoor Valley Community Bus, whose Secretary has asked for his Fuel Duty Rebate Form for the period 1 July 19X3 to 30 June 19X4 to be completed for him. This form is submitted to the Department of Transport by bus operators.

Extracts from the official Department of Transport Fuel Duty Rebate Form are set out at the end of this exercise.

*Task*

Complete the details required on the Sections of the form given, using the information available.

*Information available*

Larkmoor Valley Community Bus (LVCB) operates three services (Service Nos 1, 2 and 3, with registration numbers 6742/PF/C1, 6740/PF/C1 and 6741/PF/C1 respectively, using a single 14-seat bus which runs on unleaded petrol. LVCB has been claiming Fuel Duty Rebate in respect of each of its three services for several years.

The length of a single one way journey eligible for rebate is 24.7 kilometres for service 1, 37.2 kilometres for service 2 and 60.0 kilometres for service 3.

Details of actual dead kilometres and actual local service distances in kilometres are given below. (Dead kilometres are kilometres run empty or 'light' to or from termini, or between intermediate points on a route or between routes, which are an inherent part of the operation of the local service in question.) All of the actual local service kilometres shown are eligible.

| *Service number* | *Actual dead kms* | *Actual local service (km)* |
|---|---|---|
| 1 | 433.0 | 4,742.8 |
| 2 | 641.9 | 5,940.2 |
| 3 | 722.4 | 8,114.7 |

The bus odometer showed that total kilometres travelled by the vehicle were 23,424.7 at the end of the day on 30 June 19X3 and 45,313.1 at the end of the day on 30 June 19X4.

LVCB has a contract with a local garage under which unleaded petrol for the bus was supplied at 46.1 pence per litre for the whole of the year to 30 June 19X4. The total spent on fuel at the garage was £1,455.42.

On a few occasions, fuel was purchased at other garages. Receipts from these other garages show the following details of these purchases.

| | |
|---|---|
| 14.9.X3 | 51.8 litres @ 47.9 pence |
| 11.11.X3 | 42.1 litres @ 48.2 pence |
| 4.3.X4 | 52.7 litres @ 47.8 pence |
| 7.4.X4 | 39.2 litres @ 49.3 pence |

| For official use only |
|---|
| Operator LVCB |
| File X7/2247/N5 |

# Fuel Duty Rebate

## Section 1 - Fuel duty rebate

Actual claim for the period - from 1-7-93 to 30-6-94

Type of fuel used: UNLEADED

(A separate certified claim must be submitted in respect of each type of fuel used (eg diesel, petrol, unleaded petrol or liquid petroleum gas)).

Kilometres (Kms) for the period

| From | To | Eligible local service Kms | Dead Kms | Total eligible Kms for which rebate is claimed |
|---|---|---|---|---|
| 1.7.93 | 30.6.94 | 18797.7 | 1797.3 | 20595 |

## Section 2

Include ALL the Kms and ALL the fuel for the vehicles concerned whether run on eligible services or not.

| | | |
|---|---|---|
| a. Total Kms during this claim period of all vehicles used for at least 50% of their Kms on eligible local services. | 21888.4 | Kilometres |
| b. Total fuel issued during this claim period to all vehicles used for at least 50% of their Kms on eligible local services. | 3342.8 | Litres |

## Section 3

Analysis of actual Kms by route

| 1 Your service number | 2 Registration Numbers as given in Notices & Proceedings | 3 For services not previously claimed the issue No of the Notices & Proceedings in which they appeared | 4 Length of single one-way journey eligible for rebate (Kms) | 5 Actual local service Kms | 6 Actual dead Kms | 7 Actual total eligible Kms on which rebate is claimed (Column 5 + Column 6) |
|---|---|---|---|---|---|---|
| 1 | 6742/PF/C1 | | 24.7 km | 4742.8 | 433.0 | 5175.8 |
| 2 | 6740/PF/C1 | | 37.2 km | 5940.2 | 641.9 | 6582.1 |
| 3 | 6741/PF/C1 | | 60.0 km | 8114.7 | 722.4 | 8837.1 |
| Totals | | | | 18797.7 | 1797.3 | 20,595 |

***These totals must be the same as those entered in Section 1***

(Continue on a separate sheet if necessary; any extra sheets should be endorsed by the Certifying Auditor)

# 9 Costs, standard costs and performance

## *Objectives of this session*

This session provides practice in the following skills and techniques.

- **The use of cost per unit as a performance indicator**
- **The use of standard units of inputs and outputs**
- **Understanding productivity as a performance measure**

***Practice exercises***

## Exercise 1

Level: EASY

A direct labour employee's wage in week 5 consists of:

| | | £ |
|---|---|---|
| (a) | basic pay for normal hours worked, 36 hours at £4 per hour = | 144 |
| (b) | pay at the basic rate for overtime, 6 hours at £4 per hour = | 24 |
| (c) | overtime shift premium, with overtime paid at time-and-a-quarter ¼ × 6 hours × £4 per hour = | 6 |
| (d) | a bonus payment under a group bonus (or 'incentive') scheme: bonus for the month = | 30 |
| | Total gross wages in week 5 for 42 hours of work | 204 |

Which costs are direct? Are any indirect?

## Exercise 2

Level: EASY

(a) Suggest a cost unit appropriate to a hospital.

(b) Suggest *one* suitable cost unit and *two* cost centres for a college of further education.

## Exercise 3

Level: MODERATE

Within the costing system of a manufacturing company the following types of expense are incurred.

| *Reference number* | |
|---|---|
| 1 | Cost of oils used to lubricate production machinery |
| 2 | Motor vehicle licences for lorries |
| 3 | Depreciation of factory plant and equipment |
| 4 | Cost of chemicals used in the laboratory |
| 5 | Commission paid to sales representatives |
| 6 | Salary of the secretary to the finance director |
| 7 | Trade discount given to customers |
| 8 | Holiday pay of machine operatives |
| 9 | Salary of security guard in raw material warehouse |
| 10 | Fees to advertising agency |
| 11 | Rent of finished goods warehouse |
| 12 | Salary of scientist in the laboratory |
| 13 | Insurance of the company's premises |
| 14 | Salary of supervisor working in the factory |
| 15 | Cost of typewriter ribbons in the general office |
| 16 | Protective clothing for machine operatives |

*Tasks*

(a) Place each expense within the following classifications.

Production overhead
Selling and distribution overhead
Administration overhead
Research and development overhead

Each type of expense should appear only once in your answer. You may use the reference numbers in your answer.

(b) Give three reasons why direct production labour cost might be regarded as a fixed cost rather than as a variable cost.

## Exercise 4

Level: MODERATE

A company has established standard times of operations for the calculations of standard product costs. Suggest one other use of these standard times.

## Exercise 5

Level: MODERATE

The standard time allowed for product X is 2 hours and the standard labour rate is £5.00 per hour. Last month the output of product X was 1,000 units and the actual hours worked were 1,850. What was the value in standard hours of last month's production?

## Exercise 6

Level: MODERATE

Five employees work in the production department of Products Ltd. The rate of pay for each is £8 per hour in normal time and £10.75 per hour in overtime.

Data for the department covering a four week period is as follows.

| | *Hours* |
|---|---|
| Contractual hours (5 × 4 × 37.5) | 750 |
| Public holidays | 37.5 |
| Annual holidays | 105 |
| Certified absence through sickness | 45 |
| Other absences | 15 |
| Overtime hours worked | 108 |

Available hours are the number of hours for which workers are available for work. Disregarding employer's national insurance contributions, calculate the total cost per available hour for the department in the four-week period.

## Exercise 7

Level: MODERATE

A company currently remunerates its factory workers on a time basis and is now considering the introduction of alternative methods of remuneration. The following information relates to two employees for one week.

| | *Y* | *Z* |
|---|---|---|
| Hours worked | 44 | 40 |
| Rate of pay per hour | £3.50 | £4.50 |
| Units of output achieved | 480 | 390 |

The time allowed for each unit of output is seven standard minutes. For purposes of piecework calculations each minute is valued at £0.05.

*Tasks*

(a) Calculate the earnings of each employee where earnings are based on the following.

(i) Piecework rates with earnings guaranteed at 80% of pay calculated on an hourly basis.

(ii) Premium bonus scheme in which bonus (based on 75% of time saved) is added to pay calculated on an hourly basis.

(b) Describe two situations in which the time basis of remuneration is likely to be more appropriate than piecework schemes.

## Exercise 8

Level: MODERATE

The following information relates to two hospitals for the year ended 31 December 19X5.

| | *St Matthew's* | *St Mark's* |
|---|---|---|
| Number of in-patients | 15,400 | 710 |
| Average stay per in-patient | 10 days | 156 days |
| Total number of out-patient attendances | 130,000 | 3,500 |
| Number of available beds | 510 | 320 |
| Average number of beds occupied | 402 | 307 |

| Cost analysis | St Matthew's In-patients £ | St Matthew's Out-patients £ | St Mark's In-patients £ | St Mark's Out-patients £ |
|---|---|---|---|---|
| A *Patient care services* | | | | |
| 1 Direct treatment services and supplies (eg nursing staff) | 6,213,900 | 1,076,400 | 1,793,204 | 70,490 |
| 2 Medical supporting services | | | | |
| 2.1 Diagnostic (eg pathology) | 480,480 | 312,000 | 22,152 | 20,650 |
| 2.2 Other services (eg occupational therapy) | 237,160 | 288,600 | 77,532 | 27,790 |
| B *General services* | | | | |
| 1 Patient related (eg catering) | 634,480 | 15,600 | 399,843 | 7,700 |
| 2 General (eg administration) | 2,196,760 | 947,700 | 1,412,900 | 56,700 |

*Note*. In-patients are those who receive treatment whilst remaining in hospital. Out-patients visit hospital during the day to receive treatment.

*Tasks*

(a) Prepare separate statements for each hospital for each cost heading.

(i) Cost per in-patient day, £ to two decimal places.

(ii) Cost per out-patient attendance, £ to two decimal places.

(b) Calculate for each hospital the bed-occupation percentage.

(c) Comment briefly on your findings.

**Exercise 9** Level: MODERATE

What is a significant digit code? Give examples.

**Exercise 10** Level: MODERATE

What is the difference between 'production' and 'productivity'? (Answer in approximately 50 words.)

**Exercise 11** Level: ADVANCED

Lawry Ltd distributes its goods to a regional dealer using a single lorry. The dealer's premises are 40 kilometres away by road. The lorry has a capacity of 10½ tonnes, and makes the journey twice a day fully loaded on the outward journeys and empty on the return journeys. The following information is available for a 4-week budget control period, period 8, during 19X4.

| | |
|---|---|
| Petrol consumption | 8 kilometres per 5 litres petrol |
| Petrol cost | £0.36 per litre |
| Oil | £8 per week |
| Driver's wages and national insurance | £140 per week |
| Repairs | £72 per week |
| Garaging | £4 per day (based on a 7-day week) |
| Cost of lorry when new (excluding tyres) | £18,750 |
| Life of the lorry | 80,000 kilometres |
| Insurance | £650 per annum |
| Cost of a set of tyres | £1,250 |
| Life of a set of tyres | 25,000 kilometres |
| Estimated sale value of lorry at end of its life | £2,750 |
| Vehicle licence cost | £234 per annum |
| Other overhead costs | £3,900 per annum |

The lorry operates on a five-day week.

*Task*

You are asked to carry out the following tasks.

(a) Prepare a statement to show the total costs of operating the vehicle in period 8, 19X4 analysed into running costs and standing costs.

(b) Calculate the vehicle cost per kilometre, and the cost per tonne/kilometre in the period.

(c) Using the costs you have calculated, what would be the charge, to cover full costs, for a special delivery of 6 tonnes on each of an outward and a return journey (so the lorry is loaded both going out and returning) to a destination 120 kilometres away, if costs are estimated:

  (i) on a kilometres travelled basis;
  (ii) on the basis of tonne/kilometres carried?

## Class Exercise 1

Level: MODERATE

(a) Explain what you understand by the term 'cost unit'.

(b) What might be an appropriate cost unit for each of the following?

  (i) Steelworks
  (ii) Hospital
  (iii) Professional accounting office
  (iv) Sales representatives' expenses within a specific organisation
  (v) Restaurant

## Class Exercise 2

Level: MODERATE

A warehousing department of a company uses the following two indicators.

$$\text{Operating efficiency \%} = \frac{\text{Holding costs}}{\text{Value of issues}}$$

$$\text{Activity efficiency \%} = \frac{\text{Average stock value}}{\text{Sales turnover}}$$

(a) Does a fall in operating efficiency % mean that operating efficiency has improved or worsened?

Improved/Worsened

(Circle your choice.)

(b) Does a fall in activity efficiency % means that activity efficiency has improved or worsened?

Improved/Worsened

(Circle your choice.)

# 10 Reporting performance. Analysing results

## *Objectives of this session*

This session provides practice in the following skills and techniques.

- **Accounting for transactions between separate units of the organisation**
- **Consolidating information about costs and revenues derived from different units of the organisation in standard form**
- **Analysis of results by different divisions, services, departments, products, processes or sales areas**

### Exercise 1

Level: EASY

Explain, in approximately 100 words, the terms 'profit centre' and 'transfer price'.

### Exercise 2

Level: MODERATE

Iron Foundry Division produces cast iron moulds which are transferred to Steel Division within the same group for use in the manufacture of steel rods for sale to the oil industry.

The iron foundry has a smelting process from which molten iron is drawn and further processed to produce the cast iron moulds which each weigh 20 tonnes. The iron smelters may be operated at one of three capacity levels. The total annual operating costs of the smelting process (including raw material) are as follows.

| Capacity | 100% | 80% | 60% |
|---|---|---|---|
| Output (tonnes) | 250,000 | 200,000 | 150,000 |
| Total annual operating cost (£'000) | 45,500 | 37,000 | 28,500 |

Within the smelting process, the variable costs per tonne are constant for all capacity levels. The capacity costs include a wholly fixed element and some stepped costs which fall by £1,000,000 for each 20% fall in capacity from the 100% capacity level.

In addition to the smelting process costs, the Iron Foundry Division incurs other costs. There are (i) variable production costs of £450 per mould and (ii) fixed production costs for the additional processes of £2,500,000 at 100% capacity, falling by £250,000 at 80% capacity and a further £500,000 at 60% capacity. Iron Foundry Division also has £3,500,000 of group costs apportioned to it irrespective of the capacity level at which it operates.

Transfers of moulds to Steel Division represent the sole business of Iron Foundry Division. Moulds are transferred at total cost (based on capacity level utilised) plus 20% markup.

*Task*

You are required to prepare a summary showing the cost analysis and transfer price per mould at capacity levels of 100%, 80% and 60%.

### Exercise 3

Level: MODERATE

Allmain Ltd is a retailer of electrical goods. It operates from a single retail outlet in which 50% of the floor space is occupied by the white goods department which employs three members of staff, with the remaining floor space being split equally between the TV department and the audio department, which employ one and two members of staff respectively.

VAT of 17½% is chargeable on all sales, which were as follows together with cost of sales figures in the quarter ending 31 March 19X3. (The figures exclude VAT.)

| *Department* | *Sales (net of VAT)* | *Cost of sales* |
|---|---|---|
| | £ | £ |
| White goods | 44,500 | 28,500 |
| TV | 25,850 | 16,200 |
| Audio | 20,900 | 13,850 |

Expenses were as follows.

| | £ |
|---|---|
| Selling and distribution | 10,250* |
| Administration | 9,480 |
| Heating and lighting | 2,211 |
| Rent and rates | 5,200 |

*Of which £5,362 related to white goods, £2,252 to TV and £2,636 to audio.

Administration costs are allocated in the ratio 3:2:2 between white goods, TV and audio departments. Heating and lighting, and rent and rates, are allocated in proportion to the floor space occupied by each department.

*Tasks*

(a) Prepare the figures to be included in the departmental management accounts for the quarter ending 31 March 19X3, showing the following for each department and overall.

Sales
Gross profit
Expenses
  Selling and distribution
  Administration
  Heating and lighting
  Rent and rates
Net profit before interest and taxation

(b) Calculate the gross profit percentage and the net profit percentage for each department and overall.

*Note on methods*

$$\text{Gross profit percentage} = \frac{\text{Gross profit}}{\text{Sales}} \times 100$$

$$\text{Net profit percentage} = \frac{\text{Net profit before interest and taxation}}{\text{Sales}} \times 100$$

(c) Indicate what figures might be shown in the management accounts alongside the figures you have calculated for the purposes of comparison.

## Exercise 4 — Level: MODERATE

The company for whom you work as a trainee accountant is a distributor of office equipment and operates through three departments, namely, Communications Equipment, Data Processing Equipment and Office Furniture. The directors have decided to publish a house magazine for distribution to staff and you have been asked by the chief accountant to suggest appropriate forms of diagrammatic presentation for conveying financial information in a meaningful but non-technical manner. Selected for inclusion in the first issue of the magazine is information concerning:

(a) total sales income for each of the past five years;

(b) the value of sales by each department for each of the past five years;

(c) the proportions of total sales contributed by the various geographical areas, namely United Kingdom (Southern, Midlands and Northern Regions), and Export (Europe and Other countries), for the year recently ended.

*Task*

Submit sketches of appropriate types of diagram for each of the above and add brief comments explaining your choices.

## Information for Exercises 5 to 8

You are employed by Delicious Confectionery Ltd, a company whose chocolate department sells six different types of chocolate bar. These bars are referred to in management information using the abbreviations WIZ, PER, MRL, WLD, BKR and CRK. Value added tax at 17½% is charged on all sales.

Your manager presents you with costing statements for the department for the year as set out below.

| | *WIZ* | *PER* | *MRL* | *WLD* | *BKR* | *CRK* |
|---|---|---|---|---|---|---|
| | £ | £ | £ | £ | £ | £ |
| Direct labour | 20,248 | 7,567 | 14,521 | 4,499 | 39,661 | 22,079 |
| Direct materials | 14,210 | 6,991 | 11,100 | 5,217 | 19,147 | 12,269 |
| Variable overheads | 9,410 | 7,292 | 9,622 | 6,414 | 15,003 | 12,241 |
| | 43,868 | 21,850 | 35,243 | 16,130 | 73,811 | 46,589 |
| Fixed costs | 16,320 | 8,160 | 10,200 | 8,160 | 20,400 | 12,240 |
| Total costs | 60,188 | 30,010 | 45,443 | 24,290 | 94,211 | 58,829 |
| Sales (excluding VAT) | 72,421 | 31,229 | 41,522 | 27,611 | 101,019 | 52,722 |
| Profit/(loss) | 12,233 | 1,219 | (3,921) | 3,321 | 6,808 | (6,107) |

She is concerned that production of MRL and CRK should cease.

### Exercise 5 — Level: EASY

Present the data shown above in an alternative format, to show the contribution which each product type makes to fixed costs, and the contribution/sales percentage. Round figures to the nearest tenth of one thousand. Also show the total figures for the whole company.

### Exercise 6 — Level: MODERATE

This Exercise follows on from Exercise 5.

(a) Use graphical presentation techniques (charts) to show how the relative sizes of sales and contribution for Delicious Confectionery Ltd's products compare and the direct labour, direct materials and variable overheads for each product. This can be done by showing for each product how:
Contribution = sales – (direct labour + direct materials + variable overheads)

(b) Show on another chart the total net profit of the company. This can be done by showing on the chart how:
Net profit = total of each product's contributions - total fixed costs

### Exercise 7 — Level: MODERATE

Prepare a revised statement in the same format as that used in Exercise 5 showing what would have been the position if there had been no production of MRL and CRK during the year. Assume that all direct and variable costs for MRL and CRK are now eliminated, and that the total of fixed costs is unchanged and is to be allocated to the remaining product lines in the same proportions as it is now.

### Exercise 8 — Level: MODERATE

(a) Prepare a chart like that prepared in Exercise 6(b) showing total net profit or loss if production of MRL and CRK ceases.

(b) Comment briefly on your findings about what happens if production of MRL and CRK is stopped.

### Class Exercise 1 — Level: EASY

Fill in the words missing from the following statements.

(a) A price charged by one process or department to another or from one member of a group of companies to another is called a ______________.

(b) A difference between planned sales and actual sales is termed a ____________ .

(c) Prime cost is the total of ____________ costs.

### Class Exercise 2 — Level: MODERATE

The Chief Accountant of your company has handed to you the schedule printed below with a request for you to apportion the various expenses on the bases stated in order to ascertain the overhead cost of running each of the four production departments for the financial year just ended.

XYZ Office Furniture Ltd
Production departments' overhead costs
Year ended 30 November 19X9

| *Expense* | *basis (see below)* | *Total* | *Machining* | *Assembly 1* | *Assembly 2* | *Spraying* |
|---|---|---|---|---|---|---|
| | | £ | £ | £ | £ | £ |
| Canteen | 4 | 48,300 | | | | |
| Consumable stores | 2 | 4,485 | | | | |
| Depreciation | 3 | 103,500 | | | | |
| Indirect wages | 4 | 56,350 | | | | |
| Insurance | 3 | 4,140 | | | | |
| Lighting, heating, power | 1 | 7,920 | | | | |
| Plant maintenance | 2 | 19,435 | | | | |
| Rent and rates | 1 | 82,800 | | | | |
| | | 326,930 | | | | |

Apportionment bases

| | | | | | |
|---|---|---|---|---|---|
| 1 | - floor area sq metres | 800 | 1,200 | 1,000 | 600 |
| 2 | - number of machines | 6 | 1 | 2 | 4 |
| 3 | - asset values £'000 | 40 | 60 | 50 | 30 |
| 4 | - number of employees | 12 | 25 | 18 | 15 |

*Task*

Produce a schedule in the above form to meet the Chief Accountant's requirement.

# 11 Measuring performance

## *Objectives of this session*

This session provides practice in the following skills and techniques.

- **Using performance indicators of resource utilisation and profitability**
- **Calculating accurately ratios and performance indicators in accordance with agreed methodology**
- **Using relevant performance and quality measures**

### Information for Exercises 1 and 2

The following (fictitious) figures relate to a public sector rail passenger service operation.

| | *19X1* | *19X2* | *19X3* | *19X4* | *19X5* |
|---|---|---|---|---|---|
| Profit/(loss) as a percentage of receipts | –16.0 | –12.4 | +7.9 | +6.0 | +4.6 |
| Receipts per train mile (£) | 12.18 | 13.41 | 14.26 | 15.42 | 16.49 |
| Total operating expenses per train mile (£) | 14.33 | 15.26 | 13.28 | 15.42 | 16.20 |
| On-board services sales per £'000 of direct operating costs (£) | 2,291 | 2,185 | 2,645 | 2,843 | 2,560 |

An index for general inflation over the period is as follows.

| *Year* | *Inflation index* |
|---|---|
| 19X1 | 97.8 |
| 19X2 | 101.9 |
| 19X3 | 106.9 |
| 19X4 | 115.2 |
| 19X5 | 126.1 |

### Exercise 1

Level: EASY

A table of performance indicators is to be prepared adjusting the above figures *where appropriate* to real terms (based on 19X5 pounds).

*Tasks*

(a) Identify how any of the above figures should be adjusted and carry out any adjustment necessary, using the inflation index given.

(b) Comment briefly on your methods.

### Exercise 2

Level: MODERATE

(a) Calculate receipts per £'000 of total operating expenses from the information shown above, showing your workings clearly.

(b) Answer briefly the following question from your colleague: 'Shouldn't the figures you've calculated [in (a)] be adjusted for the effect of inflation?'

### Exercise 3

Level: MODERATE

The figures below relate to a retailing division of a diversified company at which you are employed.

| | *19X1* | *19X2* | *19X3* | *19X4* |
|---|---|---|---|---|
| | £'000 | £'000 | £'000 | £'000 |
| Sales | 1,288 | 1,342 | 1,378 | 1,473 |
| Cost of sales | 729 | 792 | 859 | 928 |
| Gross profit | 559 | 550 | 519 | 545 |
| Operating expenses | 245 | 250 | 290 | 310 |
| Net profit before interest and taxation | 314 | 300 | 229 | 235 |
| Number of employees | | | | |
| Selling | 18 | 19 | 20 | 20 |
| Other | 5 | 7 | 8 | 8 |
| Retail Prices Index (RPI) average | 202 | 207 | 214 | 217 |

It was remarked at a recent management meeting that the results for 19X4 continue an unbroken record of sales growth since 19X1. However, it was also questioned whether the record of sales volume growth per employee was so good. In particular, the performance of individual sales staff was questioned.

*Tasks*

You have been asked to produce a summary in tabular form showing:

(a) real sales growth;

(b) appropriate productivity measures (real sales per selling employee and real sales per employee);

(c) gross profit percentage;

(d) operating expenses, expressed in real terms;

(e) net profit percentage.

Comment briefly on the results.

## Information for Exercises 4 and 5

You have recently been appointed as Accounting Technician attached to the headquarters of the Alphabet Group plc, with special responsibility for monitoring the performances of the companies within the group. Each company is treated as an investment centre and every month produces an operating statement for the group headquarters. Summaries of the statements for companies X and Y, which make similar products selling at similar prices, for the last month showed a typical situation.

EXTRACT FROM COMPANY MONTHLY OPERATING STATEMENTS

| | | *X* | *Y* |
|---|---|---|---|
| | | £'000 | £'000 |
| | Sales | 600 | 370 |
| less | Variable costs | 229 | 208 |
| | = Contribution | 371 | 162 |
| less | Controllable fixed overheads | | |
| | (including depreciation on company assets) | 65 | 28 |
| | = Controllable profit | 306 | 134 |
| less | Apportioned group costs | 226 | 119 |
| | = Net profit | 80 | 15 |
| | Company assets | £6.4m | £0.9m |
| | Estimated return on capital employed | | |
| | (on annual basis) | 15% | 20% |

Although both companies are earning more than the target return on capital of 12%, there is pressure on interest rates which means that this rate must be increased soon and the board is concerned at the relatively low return achieved by X.

## Exercise 4

Level: MODERATE

Compare and discuss the relative performance of the two companies as shown in the summarised operating statements above.

## Exercise 5

Level: MODERATE

(a) Re-draft the summarised operating statements given above using residual income, an alternative performance measure to return on capital employed, and interpret them against a background of rising interest rates.

*Notes on methods*

Residual income = divisional profit less imputed interest cost.

The imputed interest cost is calculated as the cost of capital (12%) × divisional investment (company assets).

(b) Compare the use of return on capital employed and the residual income measure used in (a) to assess the performance of investment centres.

### Exercise 6

Level: MODERATE

In the public sector, individual performance targets fall under the four headings of financial performance, volume of output, quality of service and efficiency.

*Task*

Identify the heading under which each of the following measures would fall.

(a) Time taken to deal with applications in the Drivers and Vehicles Licensing Agency.

(b) Revenue from ancillary services provided by a hospital (eg shops in hospitals, television rental services) to cover costs.

(c) 20% reduction in the cost of common services over a five year period.

(d) 95% of work completed to time and to standards (Military Survey)

(e) Target of 1,300,000 placings in the year for unemployed people into jobs of which 16% are to be long term claimants, 2.4% to be people with disabilities and 34% are to be unemployed people in inner cities. (Employment Service Agency)

### Exercise 7

Level: MODERATE

Give one example each of a performance indicator which might measure:

(a) the productivity of a coal mine;
(b) the effectiveness of a newspaper advertisement for a staff vacancy.

### Exercise 8

Level: MODERATE

The Testing Office is a (fictitious) executive agency in the public (government) sector which carries out tests required by law. Since 19X0 the agency has operated a unit cost target of £26.00 per test at 19X0 prices. The agency uses a general price deflator to convert from cash to real terms. Unit costs in cash terms and the value of the general price deflator for the years 19X0 to 19X5 are as follows.

| | *Unit costs (cash)* £ | *General price deflator* |
|---|---|---|
| 19X0 | 25.78 | 1.00 |
| 19X1 | 24.57 | 1.05 |
| 19X2 | 27.58 | 1.11 |
| 19X3 | 29.97 | 1.18 |
| 19X4 | 32.06 | 1.22 |
| 19X5 | 32.13 | 1.24 |

In which of the years 19X0 to 19X5 did the agency beat its unit cost target?

### Exercise 9

Level: MODERATE

The following figures are extracted from the accounts of Hockley plc.

| | 19X2 | | 19X1 | |
|---|---|---|---|---|
| | £m | £m | £m | £m |
| Fixed assets | | 25.4 | | 17.8 |
| Current assets | 10.4 | | 17.4 | |
| Creditors: amounts falling due within one year | 10.0 | | 12.6 | |
| Net current assets | | 0.4 | | 4.8 |
| | | 25.8 | | 22.6 |
| Creditors: amounts falling due after more than one year | | (15.4) | | (16.2) |
| Provisions for liabilities and charges | | (1.6) | | (1.0) |
| | | 8.8 | | 5.4 |
| Turnover | | 35.6 | | 28.2 |
| Operating profit | | 6.0 | | 4.6 |
| Profit on ordinary activities before tax | | 5.2 | | 4.2 |
| Profit on ordinary activities after tax | | 3.6 | | 3.0 |
| Extraordinary items | | 0.4 | | 0.4 |
| Profit for the financial year | | 4.0 | | 3.4 |

The company calculates the following profitability ratios.

$$\text{Return on capital employed (ROCE)} = \frac{\text{Operating profit}}{\text{Shareholders' funds}}$$

$$\text{Profit margin} = \frac{\text{Operating profit}}{\text{Turnover}}$$

$$\text{Asset turnover} = \frac{\text{Turnover}}{\text{Shareholders' funds}}$$

Shareholders' funds are taken to be the average of the opening and closing balance sheet figures for fixed assets plus net current assets.

*Tasks*

(a) Calculate the following figures for 19X2.

(i) ROCE
(ii) Profit margin
(iii) Asset turnover

(b) What is the mathematical relationship between the three ratios calculated above?

**Class Exercise 1** Level: MODERATE

The following data relate to an express passenger coach service operator over the last three years 19X1 to 19X3. The operation faced new competition on its main routes from another coach company in 19X3.

| | 19X1 | 19X2 | 19X3 |
|---|---|---|---|
| Total passenger kilometres | 54,748,148 | 61,273,617 | 64,788,492 |
| Total loaded coach kilometres | 1,921,261 | 1,964,325 | 1,981,380 |
| Total receipts (fares) (£) | 3,119,842 | 3,799,421 | 4,145,014 |
| Total operating expenses (£) | 2,327,452 | 2,458,123 | 2,531,770 |

*Notes.* Loaded coach kilometres represent distance travelled when coaches are in service. Coaches have a full capacity of either 46 or 48.

*Tasks*

(a) From the information above, calculate the following performance indicators for each of the three years.

(i) Receipts per loaded coach kilometre (in pounds, to two decimal places)

(ii) Receipts per passenger kilometre (in pence, to one decimal place)

(iii) Passenger kilometres per loaded coach kilometre (average coach load) (in number of passengers, to one decimal place)

(iv) Total operating expenses per loaded coach kilometre (in pounds, to two decimal places)

(b) Adjust the indicators to real terms, *where it is appropriate to do so*, using the following price index.

| | *Index* |
|---|---|
| 19X1 | 93.2 |
| 19X2 | 96.1 |
| 19X3 | 100.0 |

(c) Comment briefly on trends in the performance indicators you have calculated.

### Class Exercise 2

Level: MODERATE

Among the main concepts in performance measurement in public sector agencies are *economy*, *efficiency*, *effectiveness* and *quality*.

(a) *Economy*

An economy measure describes the extent to which the cost of inputs is minimised. Economy is usually measured in terms of money saved by switching to cheaper inputs.

(b) *Efficiency*

An efficiency measure describes the relationship between the output of an agency and the associated inputs.

(c) *Effectiveness*

An effectiveness measure reveals the extent to which objectives have been met: it makes no reference to cost.

(d) *Quality*

A quality measure describes the usefulness or value of a service. A quality of service measure relates to the delivery of that service to the recipient. (HM Treasury)

The information which follows concerns Wennsmead Hospital, a fictitious hospital.

(a) 90 per cent of those on which THR (total hip replacement) operations are performed are fully ambulant for at least 5 years following surgery.

This is a performance measure of:

economy/efficiency/effectiveness/quality.

(Choose one only.)

(b) Average THR cost (unit cost of output) is £5,500.

This is a performance measure of:

economy/efficiency/effectiveness/quality.

(Choose one only.)

(c) The average waiting time for THR after being put on the waiting list is three months.

This is a performance measure of:

economy/efficiency/effectiveness/quality.

(Choose one only.)

# 12 The VAT charge and VAT records

## *Objectives of this session*

This session provides practice in the following skills and techniques.

- **Computing the VAT on a series of transactions**
- **Completing a VAT return from a set of invoices**
- **Identifying valid and invalid tax invoices**
- **Identifying the records which must be kept for VAT purposes**

### Exercise 1

Level: EASY

In January 19X3, Roger paints a picture using materials which he acquired at negligible cost. In March 19X3, he sells it to Susan for £400 excluding VAT.

Susan immediately buys materials to frame the picture from Thomas for £70.50 including VAT, and frames it. She sells it to Victor in May 19X3 for £700 excluding VAT. Victor keeps the picture.

Roger, Susan and Thomas are all registered for VAT and account for VAT quarterly. Roger and Thomas have tax periods ending at the end of June, September, December and March and Susan's tax periods end at the end of August, November, February and May.

*Task*

Show all payments to HM Customs & Excise arising from these transactions, and the due dates.

### Exercise 2

Level: MODERATE

Bernini plc has made sales and purchases as indicated by the following documents.

BERNINI PLC

| | |
|---|---|
| Jacob Ltd | 1 Long Lane |
| 45 Broad Street | Anytown |
| Newtown | AN4 5QP |
| NE7 2LH | VAT reg no GB 212 7924 36 |

Invoice no. 324
Date: 4 July 19X5
Tax point: 4 July 19X5

| | *VAT rate* % | £ |
|---|---|---|
| Sale of 300 pens | 17.5 | 600.00 |
| Sale of 400 calculators | 17.5 | 2,500.00 |
| Total excluding VAT | | 3,100.00 |
| Total VAT at 17.5% | | 542.50 |
| Total payable within 30 days | | 3,642.50 |

BERNINI PLC

| | |
|---|---|
| Brahms GmbH | 1 Long Lane |
| Peterstr 39 | Anytown |
| Hamburg | AN4 5QP |
| Germany | VAT reg no GB 212 7924 36 |

VAT reg no DE 99369326 5
Invoice no. 325
Date: 5 July 19X5
Tax point: 5 July 19X5

| | *VAT rate* % | £ |
|---|---|---|
| Sale of 500 rulers | 0.0 | 50.00 |
| Sale of 2,000 calculators | 0.0 | 12,500.00 |
| Total excluding VAT | | 12,550.00 |
| Total VAT at 0.0% | | 0.00 |
| Total payable within 30 days | | 12,550.00 |

BERNINI PLC

Michael plc
12 Narrow Road
Oldtown
OL4 7TC

1 Long Lane
Anytown
AN4 5QP
VAT reg no GB 212 7924 36

Invoice no. 326
Date: 24 August 19X5
Tax point: 24 August 19X5

| | *VAT rate* % | £ |
|---|---|---|
| Sale of 700 staplers | 17.5 | 756.00 |
| Sale of 3,000 rulers | 17.5 | 300.00 |
| Total excluding VAT | | 1,056.00 |
| Total VAT at 17.5% | | 184.80 |
| Total payable within 30 days | | 1,240.80 |

BERNINI PLC

Jacob Ltd
45 Broad Street
Newtown
NE7 2LH

1 Long Lane
Anytown
AN4 5QP
VAT reg no GB 212 7924 36

Credit note no. 28
Date: 18 September 19X5

| | *VAT rate* % | £ |
|---|---|---|
| Return of defective goods: 30 calculators (invoice no. 324, date 4 June 19X5) | 17.5 | 187.50 |
| Total credited excluding VAT | | 187.50 |
| Total VAT credited at 17.5% | | 32.81 |
| Total credited including VAT | | 220.31 |

ANGELO PLC

78 Madras Road, London NW14 2JL
VAT registration number 187 2392 49

Invoice to: Bernini plc
1 Long Lane
Anytown
AN4 5QP

Date: 3 August 19X5
Tax point: 3 August 19X5
Invoice no. 873

| | £ |
|---|---|
| Sale of 10,000 pens | 4,200.00 |
| VAT at 17.5% | 735.00 |
| Amount payable | 4,935.00 |
| Terms: strictly net 30 days | |

INVOICE
QUANTUM LTD

To: Bernini plc
1 Long Lane
Anytown
AN4 5QP

472 Staple Street
London
SE4 2QB

VAT reg no 162 4327 56
Date: 7 September 19X5
Tax point: 7 September 19X5
Invoice no. 634

| | *VAT rate* | *Net* | *VAT* | *Gross* |
|---|---|---|---|---|
| | % | £ | £ | £ |
| Sale of 600 calculators | 17.5 | 2,700.00 | 472.50 | 3,172.50 |
| Sale of 1,000 rulers | 17.5 | 80.00 | 14.00 | 94.00 |
| | | 2,780.00 | 486.50 | 3,266.50 |

£3,266.50 is payable by 7 October 19X5. Interest will be charged thereafter at 1.5% per month.

Input VAT for the VAT period ended 30 June 19X5 was overstated by £800.

*Task*

Complete the following VAT return for Bernini plc.

**Value Added Tax Return**
For the period
01 07 X5 to 30 09 X5

For Official Use

Registration number: 212 7924 36

Period: 09 X5

You could be liable to a financial penalty if your completed return and all the VAT payable are not received by the due date.

Due date: 31 10 X5

For Official Use

BERNINI PLC
1 LONG LANE
ANYTOWN
AN4 5QP

Your VAT Office telephone number is 0123-4567

Before you fill in this form please read the notes on the back and the VAT Leaflet *"Filling in your VAT return"*. Fill in all boxes clearly in ink, and write 'none' where necessary. Don't put a dash or leave any box blank. If there are no pence write "00" in the pence column. Do not enter more than one amount in any box.

| For official use | | Box | £ | p |
|---|---|---|---|---|
| | VAT due in this period on sales and other outputs | 1 | | |
| | VAT due in this period on acquisitions from other EC Member States | 2 | | |
| | Total VAT due (the sum of boxes 1 and 2) | 3 | | |
| | VAT reclaimed in this period on purchases and other inputs (including acquisitions from the EC) | 4 | | |
| | Net VAT to be paid to Customs or reclaimed by you (Difference between boxes 3 and 4) | 5 | | |
| | Total value of sales and all other outputs excluding any VAT. Include your box 8 figure | 6 | | 00 |
| | Total value of purchases and all other inputs excluding any VAT. Include your box 9 figure | 7 | | 00 |
| | Total value of all supplies of goods and related services, excluding any VAT, to other EC Member States | 8 | | 00 |
| | Total value of all acquisitions of goods and related services, excluding any VAT, from other EC Member States | 9 | | 00 |

**Retail schemes.** If you have used any ot the schemes in the period covered by this return, enter the relevant letter(s) in this box.

If you are enclosing a payment please tick this box.

DECLARATION: You, or someone on your behalf, must sign below.

I, .................................................................. declare that the
(Full name of signatory in BLOCK LETTERS)
information given above is true and complete.

Signature.................................................. Date .................. 19 ..........

**A false declaration can result in prosecution.**

## Exercise 3

Level: ADVANCED

Klopstock Ltd holds the following invoices from suppliers.

(a)

ALTONA plc

VAT reg no 337 4849 26

Klopstock Ltd
32 Verse Street
Greentown
GN4 8PJ

Invoice no. 3629
Date: 6 May 19X7
Tax point: 6 May 19X7

| | £ |
|---|---|
| Sale of 12,500 tea services | 50,000 |
| VAT at 17.5% | 8,750 |
| Total | 58,750 |

Terms: strictly net 14 days

(b)

HEINE LTD

1 Market Square
Bluetown
BL1 8VA

Klopstock Ltd
32 Verse Street
Greentown
GN4 8PJ

Invoice no.
Date: 12 June 19X7
Tax point: 12 June 19X7

| | *Net* | *VAT* | *Total* |
|---|---|---|---|
| | £ | £ | £ |
| 4,000 cups | 2,000.00 | 350.00 | 2,350.00 |
| 8,000 saucers | 2,500.00 | 437.50 | 2,937.50 |
| 3,500 cookery books | 5,880.00 | 0.00 | 5,880.00 |
| | 10,380.00 | 787.50 | 11,167.50 |

5% discount if paid within 21 days.

(c)

MANN & CO
36 Lubeck Street, Gatestown. GN2 SY4

VAT reg no 499 3493 27

Date: 15 June 19X7

30 wine glasses sold for £35.25 including VAT at 17.5%.

(d)

| VAT reg no 446 9989 57 | | | KLEIST PLC |
|---|---|---|---|
| Date: 16 June 19X7 | | | 254 Metric Street |
| Tax point: 16 June 19X7 | | | Ruletown |
| Invoice no. 328 | | | RL3 7CM |
| Klopstock Ltd | | | |
| 32 Verse Street | | | |
| Greentown | | | |
| GN4 8PJ | | | |
| *Sales of goods* | | | |
| *Type* | *Quantity* | *VAT rate* % | *Net* £ |
| Plates | 700 | 17.5 | 700.00 |
| Mats | 800 | 17.5 | 240.00 |
| Leaflets | 4,000 | 0.0 | 200.00 |
| Booklets | 1,200 | 0.0 | 120.00 |
| | | | 1,260.00 |
| VAT at 17.5% | | | 156.28 |
| Payable within 60 days | | | 1,416.28 |
| Less 5% discount if paid within 14 days | | | 63.00 |
| | | | 1,353.28 |

*Task*

For each of the above invoices, state whether it is a valid VAT invoice. Give your reasons.

## Exercise 4

Level: MODERATE

Marc runs a hardware shop supplying both tradespeople and the general public, and is registered for VAT. He does not use the cash accounting scheme or any retail scheme. All his purchases and sales are standard rated.

Marc's transactions within a single VAT period included the following.

(a) A retail cash sale for £56.40 including VAT, made using a till. The customer was registered for VAT.

(b) A retail sale on credit for £39.95 including VAT. The debtor paid by cheque two weeks later. The customer was not registered for VAT.

(c) A purchase for £270 plus VAT, paid for by cheque immediately.

*Task*

State what records should be kept reflecting the impact of these transactions, and what they should show.

### Class Exercise 1

Level: MODERATE

Grove Ltd had the following transactions in the quarter ended 31 July 19X7.

| *Date* | *Type* | *Net amount* | *VAT rate* |
|---|---|---|---|
| | | £ | % |
| 2 May | Purchase | 4,200 | 17.5 |
| 7 May | Purchase | 6,700 | 17.5 |
| 12 May | Sale | 10,000 | 0.0 |
| 12 May | Sale | 3,900 | 17.5 |
| 22 May | Sale | 12,800 | 17.5 |
| 29 May | Sale | 1,400 | 0.0 |
| 7 June | Purchase | 20,000 | 0.0 |
| 8 June | Purchases returned | 500 | 17.5 |
| 20 June | Sale | 2,300 | 0.0 |
| 23 June | Sale | 5,500 | 17.5 |
| 4 July | Sales returned | 800 | 0.0 |
| 8 July | Purchase | 730 | 17.5 |
| 14 July | Purchases returned | 120 | 0.0 |
| 22 July | Sale | 1,700 | 0.0 |
| 31 July | Sales returned | 340 | 17.5 |

All returns of goods are evidenced by credit notes for both the net price and (where applicable) the VAT. All returns related to current period transactions, except for the return on 8 June.

On the previous period's VAT return, output VAT was overstated by £1,450 and input VAT was understated by £520.

*Task*

Prepare Grove Ltd's VAT account for the quarter.

### Class Exercise 2

Level: ADVANCED

Valley Ltd has incurred the following expenses. Only the documentation noted is held. All amounts are shown including VAT.

| *Ref* | *Item* | *Documentation* | *Amount* |
|---|---|---|---|
| | | | £ |
| (a) | Purchases of goods | Full VAT invoice (Valley Ltd's registration number not shown) | 82.25 |
| (b) | Purchases of goods | Less detailed VAT invoice | 105.75 |
| (c) | Car park charge | None | 10.00 |
| (d) | Purchases of goods | Full VAT invoice (Valley Ltd's address not shown) | 869.50 |
| (e) | Purchases of goods | Less detailed VAT invoice | 98.70 |
| (f) | Computer repair services | Full VAT invoice (total price excluding VAT not shown) | 383.05 |

*Task*

Compute the amount of VAT which Valley Ltd may recover as input VAT.

# 13 The computation and administration of VAT

### *Objectives of this session*

This session provides practice in the following skills and techniques.

- **Preparing a VAT invoice for several different supplies**
- **Computing deductible input VAT when some exempt supplies are made**
- **Preparing a VAT return from a list of transactions**
- **Computing the default surcharge**

## Exercise 1

Level: EASY

Pippa Ltd supplied the following goods and services to Gold Ltd on 12 May 19X2. All amounts exclude any VAT. All amounts are totals, not unit costs.

| | Quantity | £ |
|---|---|---|
| Personal computer | 1 | 980 |
| Microscopes | 3 | 360 |
| Books | 20 | 200 |
| Periodicals | 500 | 450 |
| Insurance | | 1,200 |
| Medical treatment services | | 400 |

*Task*

Complete the following invoice for all these supplies, giving only the figures which must be shown on VAT invoices and the overall totals with and without the cash discount.

PIPPA LIMITED
32 Hurst Road,
London NE20 4LJ
VAT reg no 730 4148 37

To: Gold Ltd
75 Link Road
London NE25 3PQ

Date: 12 May 19X2
Tax point: 12 May 19X2
Invoice no. 2794

| *Item* | *Quantity* | *VAT rate* % | *Net* £ | *VAT* £ |
|---|---|---|---|---|
| *Sales of goods* | | | | |

*Terms: 30 days, 4% discount if paid within 10 days.*

## Exercise 2

Level: MODERATE

Worth plc had the following sales and purchases in the three months ended 31 December 19X2. All amounts exclude any VAT, and all transactions were with United Kingdom traders.

| | £ |
|---|---|
| Sales | |
| Standard rated | 450,000 |
| Zero rated | 237,000 |
| Exempt | 168,000 |
| Purchases | |
| Standard rated | |
| Attributable to taxable supplies | 300,000 |
| Attributable to exempt supplies | 75,000 |
| Unattributable | 240,000 |
| Zero rated | 4,200 |
| Exempt | 7,900 |

*Task*

Compute the figures which would be entered in boxes 1 to 5 of Worth plc's VAT return for the period.

## Exercise 3

Level: MODERATE

Suzanne Smith is a trader who uses the cash accounting scheme. Some of her sales are standard rated, some are zero rated and some are exempt. Transactions for which the sale, the purchase or the receipt or payment of cash fell in the three months ended 31 August 19X4 are as follows. All amounts include any VAT. No input VAT is attributable to any particular type of supply. There are no transactions with anyone outside the United Kingdom.

| *Date of transaction* | *Date cash received or paid* | *VAT rate* % | *Amount* £ |
|---|---|---|---|
| *Sales* | | | |
| 14.5.X4 | 2.6.X4 | 17.5 | 270.35 |
| 29.5.X4 | 15.6.X4 | 17.5 | 420.00 |
| 2.6.X4 | 2.6.X4 | 17.5 | 620.74 |
| 4.6.X4 | 7.6.X4 | 0.0 | 540.40 |
| 10.6.X4 | 22.6.X4 | 0.0 | 680.18 |
| 14.6.X4 | 14.6.X4 | 17.5 | 200.37 |
| 27.6.X4 | 4.7.X4 | Exempt | 180.62 |
| 4.7.X4 | 12.7.X4 | 0.0 | 235.68 |
| 10.7.X4 | 12.7.X4 | 17.5 | 429.32 |
| 21.7.X4 | 21.7.X4 | Exempt | 460.37 |
| 31.7.X4 | 20.8.X4 | Exempt | 390.12 |
| 3.8.X4 | 3.8.X4 | 0.0 | 220.86 |
| 12.8.X4 | 2.9.X4 | Exempt | 800.28 |
| 20.8.X4 | 23.8.X4 | 17.5 | 350.38 |
| 25.8.X4 | 5.9.X4 | 17.5 | 380.07 |
| *Purchases* | | | |
| 20.5.X4 | 4.6.X4 | 17.5 | 521.44 |
| 3.6.X4 | 3.6.X4 | 17.5 | 516.13 |
| 22.6.X4 | 1.7.X4 | 0.0 | 737.48 |
| 1.7.X4 | 4.7.X4 | 17.5 | 414.68 |
| 12.7.X4 | 12.7.X4 | Exempt | 280.85 |
| 4.8.X4 | 1.9.X4 | 17.5 | 779.13 |
| 23.8.X4 | 7.9.X4 | 17.5 | 211.73 |

Suzanne also took fuel from the business (without payment) for use in her 1,700 cc petrol engined car, which she does not drive for business purposes. The scale charge is £252.

*Task*

Complete the following VAT return for Suzanne Smith.

**Value Added Tax Return**
For the period
01 06 X4 to 31 08 X4

For Official Use

Registration number: 483 8611 98
Period: 08 X4

You could be liable to a financial penalty if your completed return and all the VAT payable are not received by the due date.

MS S SMITH
32 CASE STREET
ZEDTOWN
ZY4 3JN

Due date: 30 09 X4

For Official Use

Your VAT Office telephone number is 0123-4567

Before you fill in this form please read the notes on the back and the VAT Leaflet *"Filling in your VAT return"*. Fill in all boxes clearly in ink, and write 'none' where necessary. Don't put a dash or leave any box blank. If there are no pence write "00" in the pence column. Do not enter more than one amount in any box.

| For official use | | Box | £ | p |
|---|---|---|---|---|
| | VAT due in this period on sales and other outputs | 1 | | |
| | VAT due in this period on acquisitions from other EC Member States | 2 | | |
| | Total VAT due (the sum of boxes 1 and 2) | 3 | | |
| | VAT reclaimed in this period on purchases and other inputs (including acquisitions from the EC) | 4 | | |
| | Net VAT to be paid to Customs or reclaimed by you (Difference between boxes 3 and 4) | 5 | | |
| | Total value of sales and all other outputs excluding any VAT. Include your box 8 figure | 6 | | 00 |
| | Total value of purchases and all other inputs excluding any VAT. Include your box 9 figure | 7 | | 00 |
| | Total value of all supplies of goods and related services, excluding any VAT, to other EC Member States | 8 | | 00 |
| | Total value of all acquisitions of goods and related services, excluding any VAT, from other EC Member States | 9 | | 00 |
| | **Retail schemes.** If you have used any ot the schemes in the period covered by this return, enter the relevant letter(s) in this box. | | | |

If you are enclosing a payment please tick this box.

DECLARATION: You, or someone on your behalf, must sign below.

I, .................................................................... declare that the
(Full name of signatory in BLOCK LETTERS)
information given above is true and complete.

Signature.................................................... Date .................. 19 ..........

**A false declaration can result in prosecution.**

### Exercise 4

Level: ADVANCED

Lazy Ltd often submits its VAT returns and payments late, as shown in the following schedule.

| *Quarter ended* | *VAT due* | *Return and payment* |
|---|---|---|
| | £ | |
| 30.6.X2 | 4,000 | On time |
| 30.9.X2 | 2,500 | Late |
| 31.12.X2 | 5,000 | On time |
| 31.3.X3 | 4,000 | On time |
| 30.6.X3 | 5,000 | Late |
| 30.9.X3 | 4,500 | Late |
| 31.12.X3 | 7,000 | On time |
| 31.3.X4 | 3,500 | Late |
| 30.6.X4 | 4,500 | Late |
| 30.9.X4 | 500 | Late |
| 31.12.X4 | 3,600 | On time |

*Task*

Compute the default surcharges arising from the above.

### Class Exercise 1

Level: MODERATE

In the quarter ended 31 December 19X5, Roland plc made sales as follows. All amounts given exclude any VAT.

| | £ |
|---|---|
| Standard rated sales | 3,100,000 |
| Zero rated sales | 670,000 |
| Exempt sales | 1,920,000 |

The VAT on purchases attributable to standard rated and zero rated sales was £400,000. The VAT on purchases attributable to exempt sales was £160,000. In addition, VAT on purchases not attributable to any particular type of sale was £37,000.

The company also supplied itself with standard rated stationery (not related to any particular type of supply) costing £40,000 before VAT, a typical quarterly figure. Materials used to make those supplies cost £9,400 including VAT at the standard rate.

*Task*

Compute the amount payable to or recoverable from HM Customs & Excise in respect of the quarter.

### Class Exercise 2

Level: ADVANCED

In one VAT period, Heimat plc has the following transactions in goods which would be standard rated if supplied in the UK. All amounts exclude any VAT, and all goods sold are sent to the buyers' countries by Heimat plc.

(a) Buys goods from a UK supplier for £12,000

(b) Sells goods to an Italian customer for £7,300. The customer's VAT registration number is shown on the invoice

(c) Sells goods to a Danish customer for £470. The customer is not registered for VAT, and the relevant Danish VAT rate is 25%

(d) Sells goods to an Australian customer for £2,500

(e) Buys goods from a VAT registered German supplier for £3,000. The invoice shows Heimat plc's VAT registration number and the goods are transferred to the UK

*Task*

Compute the VAT payable to or recoverable from HM Customs & Excise for the period.

# *Solutions to practice exercises*

## SOLUTIONS TO SESSION 1 PRACTICE EXERCISES

Suggested solutions to Practice Exercises 1 to 5 in this session are set out below. There are often different ways to reach a satisfactory solution to an exercise and there may be no single right answer. Having completed the exercises for yourself, compare your approach to ours and identify any errors you may have made.

### Solution to Exercise 1

(a) The implication is that the business is organised primarily on a geographical basis.

(b) The junior manager might report, not to an area boss responsible for all the business's activities in an area, but directly to a regional or central finance department.

### Solution to Exercise 2

It sounds as if Autobuttle Ltd employs a matrix management structure. In this, authority is divided. The example highlights one of the disadvantages (dual authority) of matrix structures but there are advantages in flexibility, too.

### Solution to Exercise 3

Non-profit orientated organisations, like clubs or charities, need to prepare accounts to keep a record of the sums received from supporters and paid to beneficiaries. Also, if such an organisation pays out more than it receives it will eventually cease to function. Reports are used to assess performance, and to communicate information. Moreover, non profit making organisations still have assets and liabilities. Charities need to send returns to the Charities Commission.

### Solution to Exercise 4

(a) Accounting systems are used to record and manipulate data, and to report information.

(b) An organisation's bank will obviously know about the organisation's cash transactions. However the bank will also wish to know about the organisation's trading activity generally. This information gives a general indication as to the security of any loans or overdrafts.

### Solution to Exercise 5

The example given might be, for example, a return made to a trade association or a return to a government agency, such as Census of Production returns required by the Office for National Statistics.

## SOLUTIONS TO SESSION 2 PRACTICE EXERCISES

Suggested solutions to Practice Exercises 1 to 5 in this session are set out below. There are often different ways to reach a satisfactory solution to an exercise and there may be no single right answer. Having completed the exercises for yourself, compare your approach to ours and identify any errors you may have made.

### Solution to Exercise 1

Your solution should cover the points set out below.

Good information is:

(a) relevant to the needs of the user;
(b) relevant to the purpose of the user;
(c) complete for its purpose, and not including irrelevant matter;
(d) accurate within the requirements of the user;
(e) reliable, and capable of verification;
(f) timely, given its purpose;
(g) communicated in an appropriate manner;
(h) cost-effective.

### Solution to Exercise 2

(a) There is no 'definitive' list, but your answer probably included most of the following outside agencies.

- (i) Inland Revenue.
- (ii) Customs and Excise.
- (iii) Department of Trade and Industry (Companies House).
- (iv) The organisation's bankers.
- (v) Local government agencies (eg planning departments; grant-awarding agencies).
- (vi) Shareholders.

(b) Your answer will of course depend upon the organisation which you chose. For example, if you work for a health authority, you should know that the authority must make returns to the Department of Health. If you worked for a bank, you would probably know that the bank must make certain returns to the Bank of England, while a building society must report to the Building Societies Commission. In some industries, trade associations require members to submit regular returns to confirm that they continue to meet the requirements of membership.

(c) Your answer probably included some of the following examples.

- (i) If you are a taxpayer, the Inland Revenue may require you to complete an annual tax return.
- (ii) The law requires householders in Britain to complete forms listing residents for the purposes of the electoral register.
- (iii) Every ten years, householders are required (again, by law) to complete census return forms. The last Census was in 1991.
- (iv) If you need to make an insurance claim, your insurer will require you to complete a form, with a detailed report on the accident, damage or loss which has occurred.
- (v) The Association of Accounting Technicians expects you to maintain Student Record Sheets and an Accounting Portfolio.

### Solution to Exercise 3

Obviously your answer will depend upon the type of department you work in, and its particular procedures.

Bear in mind that many management reports include a lot of numbers, with perhaps very little commentary. A common fault with internal reports is to include too much detail, with numbers shown with too many digits.

## Solution to Exercise 4

Your answer could include three items from the following list, although other items might also be given.

(a) Numbers employed.
(b) Numbers of starters and leavers.
(c) Hours worked.
(d) Vacancies.
(e) Numbers of absentees.

## Solution to Exercise 5

(a) The processing of information (or data) consists of four main stages.

(i) *Receipt or gathering of the data* - ie 'input' to the system. There are various sources of information, and relevant data will have to be obtained, selected and put into a format that will be useful for further processing. In the preparation of an employee's wage payment slip, for example, time sheets or machine logs will be consulted to see how much work the employee has put in: relevant details (hours worked, units produced) will be selected. Information will be gathered from payroll records as to the appropriate wage system and scale for the employee.

(ii) *Recording and manipulation of the data.* Whether done manually, or by a computer, this will involve 'inputting' data into 'hard' form, and then analysing or handing it in various ways: selection, sorting and arrangement, calculation, reproduction etc. In our example, of the pay advice slip, hours worked will be recorded alongside pay rate per hour, together with deductions for tax and national insurance, bonuses and allowances etc. Calculations will then be made as to total taxable pay, amount of tax payable on it, and so the net amount which the employee will 'take home'. The information will be copied so that both the employer and the employee have it.

(iii) *Storage of information.* Basically, this means 'filing' although again a computer can do it without requiring paper output and storage. Storage also implies 'retrieval', since information should only be kept for a reason - ie that it will be needed for further processing one day. Our employee's wage slip will go into the organisation's files (or computer) and will be retrieved when the organisation is preparing P60 forms at the end of the tax year, and/or putting together a report on the growth of its total wage bill over 5 years etc. (It will also go into the employee's home 'files', so that he can check the details against his P60 certificate, plan his own budget for the coming months based on past take-home pay etc).

(iv) *Communication of information.* Relevant interested parties are finally supplied with the information. The employee gets his pay advice slip with his pay packet.

These four stages can be portrayed in a diagram as below.

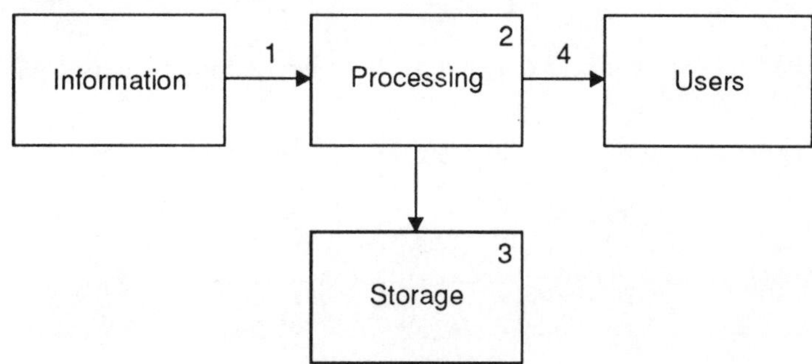


(b) *Internal demand*

*[Three of :]*

(i) Records of transactions for confirmation, later analysis etc.

(ii) Information for planning and decision making. For example, the volume of last month's sales may influence the level of this month's stock holding.

(iii) Routine information for operating decisions. For example, a customer placing an order, where the information about quantities, prices, delivery dates/addresses etc initiates action; or the information about hours worked or units produced which goes into payroll calculations.

(iv) Information about performance to be compared with plans, budgets and forecasts for the purposes of control and correction.

Each of these *types* of demand will offer many different specific examples.

*External demand*

*[Three of :]*

(i) Customers, who require delivery information, invoices and/or statements requesting payment, information about the product in order to decide whether to buy it etc.

(ii) Suppliers and sub-contractors, who require instructions, purchase orders, confirmation etc.

(iii) Parties interested in the financial performance of the organisation - eg the shareholders, investors etc.

(iv) Outside agencies requiring information for surveys, or for their own activities - eg the Inland Revenue (tax), HM Customs and Excise (VAT), DSS (National Insurance contributions), Health and Safety Executive.

## SOLUTIONS TO SESSION 3 PRACTICE EXERCISES

Suggested solutions to Practice Exercises 1 to 7 in this session are set out below. There are often different ways to reach a satisfactory solution to an exercise and there may be no single right answer. Having completed the exercises for yourself, compare your approach to ours and identify any errors you may have made.

### Solution to Exercise 1

(a) The statement does not make clear whether the increase in sales is an increase in sales volume or sales value (or both). Were more pairs of footwear sold, or was the total sales revenue higher? Of course, the statement would also convey more information if a figure were put on the increase.

The words 'not as much as clothing' are ambiguous. Does this mean that sales of footwear are increasing at a slower percentage rate than sales of clothing? Or perhaps it means that the cash increase in footwear sales is lower than the cash increase in clothing sales.

(b) Turnover may have shown a spectacular rise because two years ago sales were particularly low. It should also be indicated whether the percentage rise is in cash terms, after adjustment for general inflation, or after adjustment for changes in prices in the company's industry.

### Solution to Exercise 2

(a) The number of diagrams in a textbook is a *discrete variable*, because it can only be counted in whole number steps. You cannot, for example, have 26½ diagrams or 47.32 diagrams in a book.

(b) Whether or not a can possesses a sticker is an *attribute*. It is not something which can be measured. A can either possesses the attribute or it does not.

(c) How long an athlete takes to run a mile is a *continuous variable*, because the time recorded can in theory take any value, for example 4 minutes 2.0643 seconds.

(d) The percentage obtained in an examination is a *discrete variable*, taking whole number values between 0% and 100%. The discrete values might include half percent steps, if the examination is the sort where you could be awarded ½%. But it would not be possible to score, say, 62.32%, so the variable is not continuous.

(e) The height of a telegraph pole is a *continuous variable*.

### Solution to Exercise 3

(a), (b) and (d).

*Economic Trends* and the *Monthly Digest of Statistics* are both sources of secondary data provided by the government. Historic sales data were not collected specifically for the preparation of forecasts, therefore they are also secondary data. Data collected through personal interview for a particular project are primary data.

### Solution to Exercise 4

(a) *The Annual Abstract of Statistics*

Most government statistics of economic and business data are brought together into a main reference book, the *Annual Abstract of Statistics* published by the Office for National Statistics (ONS). The information is provided by a number of government departments. Notes and definitions of the statistical data provided are contained in the publication.

(b) *The Monthly Digest of Statistics*

This is an abbreviated version of the *Annual Abstract* and is published monthly.

(c) *Financial Statistics*

This is published monthly by the ONS. It gives a range of useful financial and monetary statistics for the UK including:

(i) financial statistics of central government and local authority borrowings;
(ii) banking statistics;
(iii) income and profits of companies and capital issues;
(iv) interest rates;
(v) gold and foreign currency reserves;
(vi) the balance of payments.

(d) *Economic Trends*

This is also published monthly by the ONS. It contains figures and graphs on topics which include production, labour, external trade, investment, prices, wages and earnings.

(e) *The Employment Gazette*

This is published monthly by the ONS. It provides figures on labour and on prices including:

(i) retail prices;
(ii) employment;
(iii) unemployment;
(iv) unfilled job vacancies;
(v) wage rates;
(vi) overtime and short time working;
(vii) stoppages at work.

## Solution to Exercise 5

(a) *Employment Gazette*, published monthly by the ONS.

(b) The *Monthly Digest of Statistics*, published monthly by the ONS.

(c) The *Balance of Payments* ('the pink book') published annually by the ONS.

(d) *Population Trends*, published quarterly by the ONS.

(e) Employment Gazette (see (a)).

## Solution to Exercise 6

(a) Regional employment statistics could help the company in deciding where to locate a new factory.

(b) Earnings data will show the company's management how the company employees' wages compare with the national or regional averages.

## Solution to Exercise 7

(a) The RPI indicates the general level of price inflation for consumers, and therefore provides a yardstick by which the prices faced by the company can be assessed, including input prices such as materials and labour as well as selling prices.

(b) The RPI is secondary data because it has been compiled by the government from price survey information and not for the company's own purposes.

## SOLUTIONS TO SESSION 4 PRACTICE EXERCISES

Suggested solutions to Practice Exercises 1 to 4 in this session are set out below. There are often different ways to reach a satisfactory solution to an exercise and there may be no single right answer. Having completed the exercises for yourself, compare your approach to ours and identify any errors you may have made.

### Solution to Exercise 1

(a) The graph is extremely unclear and could be improved in the following ways.

(i) The axes are not labelled. The horizontal axis (the x axis) should represent the independent variable, being time in this case. So it should be labelled 19X0, 19X1, ... 19X5. Similarly the vertical axis (the y axis) should represent the dependent variable, being profits in this case.

(ii) An indication should be given of whether the profits have been adjusted in any way. In particular, it would be useful to have profit figures adjusted for inflation, so that the changes in profits shown by the graph are all changes in real terms.

(iii) The graph has no heading. Every graph should have a title explaining what variables are being displayed against each other. In the given case the heading could be 'Profits of divisions W, X, Y and Z during the period 19X0 to 19X5'.

(iv) Crosses should be marked on the graph to indicate the points plotted. The given graph merely has smooth curves which presumably pass through where the crosses should be. Marking the actual points will help the reader of the graph to judge how much estimation has been carried out in trying to draw the best curves through the points.

(v) A graph should not be overcrowded with too many lines. Graphs should always give a clear, neat impression. The given graph has too many lines on it for a clear impression to be given.

(vi) If the data to be plotted are derived from calculations, there should be a neat table showing the actual figures accompanying the graph, stating the source of the figures. No such information is given here.

(b) We wish to show a time series of information for four divisions over a six year period. Possible methods of presenting the data are:

(i) pie charts;
(ii) component bar charts;
(iii) simple historigrams (like the graph in the question but properly constructed).

On balance, a vertical component bar chart would seem to be the most suitable in this instance. This would show how total profits (of all divisions together) have changed from year to year and what are the components of each year's total.

### Solution to Exercise 2

*Tutorial note.* Your answers to parts (b) and (c) may have been slightly different from those given here, but they should not have been very different, because the data points lay very nearly along a straight line.

(a) *SPG Ltd - Scatter diagram of production and factory costs, November 19X8-October 19X9*

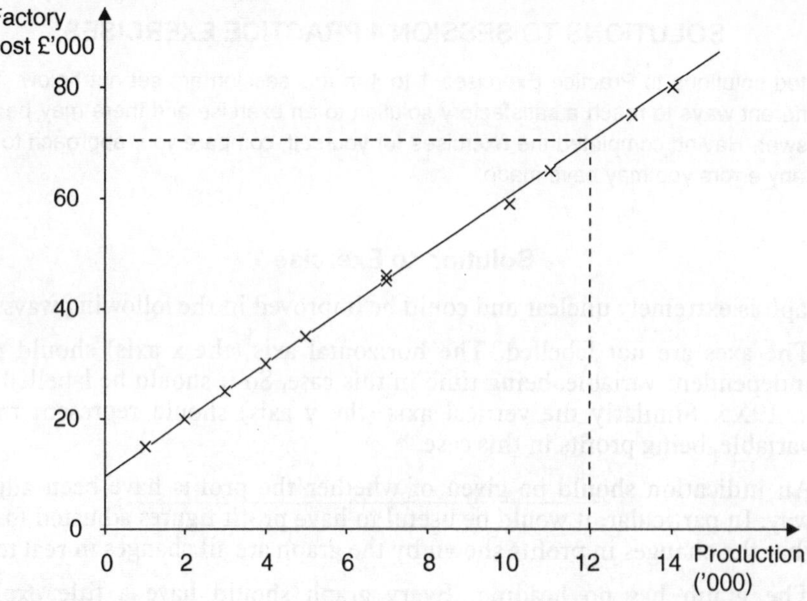


(b) (i) **The estimated factory cost for a production of 12,000 spodgets is £70,000.**

(ii) **The monthly fixed costs are indicated by the point where the line of best fit meets the vertical axis (costs at zero production). The fixed costs are estimated as £10,000 a month.**

## Solution to Exercise 3

*Tutorial note.* **You may have found cost curve II and the curve for total costs difficult to draw neatly. In such cases you may find it best to join the dots with straight lines and add a note that ideally a smooth curve should be drawn.**

(a)

| *Maximum stock* | *Cost I* | *Cost II* | *Total cost* |
|---|---|---|---|
| | | <u>*225,000*</u> | |
| *x* | *2.5x* | *x* | *I + II* |
| | £ | £ | £ |
| 50 | 125 | 4,500 | 4,625 |
| 100 | 250 | 2,250 | 2,500 |
| 200 | 500 | 1,125 | 1,625 |
| 250 | 625 | 900 | 1,525 |
| 300 | 750 | 750 | 1,500 |
| 350 | 875 | 642.9 | 1,517.9 |
| 400 | 1,000 | 562.5 | 1,562.5 |
| 500 | 1,250 | 450 | 1,700 |
| 600 | 1,500 | 375 | 1,875 |

(b) **In the graph, the straight line for cost I shows that this cost rises linearly with x. The curve for cost II shows that this cost falls as x rises, though the rate of fall gradually diminishes. The total cost curve falls then rises. The optimum value of x is where total costs are minimised, at x = 300.**

(c) **See graph. A curve for the total costs would have exactly the same shape as the curve for costs I and II, but would be £600 higher for all values of x.**

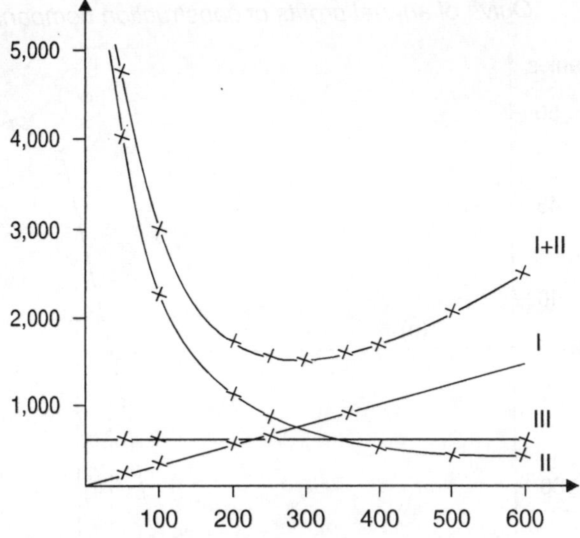


## Solution to Exercise 4

*Tutorial note.* Part (c) illustrates the fact that figures other than quartiles can be obtained from an ogive. The value exceeded by any required proportion of the population can be found.

(a)

| *Profit £m* *Under* | *No. companies (frequency)* | *'Less than' cumulative frequency* |
|---|---|---|
| −5 | 2 | 2 |
| 0 | 0 | 2 |
| 5 | 2 | 4 |
| 10 | 3 | 7 |
| 15 | 6 | 13 |
| 20 | 11 | 24 |
| 25 | 13 | 37 |
| 30 | 9 | 46 |
| 35 | 4 | 50 |
| | 50 | |

See the graph below.

(b) First quartile: 25% of companies have a profit less than this. $Q_1$ is £14,600,000.

Second quartile or median: 50% of companies have a profit less than this. $Q_2$ is £20,400,000.

Third quartile: 75% of companies have a profit less than this. $Q_3$ is £25,700,000.

(c) The top 10% of companies by profit are the top five companies.

The 90th percentile profit is £29,400,000.

(d) 5.8 companies achieved a profit of less than £8,000,000.

19.6 companies achieved a profit of less than £18,000,000.

19.6 − 5.8 = 13.8 companies achieved a profit between £8,000,000 and £18,000,000.

Thus, 10 × 13.8 = 138 companies out of 500 are estimated to have had an annual profit between £8,000,000 and £18,000,000 in 19X8.

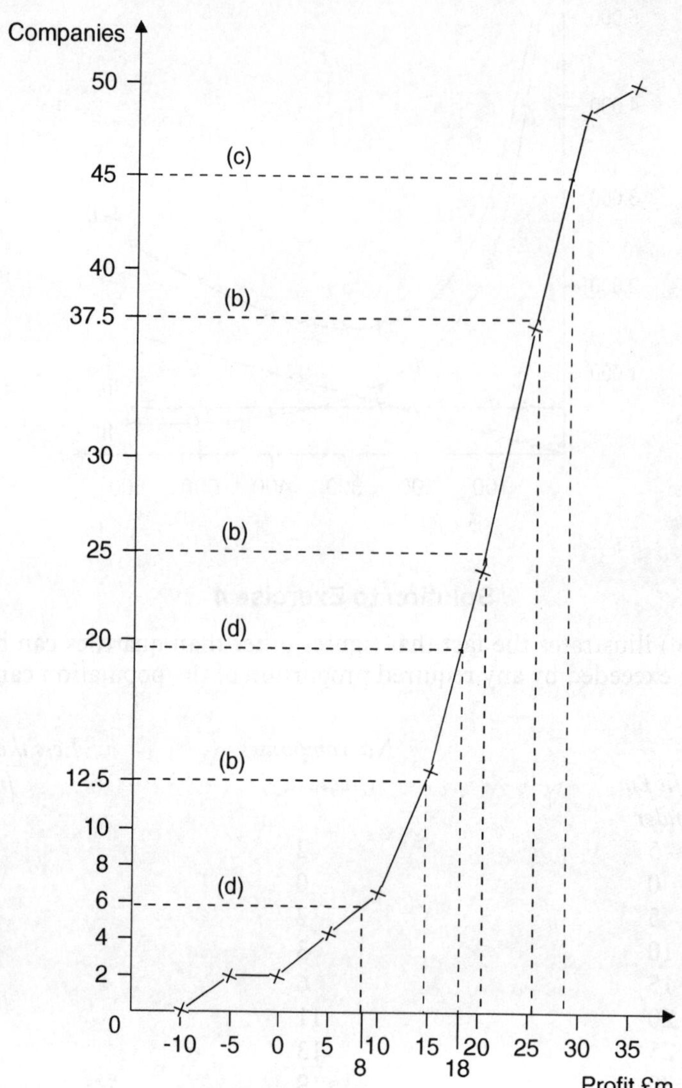

Ogive of annual profits of construction companies
Companies
50
45
40
37.5
30
25
20
12.5
10
8
6
4
2
0
(c)
(b)
(b)
(d)
(b)
(d)
-10
-5
0
5
10
15
20
25
30
35
8
18
Profit £m

## SOLUTIONS TO SESSION 5 PRACTICE EXERCISES

Suggested solutions to Practice Exercises 1 to 12 in this session are set out below. There are often different ways to reach a satisfactory solution to an exercise and there may be no single right answer. Having completed the exercises for yourself, compare your approach to ours and identify any errors you may have made.

### Solution to Exercise 1

The main rules of good tabular presentation are as follows.

(a) The table should be given a clear title.

(b) Each column should be clearly labelled, with a description as well as the units in which the items are being measured.

(c) There must not be too many columns, or else the reader of the table will become confused. A maximum of ten columns could be a guideline to follow.

(d) Where appropriate there should be clear sub-totals.

(e) A total column may be presented. This would normally be the extreme right hand column.

(f) A total figure at the bottom of each column of figures is often advisable.

(g) Figures should not be given to too many significant figures. An element of rounding will often make the table easier to follow, with significant information being highlighted.

(h) The source of the data should be stated, so that the reader could refer to that source if he wished to take his analysis further.

### Solution to Exercise 2

*New telephone installations (by company)*

| *Company* | *Installations (thousands)* | | | |
|---|---|---|---|---|
| | *1960* | *1970* | *1980* | *1990* |
| A Co Ltd | 1,810 | 3,248 | 5,742 | 4,932 |
| B Co Ltd | 2,114 | 1,288 | 3,038 | 3,138 |
| C Co Ltd | 448 | 1,618 | 2,228 | 1,506 |
| Others | 874 | 676 | 1,646 | 618 |
| Total | 5,246 | 6,830 | 12,654 | 10,194 |

### Solution to Exercise 3

(a)

| *Company* | *Installations (percentages)* | | | |
|---|---|---|---|---|
| | *1960* | *1970* | *1980* | *1990* |
| A Co Ltd | 34.5 | 47.6 | 45.4 | 48.4 |
| B Co Ltd | 40.3 | 18.8 | 24.0 | 30.8 |
| C Co Ltd | 8.5 | 23.7 | 17.6 | 14.8 |
| Others | 16.7 | 9.9 | 13.0 | 6.0 |
| Total | 100.0 | 100.0 | 100.0 | 100.0 |

(b) A Co Ltd was the second largest installer in 1960, but was the market leader in 1970, 1980 and 1990, with an apparently secure grip on nearly half the market.

B Co Ltd's share of the market dropped sharply between 1960 and 1970, but the company has since been steadily recovering market share.

C Co Ltd did very well between 1960 and 1970, but has not been able to sustain its growth rate, and has lost market share since 1970.

Other companies have maintained a small and variable market share. There is no sign of a serious challenge to the three main companies.

## Solution to Exercise 4

The two dimensions of the table should be:

(a) years;
(b) each group of employees, including a category for 'others'.

It would also be possible to include percentage growth over the years.

The entries in the 'cells' of the table could be actual numbers of employees, percentages of the total work force or both.

*Analysis of employee groups at the Soyuz Insurance Company*

| | *19X0* | | *19X3* | | | *19X6* | | | *19X9* | | |
|---|---|---|---|---|---|---|---|---|---|---|---|
| | *Number empl'd* | *% of total* | *Number empl'd* | *% of total* | *% growth in total* | *Number empl'd* | *% of total* | *% growth in total* | *Number empl'd* | *% of total* | *% growth in total* |
| Sales staff | 1,176 | 28 | 2,372 | 31 | 102 | 4,840 | 38 | 104 | 7,477 | 36 | 54 |
| Actuaries | 1,260 | 30 | 2,448 | 32 | 94 | 3,185 | 25 | 30 | 4,362 | 21 | 37 |
| Accountants | 840 | 20 | 1,607 | 21 | 91 | 2,550 | 20 | 59 | 3,739 | 18 | 47 |
| Other groups | 924 | 22 | 1,223 | 16 | 32 | 2,165 | 17 | 77 | 5,192 | 25 | 140 |
| Total | 4,200 | 100 | 7,650 | 100 | 82 | 12,740 | 100 | 67 | 20,770 | 100 | 63 |

The table shows that there has been a substantial increase in the number of sales staff over the years, with the percentage of employees who are sales staff rising from under 30% in 19X0 to 36% in 19X9. There has been a decrease in the proportion of employees who are actuaries, and a small decrease in the proportion who are accountants. The managing director's concern about the rapid growth in other groups of employees might be justified. The percentage increase in their numbers between 19X6 and 19X9 suggests that efforts to control their numbers have not yet had much success.

## Solution to Exercise 5

(a) The purpose of tabulating data is to make information easier to read and interpret. It is possible to include much information in a relatively compact table, and tables are particularly suitable for numerical data. Organising data into a table with appropriate columns and row headings allows the reader to make comparisons between categories easily.

(b) *Patients seen by doctors 1990 and 1995*

| | *1990* | | | | | | *1995* | | | | | |
|---|---|---|---|---|---|---|---|---|---|---|---|---|
| | *Minor ailment* | | *Major ailment* | | *Total* | | *Minor ailment* | | *Major ailment* | | *Total* | |
| | No | % | No | % | No | % | No | % | No | % | No | % |
| Men | 234 | 9.2 | 416 | 16.3 | 650 | 25.5 | 320 | 11.0 | 430 | 14.8 | 750 | 25.8 |
| Women | 360 | 14.1 | 440 | 17.3 | 800 | 31.4 | 550 | 19.0 | 510 | 17.6 | 1,060 | 36.6 |
| Children | 616 | 24.2 | 484 | 18.9 | 1,100 | 43.1 | 720 | 24.8 | 370 | 12.8 | 1,090 | 37.6 |
| Total | 1,210 | 47.5 | 1,340 | 52.5 | 2,550 | 100.0 | 1,590 | 54.8 | 1,310 | 45.2 | 2,900 | 100.0 |

(c) (i) In 1995, a lower percentage of all patients had major ailments but a higher percentage had minor ailments than in 1990.

(ii) In 1995, a lower percentage of children but a higher percentage of women were seen by doctors than in 1990.

(iii) In 1995, a lower percentage of children patients had major ailments (33.9% as against 44.0%) and a higher percentage of women patients had minor ailments (51.9% as against 45.0%) than in 1990.

## Solution to Exercise 6

We are told what classes to use, so the first step is to identify the lowest and highest values in the data. The lowest value is £25 (in the first row) and the highest value is £73 (in the fourth row). This means that the class intervals must go up to '£70 and under £75'.

We can now set out the classes in a column, and then count the number of items in each class using tally marks.

| *Class interval* | *Tally marks* | *Total* |
|---|---|---|
| £25 and less than £30 | /// | 3 |
| £30 and less than £35 | //// | 4 |
| £35 and less than £40 | ~~////~~ ~~////~~ | 10 |
| £40 and less than £45 | ~~////~~ ~~////~~ ~~////~~ | 15 |
| £45 and less than £50 | ~~////~~ ~~////~~ ~~////~~ /// | 18 |
| £50 and less than £55 | ~~////~~ ~~////~~ ~~////~~ ~~////~~ | 20 |
| £55 and less than £60 | ~~////~~ ~~////~~ /// | 13 |
| £60 and less than £65 | ~~////~~ /// | 8 |
| £65 and less than £70 | ~~////~~ / | 6 |
| £70 and less than £75 | /// | 3 |
| | Total | 100 |

You should be able to *interpret* tabulated data, and express an interpretation in writing. In this example, an interpretation of the data is fairly straightforward.

(a) Commission per assistant for May 19X3 ranged between £25 and £75.

(b) Most commissions were in the middle of this range, with few people earning commissions in the lower and upper ends of the range.

## Solution to Exercise 7

*Tutorial note.* It is good practice to show the source of the data.

| *Superexports plc* | |
|---|---|
| *Sales for the year ended 31 October 19X0* | £'000 |
| Market | |
| European Union | 787 |
| Rest of Europe | 219 |
| North America | 285 |
| Other developed countries | 92 |
| Developing countries | 189 |
| Oil exporting countries | 145 |
| Centrally planned economies | 34 |
| | 1,751 |

*Source: company records*

## Solution to Exercise 8

| *Workings* | *Sales* | | *Degrees* |
|---|---|---|---|
| | £'000 | | |
| European Union | 787 | (787/1,751 × 360) | 162 |
| Rest of Europe | 219 | | 45 |
| North America | 285 | | 58 |
| Other developed countries | 92 | | 19 |
| Developing countries | 189 | | 39 |
| Oil exporting countries | 145 | | 30 |
| Centrally planned economies | 34 | | 7 |
| | 1,751 | | 360 |

*Superexports plc*
*Sales for the year ended 31 October 19X0*

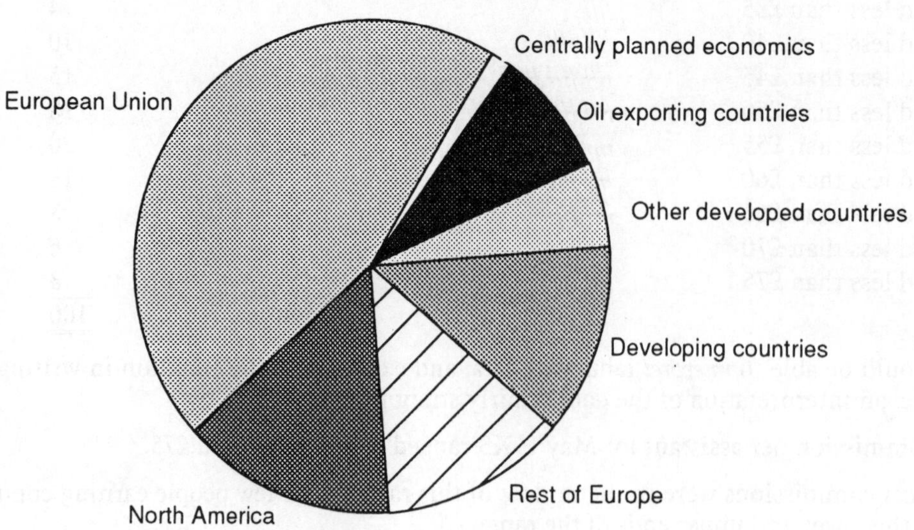


## Solution to Exercise 9

*Tutorial note.* In a percentage component bar chart, all the bars are the same height. Only proportions are indicated, not absolute magnitudes.

(a) The percentages required for the bar chart are as follows.

| *Year* | *Percentage of total units sold* | | | |
|---|---|---|---|---|
| | *P* | *Q* | *R* | *S* |
| 19X0 | 26.7 | 15.7 | 38.6 | 19.0 |
| 19X1 | 28.2 | 13.6 | 34.6 | 23.6 |
| 19X2 | 28.3 | 11.7 | 30.9 | 29.1 |

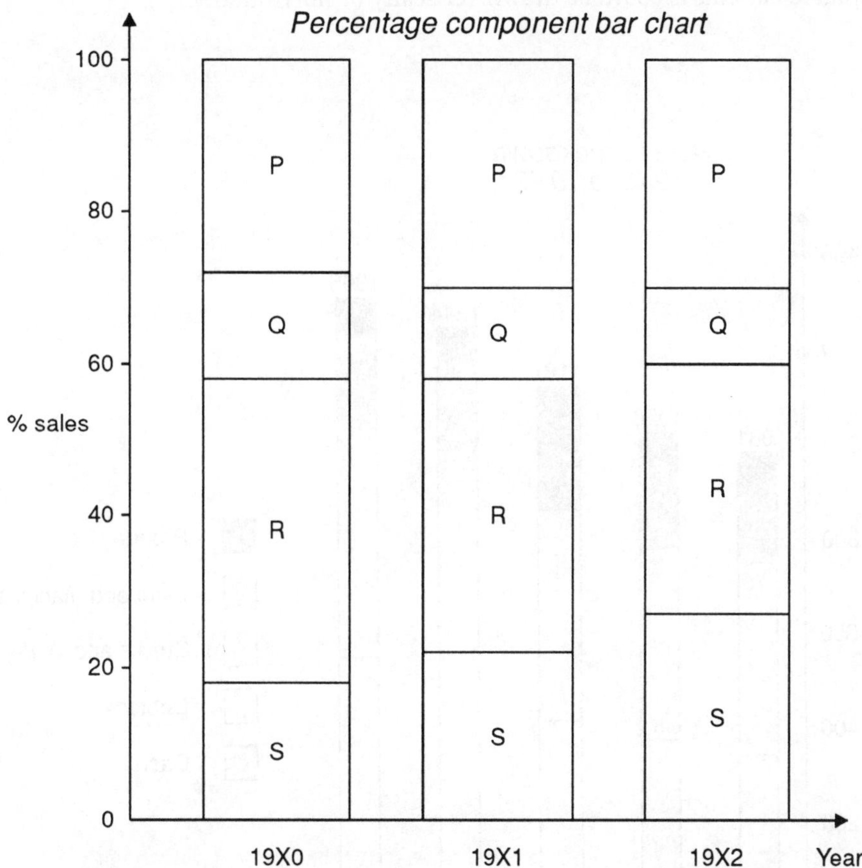


(b) Product S is clearly becoming increasingly important in relative terms and product R is becoming correspondingly less important. Product Q's sales are also falling in percentage terms, and product P's sales are growing slightly in percentage terms. All these trends are also apparent in the figures for units sold.

**Solution to Exercise 10**

In 19X0, total revenue was

$$(560 \times £3.50) + (330 \times £5.00) + (810 \times £3.00) + (400 \times £6.50) = £8,640.$$

In 19X2, total revenue was

$$(650 \times £3.50) + (270 \times £5.00) + (710 \times £3.00) + (670 \times £6.50) = £10,110.$$

The percentage increase was

$$\frac{10,110 - 8,640}{8,640} \times 100\% = 17\%$$

This increase has been achieved partly through an increased volume of sales (up from 2,100 units to 2,300 units, an increase of 9.5%) and partly through a shift in the sales mix towards the high value product S.

## Solution to Exercise 11

(a) Acceptable bar charts could be drawn vertically or horizontally.

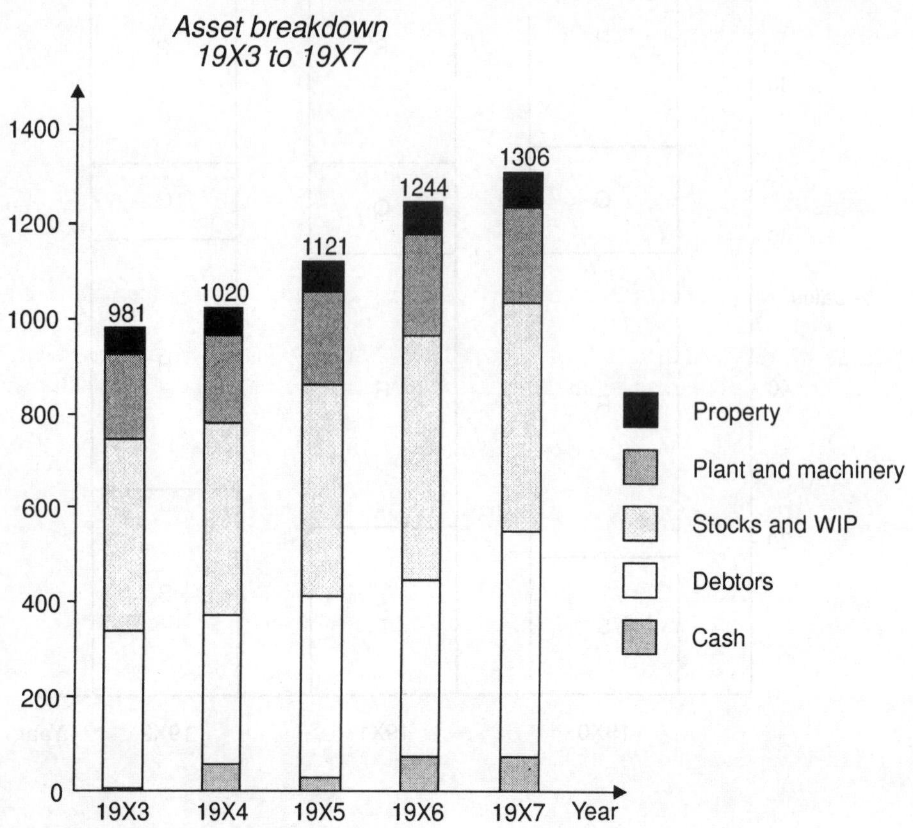


(b) The bar chart clearly shows that total assets have risen steadily over the five year period. Property remained static from 19X3 to 19X4, and showed only small increases from then on. Plant and machinery and stocks and work in progress both rose slowly from 19X3 to 19X4 and more steeply from 19X4 to 19X6, and then declined from 19X6 to 19X7. Debtors have behaved unevenly but with an increasing trend: total assets rose from 19X6 to 19X7 only because of the large increase in debtors over this period. Cash balances have also behaved unevenly but they exhibit an increasing trend over the five year period.

## Solution to Exercise 12

The correct answer is (b): multiple bar chart.

## SOLUTIONS TO SESSION 6 PRACTICE EXERCISES

Suggested solutions to Practice Exercises 1 to 10 in this session are set out below. There are often different ways to reach a satisfactory solution to an exercise and there may be no single right answer. Having completed the exercises for yourself, compare your approach to ours and identify any errors you may have made.

### Solution to Exercise 1

(a) *The mean*

The *arithmetic mean* is the best known and most widely used average. The arithmetic mean of some data is the sum of the data, divided by the number of items in the data. It is widely used because it gives a convenient and readily understood indication of the general size of the data, it takes account of all items of data and it is suitable for further mathematical analysis. On the other hand, its value can be unduly influenced by a few very large or very small items of data. The geometric mean is not often used, but it is another way of calculating an average. The geometric mean of n values is the nth root of the values multiplied together. It may be a more representative average than the arithmetic mean when the value of a variable is rising or falling at a steady rate over time.

(b) *The median*

The median is the value of the middle member of a set of data, once the data have been arranged in either ascending or descending order. It is one sort of average and it has the following properties.

(i) It is fairly easy to obtain.
(ii) It is not affected very much by extreme values.
(iii) It is not generally suitable for further statistical analysis.

The median may be more useful than the arithmetic mean in certain circumstances, for instance when determining the average salary of the employees in a company. Since a few employees might have very high salaries, the arithmetic mean could be drawn upwards by these, out of the range of salaries earned by most employees. The mean would then not be representative. The median, however, would be the item in the middle of the ranking, which would be within the range of salaries earned by most employees.

(c) *Time series*

A time series is simply a series of values recorded over time. Examples of a time series are:

(i) output at a factory each day for the last month;
(ii) monthly sales over the last two years;
(iii) the number of people employed by a company each year for the last 20 years.

Time series are often shown on a graph, with time always being the independent variable shown along the x axis, and the values at each time shown along the y axis.

The features of a time series are normally taken to be:

(i) a trend;
(ii) cyclical variations;
(iii) seasonal variations;
(iv) random variations.

### Solution to Exercise 2

The mid point of the range 'under £60' is assumed to be £55, since all other class intervals are £10. This is obviously an approximation which might result in a loss of accuracy; nevertheless, there is no better alternative assumption to use. Note that the mid points of the classes are half way between their end points, because wages can vary in steps of only 1p and so are virtually a continuous variable.

| *Mid point of class* x £ | *Frequency* f | fx |
|---|---|---|
| 55 | 3 | 165 |
| 65 | 11 | 715 |
| 75 | 16 | 1,200 |
| 85 | 15 | 1,275 |
| 95 | 10 | 950 |
| 105 | 8 | 840 |
| 115 | 6 | 690 |
| | 69 | 5,835 |

$$\text{Arithmetic mean} = \frac{£5{,}835}{69} = £84.57$$

## Solution to Exercise 3

(a) *The mean*

| *Mid point* x £ | *Frequency* f | fx | *Cumulative frequency* |
|---|---|---|---|
| 5,250 | 4 | 21,000 | 4 |
| 5,750 | 26 | 149,500 | 30 |
| 6,250 | 133 | 831,250 | 163 |
| 6,750 | 35 | 236,250 | 198 |
| 7,250 | 2 | 14,500 | 200 |
| | Σf 200 | Σfx 1,252,500 | |

$$\text{Mean} = \frac{\Sigma fx}{\Sigma f}$$

$$= \frac{1{,}252{,}500}{200} = £6{,}262.50$$

(b) The median value is the value of the 100th item.

$$\text{Median} = L + \left(\frac{R}{f} \times c\right)$$

$$= £6{,}000 + \left(\frac{100 - 30}{133} \times £500\right)$$

$$= £6{,}000 + £263.16$$

$$= £6{,}263.16$$

(c) The modal value is in the range £6,000 and less than £6,500. It is estimated as follows.

$$\text{Mode} = L + \frac{(F_1 - F_0) \times c}{2F_1 - F_0 - F_2}$$

$$= £6{,}000 + \frac{(133 - 26) \times £500}{(2 \times 133) - 26 - 35}$$

$$= £6{,}000 + \frac{£53{,}500}{205}$$

$$= £6{,}260.98$$

## Solution to Exercise 4

In order to calculate the mean handling time, we need to work with the frequency distribution for handling time.

| Handling time At least | Handling time Less than | Mid-point of range | Frequency (x) | fx (f) |
|---|---|---|---|---|
| - | 10 | 5 | 240 | 1,200 |
| 10 | 20 | 15 | 340 | 5,100 |
| 20 | 40 | 30 | 150 | 4,500 |
| 40 | 60 | 50 | 120 | 6,000 |
| 60 | 90 | 75 | 20 | 1,500 |
| 90 | 120 | 105 | 20 | 2,100 |
| 120 | 180 | 150 | 10 | 1,500 |
| | | | 900 | 21,900 |

So the mean handling time is given by:

$$\bar{x} = \frac{\Sigma fx}{\Sigma f} = \frac{21{,}900}{900} = 24.33 \text{ minutes}$$

## Solution to Exercise 5

(a) The estimated number of minutes spent handling stock each week is $\Sigma fx = 21{,}900$ minutes. Therefore the estimated number of hours is given by:

$$\frac{21{,}900}{60} = 365 \text{ man hours per week}$$

(b) There are 12 men each of whom work seven hours a day for five days a week. So the total number of hours available each week is given by:

$12 \times 7 \times 5 = 420$ hours per week

So the percentage utilisation each week (using the answer to part (a)) is:

$$\frac{365}{420} \times 100\% = 86.9\%$$

## Solution to Exercise 6

When a time series is given, an average may be taken of n consecutive values at a time (such as values for four quarters or for five years). The first n values are averaged, then the n values starting with the second value, and so on. Thus the average moves forward through the time series, and is called a moving average.

Moving averages can be used to smooth out short-term variations, and thus disclose the trend.

## Solution to Exercise 7

| Year | Sales £ | 3-year total £ | 3-year moving average £ |
|---|---|---|---|
| 1 | 100 | | |
| 2 | 110 | 318 (yrs 1, 2, 3) | 106 |
| 3 | 108 | 330 (yrs 2, 3, 4) | 110 |
| 4 | 112 | 326 (yrs 3, 4, 5) | 109 |
| 5 | 106 | | |

## Solution to Exercise 8

The underlying trend is the trend which is revealed by removing the effect of cyclical, seasonal and random variations in time series data.

## Solution to Exercise 9

*Tutorial note.* A five year moving average is found simply by adding figures five at a time and dividing the result by five. Because five is an odd number, the averages are automatically centred on actual years.

The five year moving average must first be calculated.

| *Year* | *Sales* | *Five year total* | *Five year average* |
|---|---|---|---|
| 1980 | 55 | | |
| 1981 | 52 | | |
| 1982 | 45 | 265 | 53 |
| 1983 | 48 | 280 | 56 |
| 1984 | 65 | 290 | 58 |
| 1985 | 70 | 300 | 60 |
| 1986 | 62 | 310 | 62 |
| 1987 | 55 | 320 | 64 |
| 1988 | 58 | 330 | 66 |
| 1989 | 75 | 345 | 69 |
| 1990 | 80 | 345 | 69 |
| 1991 | 77 | 360 | 72 |
| 1992 | 55 | 370 | 74 |
| 1993 | 73 | 380 | 76 |
| 1994 | 85 | | |
| 1995 | 90 | | |

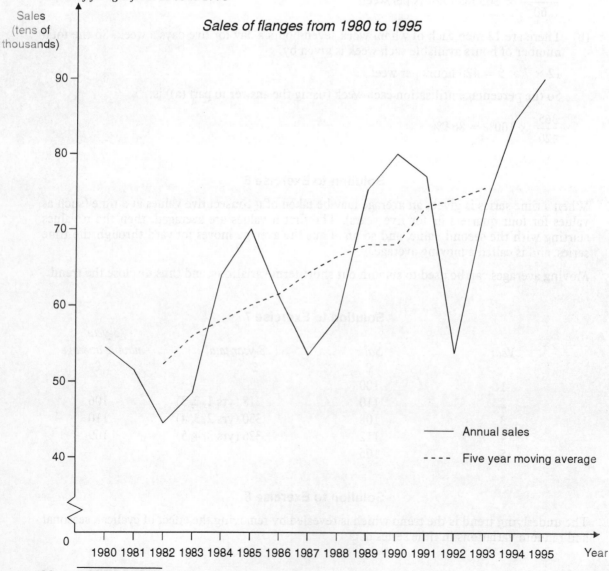

*Sales of flanges from 1980 to 1995*

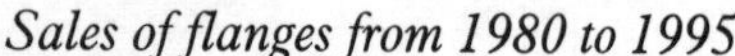

## Solution to Exercise 10

*Moving annual totals and averages*

| *Period to:* | *Moving annual total* | *Moving annual average* |
|---|---|---|
| | £'000 | £'000 |
| *19X7* | | |
| December | 103.4 | 8.62 |
| *19X8* | | |
| January | 103.5 | 8.63 |
| February | 103.7 | 8.64 |
| March | 102.7 | 8.56 |
| April | 102.5 | 8.54 |
| May | 101.9 | 8.49 |
| June | 100.7 | 8.39 |
| July | 101.3 | 8.44 |
| August | 103.8 | 8.65 |
| September | 105.1 | 8.76 |
| October | 107.3 | 8.94 |
| November | 110.6 | 9.22 |
| December | 113.7 | 9.48 |

*Notes*

(1) December 19X8 annual moving total equals total profits for 19X8.
(2) The first moving average (8.62) is plotted at July 19X7.

*Moving three monthly totals and averages*

| *Period to:* | *Moving 3-monthly total* | *Moving 3-monthly average* |
|---|---|---|
| | £'000 | £'000 |
| March 19X7 | 21.9 | 7.3 |
| April | 18.3 | 6.1 |
| May | 16.5 | 5.5 |
| June | 22.1 | 7.4 |
| July | 29.7 | 9.9 |
| August | 34.9 | 11.6 |
| September | 29.2 | 9.7 |
| October | 21.6 | 7.2 |
| November | 21.5 | 7.2 |
| December | 30.2 | 10.1 |
| January 19X8 | 33.9 | 11.3 |
| February | 30.8 | 10.3 |
| March | 21.2 | 7.1 |
| April | 17.3 | 5.8 |
| May | 14.7 | 4.9 |
| June | 20.1 | 6.7 |
| July | 28.5 | 9.5 |
| August | 36.8 | 12.3 |
| September | 33.6 | 11.2 |
| October | 27.6 | 9.2 |
| November | 28.3 | 9.4 |
| December | 38.8 | 12.9 |

*Note.* The first moving average (7.3) will be plotted as at February 19X7, as that is the mid-point of the three monthly period January 19X7 to March 19X7.

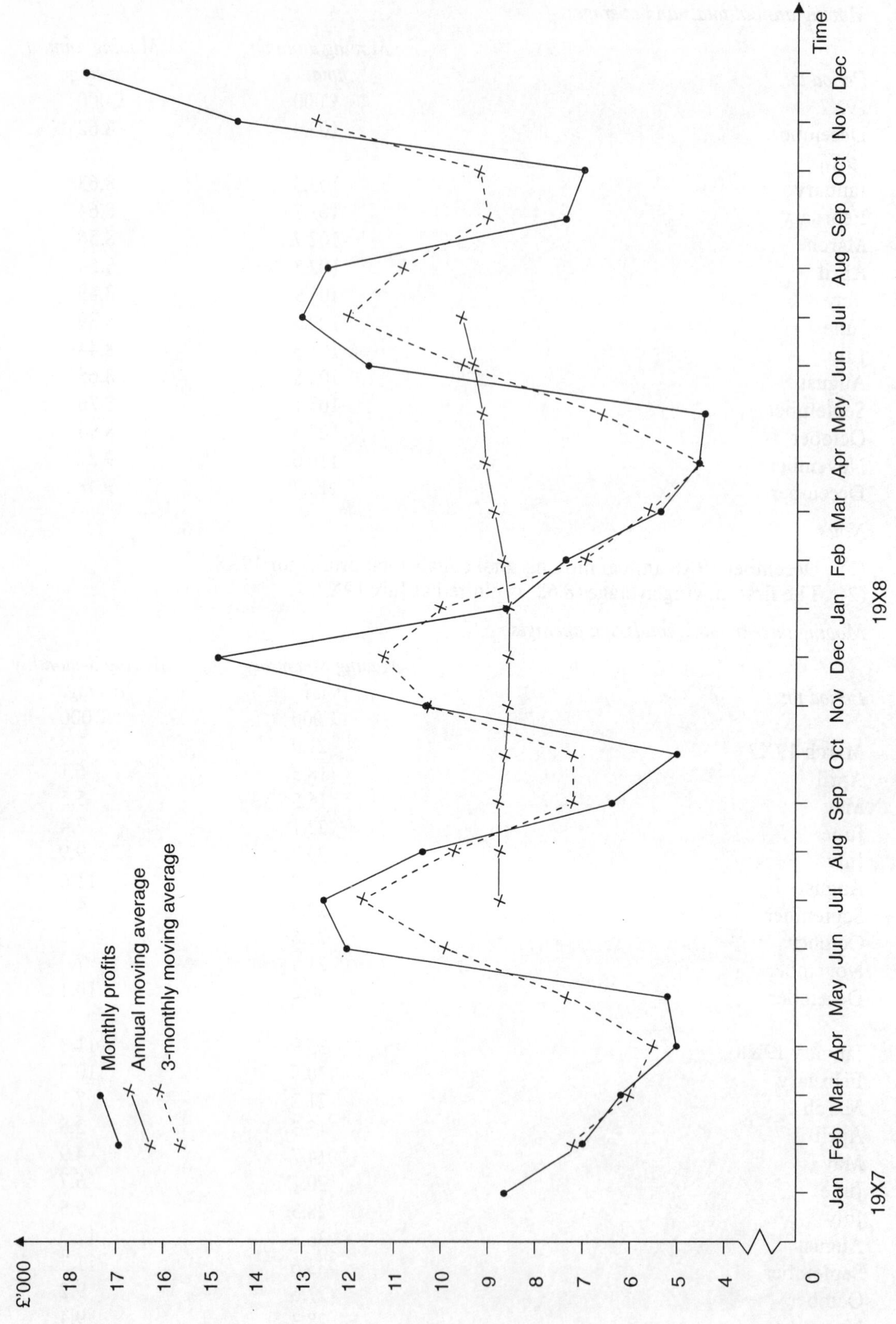


*Comment:* The three-monthly average has smoothed out the 'spiky' profit line to some extent, but it still clearly shows the summer and Christmas seasonal variations. The annual moving average has smoothed away these seasonal variations completely and shows that, after a slightly shaky start, the business is now doing well.

## SOLUTIONS TO SESSION 7 PRACTICE EXERCISES

Suggested solutions to Practice Exercises 1 to 15 in this session are set out below. There are often different ways to reach a satisfactory solution to an exercise and there may be no single right answer. Having completed the exercises for yourself, compare your approach to ours and identify any errors you may have made.

### Solution to Exercise 1

*Base period; producer price* indices.

### Solution to Exercise 2

*1992* $\frac{106}{112} \times 100 = 94.6$, rounded to 95

*1993* $\frac{120}{112} \times 100 = 107.1$, rounded to 107

### Solution to Exercise 3

*Sales expressed in terms of Year 1 prices*

| | | £'000 |
|---|---|---|
| Year 1 | | 27,500 |
| Year 2 | 29,680 × 217/228 | 28,248 |
| Year 3 | 32,535 × 217/246 | 28,700 |
| Year 4 | 34,455 × 217/268 | 27,898 |

Although sales have increased each year in absolute terms, when the effect of inflation is removed it can be seen that, in real terms, sales rose in year 2 and year 3 but fell in year 4.

### Solution to Exercise 4

| *Year* | *Sales (£'000)* | | *Index* |
|---|---|---|---|
| 19X5 | 35 | $\frac{35}{42} \times 100$ | = 83 |
| 19X6 | 42 | | 100 |
| 19X7 | 40 | $\frac{40}{42} \times 100$ | = 95 |
| 19X8 | 45 | $\frac{45}{42} \times 100$ | = 107 |
| 19X9 | 50 | $\frac{50}{42} \times 100$ | = 119 |

### Solution to Exercise 5

(a) The base year appears to be 19X2, because the index is 100. We cannot be absolutely sure about this, because the base year *could* be before 19X0 or after 19X3, and the cost of shoes in 19X2 just happened to be the same as in the base year.

(b) The index has moved from 96 points to 100 points, a rise of 4 points.

(c) $\frac{4}{96} \times 100\% = 4.17\%$

(d) $£7.50 \times \frac{113}{98} = £8.65$

## Solution to Exercise 6

Figures for sales per employee provide one indication of how efficient a supermarket chain is. This does not necessarily translate into profitability terms, since if margins (or price mark-ups) are reducing then the business may be becoming less profitable.

Over the period 1986 to 1990, sales per employee rose by 29% from £77,200 to £99,400. However, this is a rise in money terms. There was also a general rise in prices over this period of approximately 29%, using average RPI figures for the calendar years 1986 and 1990. Thus, in real terms, sales per employee have not changed much between 1986 and 1990. This means that the 'physical volume' of sales per employee has not changed much over the period.

The chart shows sales per employee in money terms. A chart such as this is intended as a visual aid to the reader: alternatively, just the figures could be included in a report. The chart gives the visual impression that there has been a significant rise in sales per employee.

Two features of the chart help to give this visual impression.

(a) The y-axis starts at 75 and not at zero.
(b) The chart is based on sales figures in money terms rather than real terms.

As commented above, the rise does not appear to have been significant in real terms and it is the figures for sales per employee in real terms which matter.

## Solution to Exercise 7

*Tutorial note.* As well as requiring you to calculate some index numbers, this question required you to explain what index numbers mean. This shows the importance of making sure that you understand *why* you are performing the calculations, instead of just learning how to do them without thinking about their meanings.

(a) (i) The price relative index numbers in Table 1 are based on prices in 19X5. The 19X7 price relative index number of 120 for material D means that the price of material D was 20% higher in 19X7 than in 19X5.

(ii) The price relative index value for material B in 19X9 was below 100. This indicates that the price of material B was lower in 19X9 than in 19X5. The index number of 90 means that the price of B was 10% lower in 19X9 than in 19X5.

(b)

| *Cost item* | | *Percentage* |
|---|---|---|
| | £'000 | % |
| A | 20 | 16 |
| B | 30 | 24 |
| C | 15 | 12 |
| D | 5 | 4 |
| Labour | 55 | 44 |
| | 125 | 100 |

## Solution to Exercise 8

| *Cost item* | *Weight* | *19X6 Index* | *19X6 Weighted index* | *19X7 Index* | *19X7 Weighted index* | *19X8 Index* | *19X8 Weighted index* | *19X9 Index* | *19X9 Weighted index* |
|---|---|---|---|---|---|---|---|---|---|
| A | 16 | 112 | 1,792 | 115 | 1,840 | 116 | 1,856 | 120 | 1,920 |
| B | 24 | 98 | 2,352 | 96 | 2,304 | 95 | 2,280 | 90 | 2,160 |
| C | 12 | 103 | 1,236 | 105 | 1,260 | 109 | 1,308 | 110 | 1,320 |
| D | 4 | 117 | 468 | 120 | 480 | 120 | 480 | 120 | 480 |
| Labour | 44 | 110 | 4,840 | 115 | 5,060 | 121 | 5,324 | 125 | 5,500 |
| | 100 | | 10,688 | | 10,944 | | 11,248 | | 11,380 |
| *Overall price index* | | (÷ 100) | 106.88 | | 109.44 | | 112.48 | | 113.80 |

The overall price index numbers show that the combined cost of materials and labour rose by 13.8% over the period from 19X5 to 19X9. The overall cost increased each year, although the rate of increase was slower between 19X8 and 19X9 than in earlier years.

The overall increase of 13.8% is an average increase which masks the relative price changes in each of the cost items. The prices of three of the items rose by 20% or more (materials A and D by 20% and labour by 25%). However material B carries 24% of the weighting and the price of B actually fell by 10% between 19X5 and 19X9. This fall, combined with the increase of only 10% in the price of material C meant that the weighted average overall cost increase was only 13.8%.

## Solution to Exercise 9

(a) False. There was sales growth in B Division over the period 19X1 to 19X5.
(b) True.

## Solution to Exercise 10

The values of items consumed in the base period are:

A £10,000
B £18,000
C £15,000

These can be cancelled down to give weights of 10, 18 and 15.

| | *Price relative × weight* | | | |
|---|---|---|---|---|
| *Period* | *A* | *B* | *C* | *Total* |
| 19X0 | 1,000 | 1,800 | 1,500 | 4,300 |
| 19X1 | 1,000 | 1,944 | 1,350 | 4,294 |
| 19X2 | 1,100 | 2,070 | 1,500 | 4,670 |

$$\text{Price index for 19X1} = \frac{4{,}294}{4{,}300} \times 100 = 99.9$$

$$\text{Price index for 19X2} = \frac{4{,}670}{4{,}300} \times 100 = 108.6$$

## Solution to Exercise 11

Based on 19X3 quantities, the change in prices in 19X4 is calculated as follows.

| | *Quantity* | *Price* | *Pence* |
|---|---|---|---|
| Cover board | 1 | 10.6p | 10.6 |
| Paper | 230 | 31p/100 | 71.3 |
| Ink | 5 | 1p | 5.0 |
| Bindings | 1 | 3p | 3.0 |
| | | | 89.9 |

89.9 ÷ 86.8 × 100 = 103.6, rounded to 104.

The index number for 19X4 prices is 104.

## Solution to Exercise 12

The base period is October 19X3.

| *Item* | *Quantity* $q_0$ | *Weighting* $w$ | $q_0w$ |
|---|---|---|---|
| Hocks | 30 | 9 | 270 |
| Nocks | 24 | 4 | 96 |
| Socks | 18 | 5 | 90 |
| | | | 456 |

To remove differences in the number of days worked, we should calculate a daily rate of output in October 19X3.

$$\frac{456}{22 \text{ days}} = 20.727 \text{ weighted units per day}$$

| *Item* | *Quantity Nov 19X3* | *Quantity Dec 19X3* | *Weighting* | | |
|---|---|---|---|---|---|
| | $q_1$ | $q_2$ | $w$ | $q_1w$ | $q_2w$ |
| Hocks | 25 | 24 | 9 | 225 | 216 |
| Nocks | 28 | 20 | 4 | 112 | 80 |
| Socks | 20 | 16 | 5 | 100 | 80 |
| | | | | 437 | 376 |

| | *November 19X3* | *December 19X3* |
|---|---|---|
| Days in month | 20 | 16 |
| Weighted units per day | 21.85 | 23.5 |

*Productivity index*

November 19X3 $\frac{21.85}{20.727} \times 100 = 105.4$

December 19X3 $\frac{23.5}{20.727} \times 100 = 113.4$

## Solution to Exercise 13

| *Group* | *Group weight* | *Group index number* | *Product* |
|---|---|---|---|
| 1 | 203 | 318.5 | 64,655.5 |
| 2 | 78 | 373.2 | 21,109.6 |
| 3 | 39 | 450.0 | 17,550.0 |
| 4 | 137 | 381.6 | 52,279.2 |
| 5 | 69 | 469.0 | 32,361.0 |
| 6 | 64 | 253.0 | 16,192.0 |
| 7 | 74 | 217.1 | 16,065.4 |
| 8 | 159 | 371.7 | 59,100.3 |
| 9 | 75 | 353.4 | 26,505.0 |
| 10 | 63 | 350.0 | 22,050.0 |
| 11 | 39 | 375.7 | 14,652.3 |
| | 1,000 | | 350,520.3 |

(a) Index number for all groups combined

$$= \frac{350{,}520.3}{1{,}000} = 350.5$$

(b) Index number for all groups excluding housing

$$= \frac{350{,}520.3 - 52{,}279.2}{1{,}000 - 137}$$

$$= \frac{298{,}241.1}{863}$$

$$= 345.6$$

## Solution to Exercise 14

*Tutorial note.* An index covering the prices of several items is an indication of the average of changes in the prices, with weights being used to allow for the relative importance of the different items.

| | | 19X5 | | 19X6 | | 19X7 | | 19X8 | |
|---|---|---|---|---|---|---|---|---|---|
| *Ingredient* | *Weight* | *Index* | *W'ted* | *Index* | *W'ted* | *Index* | *W'ted* | *Index* | *W'ted* |
| G | 6 | 103 | 618 | 107 | 642 | 115 | 690 | 120 | 720 |
| L | 5 | 104 | 520 | 111 | 555 | 118 | 590 | 123 | 615 |
| O | 4 | 107 | 428 | 113 | 452 | 117 | 468 | 121 | 484 |
| W | 3 | 102 | 306 | 106 | 318 | 110 | 330 | 118 | 354 |
| | 18 | | 1,872 | | 1,967 | | 2,078 | | 2,173 |

(a) Material cost index (19X4 = 100): 19X5 104; 19X6 109; 19X7 115; 19X8 121

Each total is divided by 18 (the sum of the weights) to derive the index number.

(b) Using 19X7 as the base year, the index for 19X8 is

$$\frac{2{,}173 \times 100}{2{,}078} = 105.$$

## Solution to Exercise 15

The index number for each year with 19X6 as the base year will be the original index number divided by 1.14, and the real wages for each year will be (money wages × 100)/index number for the year.

| Year | Index | Real wages £ |
|---|---|---|
| 19X0 | 88 | 170 |
| 19X1 | 90 | 179 |
| 19X2 | 93 | 181 |
| 19X3 | 95 | 188 |
| 19X4 | 96 | 193 |
| 19X5 | 98 | 195 |
| 19X6 | 100 | 197 |
| 19X7 | 102 | 199 |
| 19X8 | 104 | 199 |
| 19X9 | 106 | 201 |
| 19Y0 | 108 | 214 |

## SOLUTIONS TO SESSION 8 PRACTICE EXERCISES

Suggested solutions to Practice Exercises 1 to 6 in this session are set out below. There are often different ways to reach a satisfactory solution to an exercise and there may be no single right answer. Having completed the exercises for yourself, compare your approach to ours and identify any errors you may have made.

### Solution to Exercise 1

(a) The conclusions of a report might be positioned either at the end (perhaps before a 'recommendations' section and any lists of sources) or alternatively after the introduction.

(b) The terms of reference of a report are an explanation of the purpose of the report and of any limitations on its scope.

(c) To keep the main body of the report short enough to hold the reader's interest, detailed explanations and tables of figures may be put into appendices to which the main body of the report cross refers.

### Solution to Exercise 2

(a) *Tutorial note.* In essence, the informal report is more flexible about the kind of headings you can use. It is also less scrupulous about setting out the formal purposes and methodology of the investigation and report.

*Short formal report*

I Terms of reference/Introduction
II Procedure/Method
III Findings/Information
IV Conclusions/Summary
V Recommendations (if required)

*Short informal report*

I Background/Introduction/Situation
II Findings/Analysis/Information
III Action/Solution/Conclusion/Summary
IV Recommendations (if required)

(b) *Tutorial note.* Even the formal requirements of a report need not make it stiff and uninteresting to read.

Any ten of:

| | |
|---|---|
| Stated | Affirmed |
| Asserted | Proposed |
| Commented | Argued |
| Suggested | Replied |
| Claimed | Insinuated |
| Remarked | Repeated |
| Emphasised | Stressed |
| Agreed | Promised |
| Indicated | Alleged |
| Told (x) that | Informed (x) that |

(c) (i) Your Name investigated the matter. *or*

The matter was investigated.

(In a formal report, the first person should be avoided, and third person or impersonal constructions used.)

(ii) Mr Harris indicated [to Your Name] that he would investigate further.

(Direct speech should not be used, and should be changed to indirect or reported speech. It is optional whether you include the fact that Mr Harris told *you* specifically: this can be assumed, since you are the author of the report.)

(iii) He surmised [suggested/assumed] that there was a problem in the Accounts Department, since it seemed [he considered/felt/believed] that the fault did not lie with his own department.

(Direct speech becomes indirect, with the clarifying details that that requires - eg 'our' becomes 'his own department'. Just as importantly, the speaker is using words like 'must be' and 'obviously', indicating that he is making certain assumptions and is stating an *opinion* or viewpoint of his own. In a formal report, any assumptions or potential bias must be made clear so that the account is objective: verbs like 'surmised', 'assumed' and 'believed' show clearly that what follows is a *subjective* statement, not objective fact.)

(iv) Accounts appeared not to have received the complaint.

(Viewed objectively, the facts are that Accounts say they have not received the complaint: that they might be lying about this is an assumption - and accusation - on the part of the writer and should be kept out of the formal report, especially since 'pretended' is a rather loaded word.)

(v) Mr Harris considered the latitude given to the Accounts Department to be deplorable.

(Emotionally loaded words like 'outrageous', 'layabouts', 'getting away with' and 'fumed' should be avoided in favour of a more impersonal, 'calmer' style.)

(vi) Your Name indicated that he would himself undertake the task, if they lacked the initiative to do so.

(Avoid colloquial abbreviations - I'd, weren't etc - and expressions in formal written English.)

## Solution to Exercise 3

*Russia: country data*

Russia covers an area of 17.1 million square kilometres. The country comprises 76% of the territory of the former Soviet Union (FSU) but, with 148.3 million inhabitants in mid-1990, only 51% of the total population of the FSU. Average annual population growth was 0.4% during the 1980s and population density was 8.7 per square kilometre in 1990.

Russia's Gross Domestic Product at current market prices was 573.1 billion roubles in 1989. Industry accounted for 46.6% of this total, services accounted for 37.8% and agriculture accounted for 15.6%.

The value of Russia's exports was 140.9 billion roubles in 1989, of which oil and gas represented 31.2%.

## Solution to Exercise 4

*Tutorial note.* Additional knowledge of the subject matter is not required in order to summarise the information for a written report, as below. The table listed the enterprises in alphabetical order: note that a different order of presentation has been used below.

Important changes occurred in the competitive environment facing the largest public enterprises from the late 1970s up to 1990.

Changes for the Post Office were the deregulation of courier services in 1981 and the restructuring of the enterprise into separate businesses. British Telecom (BT) was affected by the liberalisation of apparatus (1981), value added services (1981) and a second terrestrial carrier in 1982.

British Coal had better defined contracts for supply to electricity generators from 1989 and reduced protection from imports of coal and from gas. British Steel was affected by the unwinding of European Community steel quotas from 1980 onwards.

Important legislation in the energy supply industries were the Energy Act (1983), the Gas Act (1985) and the Electricity Act (1986). British Gas faced partial competition in the supply of gas to industrial consumers; partial competition was also introduced in the electricity supply industry, with fuller competition in electricity supply being introduced in 1990.

The main competitive change for British Airways was route liberalisation which was introduced on North Atlantic routes in 1977, UK routes in 1982 and European routes from 1984 onwards. Domestic aviation presented increased competition for British Rail from 1982, as did the deregulation of bus services in 1986 and coach services from 1980.

## Solution to Exercise 5

(a) Your answer might have included the following.

Enrolment and application forms of many different sorts
Order forms for goods
Payment or paying-in forms at the bank
Complaint forms
Parking tickets

(b) The answer will depend upon the forms you have obtained. Look back at the tutorial text if you need guidance on the general features of 'good' forms.

## Solution to Exercise 6

You should be able to look at the completed form and see:

(a) the 'split' of time spent on the various tasks that make up your job or project each day and over a week;

(b) whether you are spending too much time on one particular part of your job or project (eg if you spent a lot more time than you'd planned on one particular task, but not others) and may need to practise more or find better ways of approaching it;

(c) whether you are realistic about the time plans you make for yourself: do you over- or under-estimate the time a task will take you?

(d) whether you work more efficiently at the beginning or end of the week (eg by Friday afternoon, do things start taking longer than planned?);

(e) how much time you're actually spending on the phone, and in non-work pursuits (including chatting to people etc) - just for interest. The results may surprise you.

## SOLUTIONS TO SESSION 9 PRACTICE EXERCISES

Suggested solutions to Practice Exercises 1 to 11 in this session are set out below. There are often different ways to reach a satisfactory solution to an exercise and there may be no single right answer. Having completed the exercises for yourself, compare your approach to ours and identify any errors you may have made.

### Solution to Exercise 1

Items (a) and (b) are direct labour costs of the items produced in the 42 hours worked in week 5.

Overtime premium, item (c), is usually regarded as an overhead expense, because it is 'unfair' to charge the items produced in overtime hours with the premium. Why should an item made in overtime be more costly just because, by chance, it was made after the employee normally clocks off for the day?

Group bonus scheme payments (d) are usually overhead costs, because they cannot normally be traced directly to individual products or jobs.

In this example, the direct labour employee costs were £168 in direct costs and £36 in indirect costs, and these costs would be coded differently, to allocate them to different cost units or overhead cost centres.

### Solution to Exercise 2

(a) Any one of the following is an acceptable answer.

- (i) Bed occupied
- (ii) Patient
- (iii) Bed-day

(b) Possible cost units:

- (i) Enrolled student
- (ii) Successful student
- (iii) Course-week

Possible cost centres:

- (i) An academic department, such as the Accounting and Finance Department
- (ii) Administration Department
- (iii) Catering Section

### Solution to Exercise 3

(a) The reference numbers for each expense can be classified as follows.

| | *Reference numbers* |
|---|---|
| Production overhead | 1, 3, 8, 9, 14, 16 |
| Selling and distribution overhead | 2, 5, 7, 10, 11 |
| Administration overhead | 6, 13, 15 |
| Research and development overhead | 4, 12 |

(b) Direct production labour cost might be regarded as a fixed cost rather than as a variable cost for the following reasons.

- (i) Direct labour may be paid a guaranteed salary, regardless of output.
- (ii) Production methods may be highly mechanised, with the result that direct labour cost is insignificant and may be approximated to a fixed cost.
- (iii) A no-redundancy policy may result in labour costs remaining fixed regardless of output.
- (iv) Union agreements featuring guaranteed manning levels can result in fixed production labour costs.

(*Tutorial note:* you need only give *three* reasons, as requested.)

## Solution to Exercise 4

Any one of the following is an acceptable answer.

(a) Calculation of wages where a piecework system is in operation.
(b) Measurement of efficiency.
(c) Production planning.

## Solution to Exercise 5

| | | |
|---|---|---|
| Standard hours | = | standard time allowed × output |
| | = | 2 hours × 1,000 units |
| | = | 2,000 standard hours |

## Solution to Exercise 6

| | | Hours | Hours | £ | Cost £ |
|---|---|---|---|---|---|
| Contractual hours | | | 750.0 | × 8.00 | 6,000 |
| Overtime hours | | | 108.0 | × 10.75 | 1,161 |
| | | | | | 7,161 |
| Absence: | Public holidays | 37.5 | | | |
| | Annual holidays | 105.0 | | | |
| | Certified sickness | 45.0 | | | |
| | Other absences | 10.0 | | | |
| | | | (202.5) | | |
| Available hours | | | 655.5 | | |

$$\text{Total cost per available hour} = \frac{7{,}161}{655.5} = £10.92$$

## Solution to Exercise 7

(a) (i) *Earnings based on piecework*

| | *Y* | *Z* |
|---|---|---|
| Hours worked | 44 | 40 |
| | £ | £ |
| Hourly rate | 3.50 | 4.50 |
| Pay calculated on an hourly basis | 154 | 180 |
| × 80% = guaranteed earnings (A) | 123.20 | 144 |
| Piecework earnings: | | |
| 480 × 7 minutes × £0.05 (B) | 168 | |
| 390 × 7 minutes × £0.05 (B) | | 136.50 |
| Earnings are the higher of (A) and (B) for each employee: | 168 | 144 |

(ii) *Earnings based on premium bonus and hourly pay*

| | *X* | *Y* |
|---|---|---|
| Std time allowed for production achieved: | | |
| 480 × 7 minutes ÷ 60 | 56 hrs | |
| 390 × 7 minutes ÷ 60 | | 45.5 hrs |
| Hours worked | 44 | 40.0 |
| Time saved (hrs) | 12 | 5.5 |
| × 75% = bonus hours | 9 | 4.125 |
| Hours worked | 44 | 40.000 |
| Total hours paid | 53 | 44.125 |
| Hourly rate | £3.50 | £4.50 |
| Earnings (hours paid × hourly rate) | £185.50 | £198.56 |

(b) The time basis of remuneration is likely to be more appropriate than piecework schemes in the following situations.

(i) When there is no basis for piecework measurement, for example in the case of administration staff.

(ii) When the quality of work is more important than quantity.

(iii) When the employee has no control over the level of output.

(iv) When the employee is learning the job.

## Solution to Exercise 8

*Tutorial note.* This is a fairly straightforward question if you understand the use of composite cost units. These are cost units which are made up of two parts and they are often used in service organisations. In the case of these hospitals the cost units are an in-patient day and an out-patient visit. The cost per in-patient would not be particularly meaningful because this cost could be very large or very small depending on the average length of stay. It would not be possible to compare the cost per in-patient for the two hospitals. The cost of one patient for one day (abbreviated to cost per patient-day) would however be comparable, and therefore useful for control purposes.

(a)

| | *St Matthew's* | | *St Mark's* | |
|---|---|---|---|---|
| | *Cost per in-patient day* | *Cost per out-patient day* | *Cost per in-patient day* | *Cost per out-patient day* |
| Number of in-patient days (*) | 154,000 | - | 110,760 | - |
| Number of out-patient attendances | - | 130,000 | - | 3,500 |
| | £ | £ | £ | £ |
| A Patient care services | | | | |
| 1 Direct treatment | 40.35 | 8.28 | 16.19 | 20.14 |
| 2 Medical support | | | | |
| 2.1 Diagnostic | 3.12 | 2.40 | 0.20 | 5.90 |
| 2.2 Other services | 1.54 | 2.22 | 0.70 | 7.94 |
| B General services | | | | |
| 1 Patient related | 4.12 | 0.12 | 3.61 | 2.20 |
| 2 General | 14.26 | 7.29 | 12.76 | 16.20 |
| Total cost | 63.39 | 20.31 | 33.46 | 52.38 |

* Number of in-patient days = number of in-patients × average stay

St Matthew's = 15,400 × 10 days = 154,000
St Mark's = 710 × 156 days = 110,760

(b) *Bed-occupation percentages*

$$\text{St Matthew's} = \frac{402}{510} \times 100\% = 78.8\%$$

$$\text{St Mark's} = \frac{307}{320} \times 100\% = 95.9\%$$

(c) *Cost per in-patient day*

St Mark's has a lower cost than St Matthew's. This is partly due to the fact that St Mark's has a higher bed-occupation percentage, which indicates that this hospital is making more efficient use of the available resources. A higher bed-occupation will mean that the fixed costs are spread over more cost units, thus reducing the unit cost.

*Cost per out-patient attendance*

St Matthew's has a lower cost in this case, probably owing to the large volume of patients. It is likely that more efficient systems are in operation to cope with the higher activity.

It is evident from the figures that the two hospitals care for very different types of patient. St Mark's deals with long stays and does not attend to many out-patients. St Matthew's in-patients stay for a short time and are far fewer in number than the out-patients. Therefore despite the use of comparable cost units, caution is necessary before reaching any firm conclusions regarding the relative costs.

## Solution to Exercise 9

Significant digit codes incorporate some digit(s) which is (are) part of the description of the item being coded.

Examples:

| | |
|---|---|
| 5000 | screws |
| 5050 | 50 mm screws |
| 5060 | 60 mm screws |
| 5075 | 75 mm screws |

## Solution to Exercise 10

*Production* is the quantity or volume of output produced. It is the number of units produced, or the actual number of units produced converted into an equivalent number of standard hours of production. 'Standard hours of production' is a concept used in standard costing.

*Productivity* is a measure of the efficiency with which output has been produced, for example production per employee.

## Solution to Exercise 11

(a)

| | |
|---|---|
| Distance travelled per day | 40 × 2 × 2 = 160 km |
| Distance travelled in the period | 160 × 5 days × 4 weeks = 3,200 km |
| Distance travelled in the period fully loaded (½ of 3,200) | 1,600 km |
| Tonnes carried, per trip | 10½ tonnes |
| Tonnes/kilometres in the period | 16,800 tonne/kilometres |

STATEMENTS OF COSTS PERIOD 8 19X4

(i) Running costs:

| | £ |
|---|---|
| Petrol (3,200 km ÷ 8 km per 5 litres × £0.36 per litre) | 720 |
| Oil (£8 × 4 weeks) | 32 |
| Repairs (£72 × 4 weeks) | 288 |
| Wages (£140 × 4 weeks) | 560 |
| Tyres cost (£1,250 ÷ 25,000 km × 3,200 km) | 160 |
| Depreciation ((£18,750 – 2,750) ÷ 80,000 km × 3,200 km) | 640 |
| Running costs | 2,400 |

Depreciation is assumed to be a running cost, charged on distance travelled, rather than a fixed charge per period.

(ii) Standing costs:

| | £ |
|---|---|
| Garaging (£4 per day × 7 days × 4 weeks) | 112 |
| Insurance (£650 ÷ 13) | 50 |
| Licence cost (£234 ÷ 13) | 18 |
| Other overheads (£3,900 ÷ 13) | 300 |
| | 480 |

(iii) Total costs:

| | £ |
|---|---|
| Running costs | 2,400 |
| Standing costs | 480 |
| Total costs, period 8 | 2,880 |

(b) Cost per km travelled $\dfrac{£2,880}{3,200 \text{ km}}$ = £0.90 per km

Cost per tonne/km $\dfrac{£2,880}{16,800 \text{ tonne / km}}$ = £0.171 per tonne/km

(c) To deliver six tonnes to a destination 120 km away, and to return loaded with a further six tonnes, 240 km would be travelled and the tonne/kilometres would be:

$240 \times 6 = 1,440$ tonne/kilometres

Charge:

| | | |
|---|---|---|
| (i) | on a kilometre basis of costs: 240 kilometres × £0.9 = | £216 |
| (ii) | on a tonne/kilometre basis of costs: 1,440 tonne/kilometres × £0.171 = | £246 |

## SOLUTIONS TO SESSION 10 PRACTICE EXERCISES

Suggested solutions to Practice Exercises 1 to 8 in this session are set out below. There are often different ways to reach a satisfactory solution to an exercise and there may be no single right answer. Having completed the exercises for yourself, compare your approach to ours and identify any errors you may have made.

### Solution to Exercise 1

In many businesses, management establish *profit centres* of operations, with each centre held accountable for making a profit, and the manager of the centre made responsible for its good or bad results. When a production department is established as a profit centre, it makes a 'profit' on the output it makes and transfers out, either to finished goods store or to another profit centre. But production departments do not sell goods, they only make them; and so if a production department is a profit centre, its 'income' must come from the goods it makes, and not from the goods sold. This is achieved, in profit centre accounting, by creating an 'artificial' selling price for goods produced and transferred. This artificial 'internal' selling price is called a *transfer price*.

### Solution to Exercise 2

| | | *Capacity level* | |
|---|---|---|---|
| | *100%* | *80%* | *60%* |
| | £'000 | £'000 | £'000 |
| Variable smelting costs (W1) | 37,500 | 30,000 | 22,500 |
| Other variable costs (W2) | 5,625 | 4,500 | 3,375 |
| | 43,125 | 34,500 | 25,875 |
| Fixed smelting costs (W1) | 8,000 | 7,000 | 6,000 |
| Other fixed costs (given) | 2,500 | 2,250 | 1,750 |
| | 53,625 | 43,750 | 33,625 |
| Group costs apportioned (given) | 3,500 | 3,500 | 3,500 |
| | 57,125 | 47,250 | 37,125 |
| 20% markup | 11,425 | 9,450 | 7,425 |
| | 68,550 | 56,700 | 44,550 |
| Per mould | £5,484 | £5,670 | £5,940 |

*Workings*

1 *Variable and fixed smelting costs*

The high-low method can be used as long as care is taken with the stepped element of fixed costs which has to be added back so that the only fall included in the calculation is that caused by variable costs. Taking the 80% and 60% levels:

$$\frac{£37,000 - £(28,500 + 1,000)}{200 - 150} = £150$$

Thus variable costs at the 100% level are 250,000 × £150 = £37.5m and so on. Fixed costs are the balance between this and the total costs given in the question.

2 Other variable costs are incurred at £450 per mould.

| | *100%* | *80%* | *60%* |
|---|---|---|---|
| Output (tonnes) | 250,000 | 200,000 | 150,000 |
| Tonnes per mould | 20 | 20 | 20 |
| Moulds | 12,500 | 10,000 | 7,500 |
| × £450 | £5,625,000 | £4,500,000 | £3,375,000 |

## Solution to Exercise 3

(a) *Allmain Limited*
*Departmental management accounts*

| | *White goods* | *TV* | *Audio* | *Total* |
|---|---|---|---|---|
| | £ | £ | £ | £ |
| Sales | 44,500 | 25,850 | 20,900 | 91,250 |
| Cost of sales | (28,500) | (16,200) | (13,850) | (58,550) |
| Gross profit | 16,000 | 9,650 | 7,050 | 32,700 |
| Expenses | | | | |
| Selling and distribution | 5,362 | 2,252 | 2,636 | 10,250 |
| Administration | 4,062 | 2,709 | 2,709 | 9,480 |
| Heating and lighting | 1,105 | 553 | 553 | 2,211 |
| Rent and rates | 2,600 | 1,300 | 1,300 | 5,200 |
| Total expenses | 13,129 | 6,814 | 7,198 | 27,141 |
| Net profit before interest and taxation | 2,871 | 2,836 | –148 | 5,559 |

(b)

| | | | | |
|---|---|---|---|---|
| Gross profit percentage | 36.0 | 37.3 | 33.7 | 35.8 |
| Net profit percentage | 6.5 | 11.0 | – 0.7 | 6.1 |

*Workings*

| | *White goods* | *TV* | *Audio* |
|---|---|---|---|
| Selling and distribution | £5,362 | £2,252 | £2,636 |
| Administration | | | |
| £9,480 × | $^3/_7$ | $^2/_7$ | $^2/_7$ |
| = | £4,062 | £2,709 | £2,709 |
| Heating and lighting, rent and rates | | | |
| £2,211/£5,200 × | ½ | ¼ | ¼ |
| Heating and lighting | £1,105 | £553 | £553 |
| Rent and rates | £2,600 | £1,300 | £1,300 |

(c) Comparative figures might include budgeted (forecast) figures, year to date figures, last year's figures and annual moving average figures.

## Solution to Exercise 4

*Tutorial note.* You should have ensured that your sketches reflected the facts given in the question. Thus the right departments and the right geographical areas should have been shown.

(a) *Total sales income for each of the past five years*

A simple bar chart, with one bar for each year, is appropriate. The bars will make the trend of total sales immediately apparent, and sales for any one year can be easily read from the vertical axis.

(b) *Sales by department for each of the last five years*

A multiple bar chart is appropriate. The trend of sales in each department will then be clearly visible. Total sales will not be obvious, but this does not matter if the simple bar chart described in part (a) is also supplied.

(c) *The proportions of sales for one year contributed by various geographical areas*

A pie chart is a good way of showing proportions rather than absolute values. Exact proportions cannot be easily read from such a chart, but a good general impression can easily be gained.

Here are sketches of all the above types of graph.

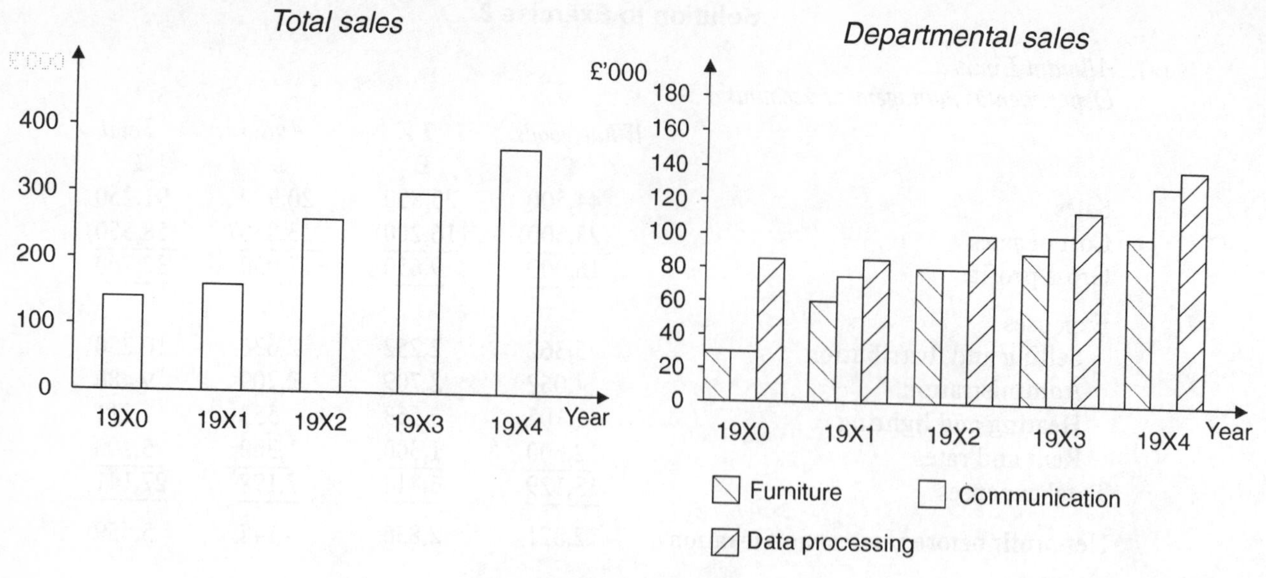


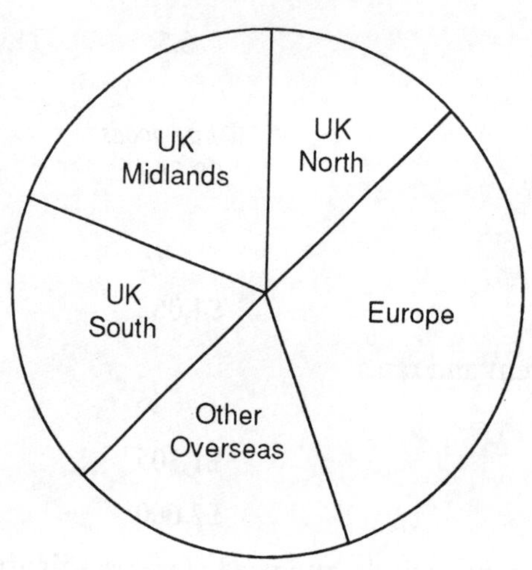


## Solution to Exercise 5

| | *WIZ* | *PER* | *MRL* | *WLD* | *BKR* | *CRK* | *Total* |
|---|---|---|---|---|---|---|---|
| | '000 | £'000 | £'000 | £'000 | £'000 | £'000 | £'000 |
| Sales | 72.4 | 31.2 | 41.5 | 27.6 | 101.0 | 52.7 | 326.4 |
| Direct labour | 20.2 | 7.6 | 14.5 | 4.5 | 39.7 | 22.1 | 108.6 |
| Direct materials | 14.2 | 7.0 | 11.1 | 5.2 | 19.1 | 12.3 | 68.9 |
| Variable overheads | 9.4 | 7.3 | 9.6 | 6.4 | 15.0 | 12.2 | 59.9 |
| | 43.8 | 21.9 | 35.2 | 16.1 | 73.8 | 46.6 | 237.4 |
| Contribution | 28.6 | 9.3 | 6.3 | 11.5 | 27.2 | 6.1 | 89.0 |
| Fixed costs | 16.3 | 8.2 | 10.2 | 8.2 | 20.4 | 12.2 | 75.5 |
| Profit/(loss) | 12.3 | 1.1 | (3.9) | 3.3 | 6.8 | (6.1) | 13.5 |
| Contribution/sales | 39.5% | 29.8% | 15.2% | 41.7% | 26.9% | 11.6% | 27.3% |

## Solution to Exercise 6

*Tutorial note.* Different presentations of the information are possible. The presentation below is similar to one suggested in the BPP Tutorial Text.

(a)

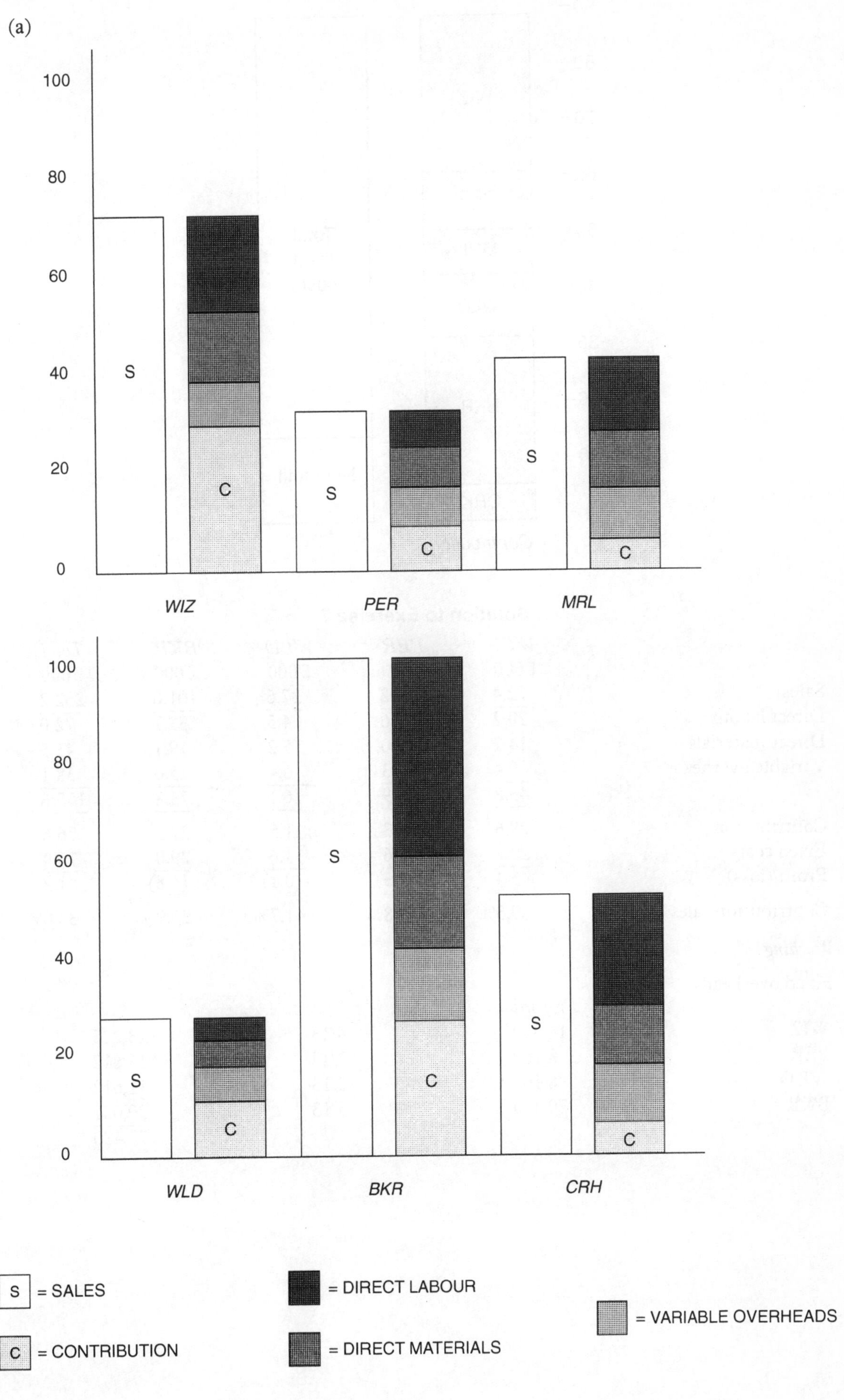
100
80
60
40
20
0
S
C
WIZ
PER
MRL
WLD
BKR
CRH
S = SALES
C = CONTRIBUTION
= DIRECT LABOUR
= DIRECT MATERIALS
= VARIABLE OVERHEADS

(b)

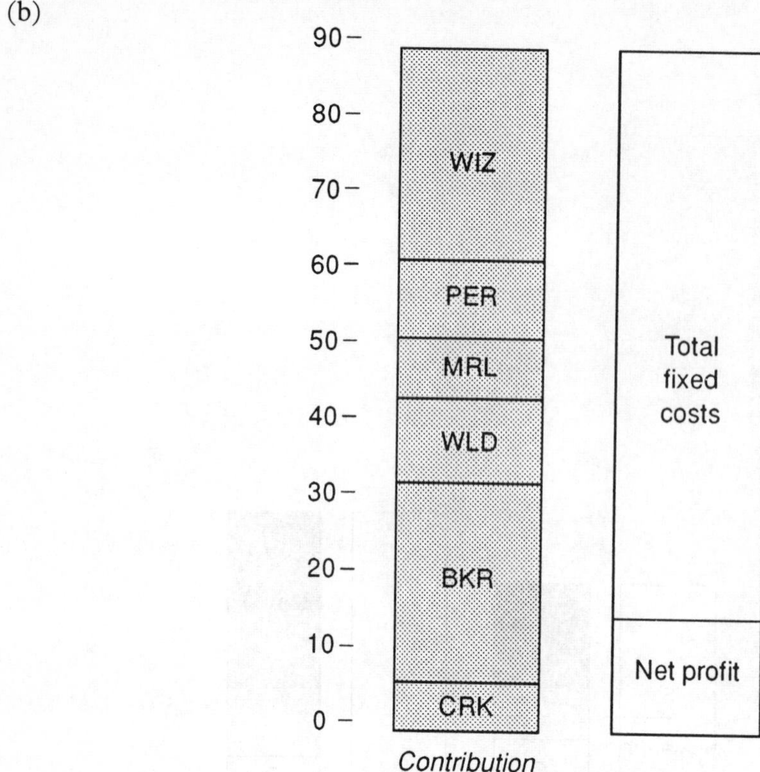


Contribution

## Solution to Exercise 7

| | *WIZ* | *PER* | *WLD* | *BKR* | *Total* |
|---|---|---|---|---|---|
| | £'000 | £'000 | £'000 | £'000 | £'000 |
| Sales | 72.4 | 31.2 | 27.6 | 101.0 | 232.2 |
| Direct labour | 20.2 | 7.6 | 4.5 | 39.7 | 72.0 |
| Direct materials | 14.2 | 7.0 | 5.2 | 19.1 | 45.5 |
| Variable overheads | 9.4 | 7.3 | 6.4 | 15.0 | 38.1 |
| | 43.8 | 21.9 | 16.1 | 73.8 | 155.6 |
| Contribution | 28.6 | 9.3 | 11.5 | 27.2 | 76.6 |
| Fixed costs | 23.2 | 11.6 | 11.6 | 29.0 | 75.4 |
| Profit/(loss) | 5.4 | (2.3) | (0.1) | (1.8) | 1.2 |
| Contribution/sales | 39.5% | 29.8% | 41.7% | 26.9% | 33.0% |

*Working*

Fixed overheads

| | *Proportions* | | £ |
|---|---|---|---|
| WIZ | 16,320 | 4/13 | 23,225 |
| PER | 8,160 | 2/13 | 11,612 |
| WLD | 8,160 | 2/13 | 11,612 |
| BKR | 20,400 | 5/13 | 29,031 |
| | | | 75,480 |

## Solution to Exercise 8

(a)

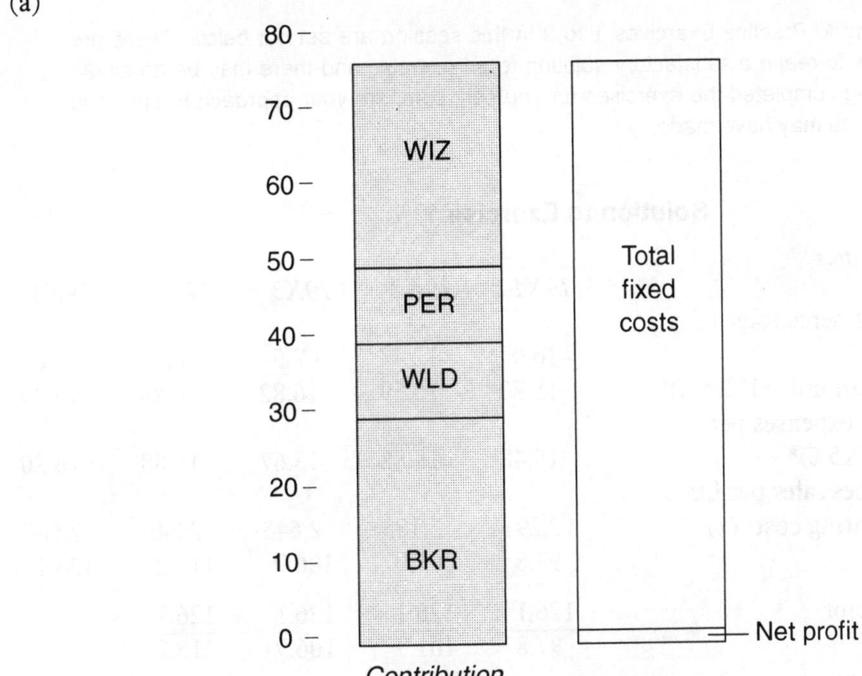


(b) Even though the statement in Exercise 5 shows MRL and CRK as giving an overall loss, eliminating their production reduces the total profit from £13,500 to £1,200. This is because both MRL and CRK made a positive contribution to fixed costs. Fixed overheads now have to be spread over a smaller range of products.

## SOLUTIONS TO SESSION 11 PRACTICE EXERCISES

Suggested solutions to Practice Exercises 1 to 9 in this session are set out below. There are often different ways to reach a satisfactory solution to an exercise and there may be no single right answer. Having completed the exercises for yourself, compare your approach to ours and identify any errors you may have made.

### Solution to Exercise 1

(a) *Performance indicators*

| | *19X1* | *19X2* | *19X3* | *19X4* | *19X5* |
|---|---|---|---|---|---|
| Profit/(loss) as a percentage of receipts | –16.0 | –12.4 | +7.9 | +6.0 | +4.6 |
| Receipts per train mile (19X5 £)* | 15.70 | 16.59 | 16.82 | 16.88 | 16.49 |
| Total operating expenses per train mile (19X5 £)* | 18.48 | 18.88 | 15.67 | 16.88 | 16.20 |
| On-board services sales per £'000 of direct operating costs (£) | 2,291 | 2,185 | 2,645 | 2,843 | 2,560 |
| Inflation index | 97.8 | 101.9 | 106.9 | 115.2 | 126.1 |
| *Conversion factor | $\frac{126.1}{97.8}$ | $\frac{126.1}{101.9}$ | $\frac{126.1}{106.9}$ | $\frac{126.1}{115.2}$ | 1 |

(b) *Comments on methods*

Inflation will affect both costs and revenues. The profit/(loss) as a percentage of receipts does not require adjustment since it is expressed as a percentage. Similarly, as on-board services sales per £'000 of direct operating costs is a ratio of revenues to costs, no adjustment is necessary: inflation will affect both sales prices and operating costs.

The other indicators (receipts per train mile, and total operating costs per train mile) are each calculated using only one monetary term (receipts and total operating costs, respectively) and are adjusted by 126.1 ÷ inflation index for the relevant year, in order to express them in real terms (19X5 £s).

### Solution to Exercise 2

(a)

| | 19X1 | 19X2 | 19X3 | 19X4 | 19X5 |
|---|---|---|---|---|---|
| $\frac{\text{Receipts per train mile} \times 1{,}000}{\text{Total operating expenses per train mile}}$ | $\frac{12{,}180}{14.33}$ | $\frac{13{,}410}{15.26}$ | $\frac{14{,}260}{13.28}$ | $\frac{15{,}420}{15.42}$ | $\frac{16{,}490}{16.20}$ |
| = Receipts per £'000 of total operating expenses (£) | 850 | 879 | 1,074 | 1,000 | 1,018 |

(b) No. Both 'sides' of the ratio, receipts and total operating expenses, will be affected by general inflation. Strictly speaking, it might be meaningful to adjust each factor by an appropriate specific price index. For example, receipts might be adjusted by an index of transport fares and total operating costs might be adjusted by an index of general industrial costs. However, such indices are not available here.

## Solution to Exercise 3

| | *19X1* | *19X2* | *19X3* | *19X4* |
|---|---|---|---|---|
| Sales (19X4 £'000s) | 1,384 | 1,407 | 1,397 | 1,473 |
| Annual real sales growth | - | 1.7% | -0.7% | 5.4% |
| Selling employees | 18 | 19 | 20 | 20 |
| Total employees | 23 | 26 | 28 | 28 |
| Sales per selling employee (19X4 £'000s) | 76.9 | 74.1 | 69.9 | 73.7 |
| Sales per employee (19X4 £'000s) | 60.2 | 54.1 | 49.9 | 52.6 |
| Gross profit percentage | 43.4% | 41.0% | 37.7% | 37.0% |
| Operating expenses (19X4 £'000s) | 263 | 262 | 294 | 310 |
| Net profit percentage | 24.4% | 22.4% | 16.6% | 16.0% |

*Comments*

Sales growth needs to be viewed in terms of real sales by adjusting for inflation. Real sales show little change in 19X2 and 19X3, followed by 5.4% growth in real sales (ie in volume terms) in 19X4.

Real sales per selling employee declined in 19X2 and 19X3 but showed some recovery in 19X4. However, real sales per employee overall has shown larger percentage falls, with only a small rise in 19X4.

Over the period 19X1 to 19X4, the gross profit percentage declined each year, standing at 37% in 19X4 against 43.4% in 19X1. Accompanying a rise in expenses in real terms, partly reflecting the increase in non-selling staff numbers, there has been a decline in the net profit percentage from 24.4% to 16.0% between 19X1 and 19X4.

It is unclear from the figures given why it should have been necessary to increase non-selling staff employed from five to eight over the period.

## Solution to Exercise 4

ROCE = Asset turnover × profit percentage

$$= \frac{\text{Sales}}{\text{Capital employed}} \times \frac{\text{Profit}}{\text{Sales}}$$

| | *X* | *Y* |
|---|---|---|
| Profit (annual basis) | £960,000 (×12) | £180,000 |
| Sales (annual basis) | £7,200,000 (×12) | £4,440,000 |

ROCE

$$X: \frac{£7.2m}{£6.4m} \times \frac{£0.96m}{£7.2m} \qquad Y: \frac{£4.44m}{£0.9m} \times \frac{£0.18m}{£4.44m}$$

| | *X* | *Y* |
|---|---|---|
| | = 1.125 times × 13.3% | = 4.933 times × 4.1% |
| | = 15% | = 20% |

| | *X* | *Y* |
|---|---|---|
| | % | % |
| Sales | 100 | 100 |
| Variable costs | 38 | 56 |
| | 62 | 44 |
| Controllable fixed costs | 11 | 8 |
| Controllable profit | 51 | 36 |
| Apportioned group costs | 38 | 32 |
| Net profit | 13 | 4 |

$$\text{Controllable annual ROCE} \qquad X: \frac{306 \times 12}{6,400} = 57.4\% \qquad Y: \frac{134 \times 12}{900} = 178.7\%$$

(a) Y achieves a higher return on capital employed (ROCE) than X, even when controllable profit is used in the calculation.

(b) Y achieves a higher asset turnover rate than X, which outweighs the effect of the lower profitability of sales, producing a higher ROCE.

(c) The higher contribution to sales ratio achieved by X suggests that its ROCE could be substantially improved if sales were increased at the same prices.

(d) The higher sales to capital employed ratio achieved by Y may indicate a different basis of operating compared with X (high sales, low profitability), but it may be due to the fact that Y is using older or fully depreciated fixed assets. It may therefore be misleading to draw firm conclusions from these ratios.

## Solution to Exercise 5

Residual income can be used as an alternative performance measure as follows.

| | | *X* | | *Y* | |
|---|---|---|---|---|---|
| | | £'000 | | £'000 | |
| (a) | Sales | 600 | | 370 | |
| | Variable costs | 229 | | 208 | |
| | Contribution | 371 | | 162 | |
| | Controllable fixed overhead | 65 | | 28 | |
| | Controllable profit | 306 | | 134 | |
| | Imputed interest | 64 | (W1) | 9 | (W2) |
| | Controllable residual income | 242 | | 125 | |
| | Apportioned group costs | 226 | | 119 | |
| | Net residual income | 16 | | 6 | |

*Workings*

1 £6.4m × 12% × $^1/_{12}$ = £64,000 per month
2 £0.9m × 12% × $^1/_{12}$ = £9,000 per month

Both companies have a positive residual income, indicating that they earn returns in excess of the target return on capital. X has a greater investment in company assets, therefore the imputed interest charge is greater.

The apparent relative performance of the two companies is now reversed - X achieves a higher residual income than Y. This is because, although X has a ROCE of only 15%, it is returning 15% on a much larger asset base and therefore the absolute profit in excess of cost of capital is greater.

(b) (i) ROCE can discourage managers from undertaking new investments since the high balance sheet values of new assets tend to depress the ROCE initially.

(ii) Residual income uses absolute values and highlights those investments which return more than the cost of capital by showing a positive residual income.

(iii) ROCE tends to be used by external analysts in assessing company performance, therefore it is important to ensure that its level is maintained. However, it must not be applied too rigidly and it is probably better used in conjunction with other performance measures.

## Solution to Exercise 6

(a) Quality of service. (This target relates to timeliness; other quality targets relate to quality of product.)

(b) Financial performance.

(c) Efficiency.

(d) Quality.

(e) Output.

## Solution to Exercise 7

(a) Monthly tonnes of coal produced per mining worker.
(b) Number of applications made as a result of the advertisement.

## Solution to Exercise 8

The correct answer is: every year except 19X4.

| | (1) Unit costs (cash) | (2) General price deflator | (3) Unit costs (real) |
|---|---|---|---|
| | £ | | £ |
| 19X0 | 25.78 | 1.00 | 25.78 |
| 19X1 | 24.57 | 1.05 | 23.40 |
| 19X2 | 27.58 | 1.11 | 24.85 |
| 19X3 | 29.97 | 1.18 | 25.40 |
| 19X4 | 32.06 | 1.22 | 26.28 |
| 19X5 | 32.13 | 1.24 | 25.91 |

(3) = (1) ÷ (2)

## Solution to Exercise 9

(a) (i) $\dfrac{6.0}{(25.8 + 22.6) \div 2} = \dfrac{6.0}{24.2} = 24.8\%$

(ii) $\dfrac{6.0}{35.6} = 16.9\%$

(iii) $\dfrac{35.6}{24.2} = 1.5$ times

(b) $\dfrac{\text{Operating profit}}{\text{Turnover}} \times \dfrac{\text{Turnover}}{\text{Shareholders' funds}} = \dfrac{\text{Operating profit}}{\text{Shareholders' funds}}$

Profit margin × Asset turnover = Return on capital employed

## SOLUTIONS TO SESSION 12 PRACTICE EXERCISES

Suggested solutions to Practice Exercises 1 to 4 in this session are set out below. There are often different ways to reach a satisfactory solution to an exercise and there may be no single right answer. Having completed the exercises for yourself, compare your approach to ours and identify any errors you may have made.

### Solution to Exercise 1

*Tutorial note.* The total collected by HM Customs & Excise is £700 × 17.5% = £122.50, the VAT on the final sale to Victor.

| *Trader* | *Working* | *Amount* | *Due date* |
|---|---|---|---|
| | | £ | |
| Roger | £400 × 0.175 | 70.00 | 30.4.X3 |
| Susan | £700 × 0.175 - £70 - £10.50 | 42.00 | 30.6.X3 |
| Thomas | £70.50 × 7/47 | 10.50 | 30.4.X3 |
| | | 122.50 | |

### Solution to Exercise 2

*Tutorial note*. All the documents in fact meet the requirements of VAT law, but you should have checked that this was so. Input VAT can only be reclaimed if the purchaser holds a valid VAT invoice. If an invoice issued by Bernini plc had shown too little VAT, the shortfall would have had to be accounted for.

The total VAT on sales and other outputs (Box 1) is as follows.

| | £ |
|---|---|
| Sale to Jacob Ltd | 542.50 |
| Sale to Brahms GmbH | 0.00 |
| Sale to Michael plc | 184.80 |
| | 727.30 |
| Less credit to Jacob Ltd | 32.81 |
| | 694.49 |

The Box 2 figure is 'None' so the Box 3 figure is the same as the Box 1 figure.

The total input VAT (Box 4) is as follows.

| | £ |
|---|---|
| Purchase from Angelo plc | 735.00 |
| Purchase from Quantum Ltd | 486.50 |
| | 1,221.50 |
| Less overstatement in previous period | 800.00 |
| | 421.50 |

The Box 5 figure is £(694.49 - 421.50) = £272.99. Because a payment will be made, the box to the left of the declaration must be ticked.

The Box 6 figure is £(3,100.00 + 12,550.00 + 1,056.00 - 187.50) = £16,518.50, to be rounded down to £16,518.

The Box 7 figure is £(4,200 + 2,780) = £6,980.

The Box 8 figure is £12,550.

The Box 9 figure is 'None'.

**Value Added Tax Return**

For the period

01 07 X5 to 30 09 X5

Registration number: 212 7924 36

Period: 09 X5

You could be liable to a financial penalty if your completed return and all the VAT payable are not received by the due date.

BERNINI PLC
1 LONG LANE
ANYTOWN
AN4 5QP

Due date: 31 10 X5

For official use

Your VAT Office telephone number is 0123-4567

Before you fill in this form please read the notes on the back and the VAT Leaflet *"Filling in your VAT return"*. Fill in all boxes clearly in ink, and write 'none' where necessary. Don't put a dash or leave any box blank. If there are no pence write "00" in the pence column. Do not enter more than one amount in any box.

For official use

| | Box | £ | p |
|---|---|---|---|
| VAT due in this period on sales and other outputs | 1 | 694 | 49 |
| VAT due in this period on acquisitions from other EC Member States | 2 | NONE | |
| Total VAT due (the sum of boxes 1 and 2) | 3 | 694 | 49 |
| VAT reclaimed in this period on purchases and other inputs (including acquisitions from the EC) | 4 | 421 | 50 |
| **Net VAT to be paid to Customs or reclaimed by you (Difference between boxes 3 and 4)** | 5 | 272 | 99 |
| Total value of sales and all other outputs excluding any VAT. Include your box 8 figure | 6 | 16,518 | 00 |
| Total value of purchases and all other inputs excluding any VAT. Include your box 9 figure | 7 | 6,980 | 00 |
| Total value of all supplies of goods and related services, excluding any VAT, to other EC Member States | 8 | 12,550 | 00 |
| Total value of all acquisitions of goods and related services, excluding any VAT, from other EC Member States | 9 | NONE | 00 |

**Retail schemes.** If you have used any ot the schemes in the period covered by this return, enter the relevant letter(s) in this box.

If you are enclosing a payment please tick this box. ✓

DECLARATION: You, or someone on your behalf, must sign below.

I, ANNE ACCOUNTANT declare that the
(Full name of signatory in BLOCK LETTERS)
information given above is true and complete.

Signature *A Accountant* Date 25 Oct 19 X5

**A false declaration can result in prosecution.**

## Solution to Exercise 3

*Tutorial note.* All the invoices except (c) look superficially plausible, but in fact (c) is the only valid invoice. This shows the importance of attention to detail in applying VAT law.

(a) The invoice from Altona plc is invalid because it does not show the supplier's address. In all other respects it meets the requirements for a valid VAT invoice.

(b) The invoice from Heine Ltd is invalid because the invoice number has been omitted, because the supplier's VAT registration number is not shown and because the type of supply (presumably a sale) is not shown.

The VAT on this invoice has been wrongly computed. VAT should be computed on the net amount after any cash discount. The correct amounts of VAT are as follows.

| | *Net less 5%* | *VAT* |
|---|---|---|
| | £ | £ |
| 4,000 cups | 1,900 | 332.50 |
| 8,000 saucers | 2,375 | 415.62 |

Finally, the invoice is invalid because the applicable rates of VAT (17.5% and 0%) are not shown.

(c) The total value of the supply by Mann & Co, including VAT, does not exceed £100, so a less detailed invoice is permissible.

The invoice is valid, because it includes all the information which must be shown on a less detailed invoice.

(d) The invoice from Kleist plc is invalid because the total value of zero rated supplies is not shown.

## Solution to Exercise 4

*Tutorial note.* Extensive records must be kept for VAT purposes. In general, these records are no more than a trader would probably keep anyway, but even if a trader could manage without some of the required records, he must still keep them.

(a) *The retail cash sale*

(i) The till roll, showing the gross sale of £56.40, must be kept.

(ii) A cash book showing the sale (or the total of the day's cash sales) must be kept.

(iii) A VAT invoice (possibly a less detailed invoice) will be issued, and a copy must be kept.

(iv) A summary of supplies must be kept, showing this sale, in such a way as to allow the trader to work out, for each VAT period:

(1) the VAT-exclusive values of standard rated supplies, zero rated supplies, exempt supplies and all supplies;

(2) the VAT chargeable on supplies.

(v) A VAT account must be kept. The VAT on the sale, £56.40 × 7/47 = £8.40, will appear on the credit (VAT payable) side of the account, probably as part of a total of VAT on several sales.

(b) *The retail credit sale*

(i) The sale must appear in the summary of supplies described in (a)(iv) above, and the VAT on the sale (£39.95 × 7/47 = £5.95) in the VAT account mentioned in (a)(v) above.

(ii) A sales day book showing the sale must be kept, and a cash book to record the eventual receipt. Records showing the debt must also be kept.

(iii) Because the customer is not registered for VAT, no VAT invoice need be issued. If one is issued (possibly a less detailed invoice), a copy must be kept.

(c) *The cash purchase*

(i) The VAT invoice received must be kept.

(ii) A cash book showing the purchase must be kept.

(iii) Any other documents relating to the purchase, such as a copy of the order or a delivery note, must be kept.

(iv) A summary of purchases must be kept, showing this purchase, in such a way as to allow the trader to work out, for each VAT period, the VAT-exclusive value of all supplies received and the VAT charged on them.

(v) The VAT on the purchase (£270 × 17.5% = £47.25) must appear (probably as part of a larger total) on the debit (VAT allowable) side of the VAT account mentioned in (a)(v) above.

## SOLUTIONS TO SESSION 13 PRACTICE EXERCISES

Suggested solutions to Practice Exercises 1 to 4 in this session are set out below. There are often different ways to reach a satisfactory solution to an exercise and there may be no single right answer. Having completed the exercises for yourself, compare your approach to ours and identify any errors you may have made.

### Solution to Exercise 1

*Tutorial note.* There were two standard rated, two zero rated and two exempt supplies, and totals were needed for each category and for the invoice as a whole. Note that the total including VAT need not be shown, but in practice it always is shown. Note also that the VAT is computed on the net amount after the 4% cash discount.

PIPPA LIMITED
32 Hurst Road, London NE20 4LJ
VAT reg no 730 4148 37

To: Gold Ltd
75 Link Road
London NE25 3PQ

Date: 12 May 19X2
Tax point: 12 May 19X2
Invoice no. 2794

| *Item* | *Quantity* | *VAT rate* | *Net* | *VAT* |
|---|---|---|---|---|
| | | % | £ | £ |
| *Sales of goods* | | | | |
| Personal computer | 1 | 17.5 | 980 | |
| Microscopes | 3 | 17.5 | 360 | |
| Total of standard rated (17.5%) supplies | | | 1,340 | 225.12 |
| Books | 20 | 0.0 | 200 | |
| Periodicals | 500 | 0.0 | 450 | |
| Total of zero rated (0%) supplies | | | 650 | 0.00 |
| *Supplies of services* | | | | |
| Insurance | | Exempt | 1,200 | |
| Medical treatment services | | Exempt | 400 | |
| Total of exempt supplies | | | 1,600 | |
| Total invoice price excluding VAT | | | 3,590 | |
| Total VAT | | | | 225.12 |

| | £ |
|---|---|
| Total payable within 30 days | 3,815.12 |
| Less cash discount for payment within 10 days | 143.60 |
| Total payable if paid within 10 days | 3,671.52 |

*Terms: 30 days, 4% discount if paid within 10 days.*

### Solution to Exercise 2

*Tutorial note*. Because Worth plc makes some exempt supplies, not all the VAT on purchases can be recovered. The VAT on purchases which is not attributable to either taxable supplies or exempt supplies must be apportioned.

(a) *Box 1: VAT due on outputs*

The figure is £450,000 × 17.5% = £78,750.00

(b) *Box 2: VAT due on acquisitions*

None.

(c) *Box 3: sum of Boxes 1 and 2*

£78,750.00

(d) *Box 4: VAT reclaimed on inputs*

The figure is £86,520.00, as follows.

Apportionment percentage = (450 + 237)/(450 + 237 + 168) = 80.35%, rounded up to 81%.

| | £ |
|---|---|
| Tax on purchases attributable to taxable supplies £300,000 × 17.5% | 52,500.00 |
| Tax on unattributable purchases | |
| £240,000 × 17.5% × 81% | 34,020.00 |
| | 86,520.00 |

(e) *Box 5: net VAT to be paid or reclaimed*

The amount reclaimable is £(86,520.00 - 78,750.00) = £7,770.00.

## Solution to Exercise 3

*Tutorial note*. You first had to compute the relevant totals, then you had to check the position on partial exemption.

| *Date cash received* | *Standard rated turnover* | *Zero rated turnover* | *Exempt turnover* | *VAT at 7/47* |
|---|---|---|---|---|
| | £ | £ | £ | £ |
| 2.6.X4 | 270.35 | | | 40.26 |
| 15.6.X4 | 420.00 | | | 62.55 |
| 2.6.X4 | 620.74 | | | 92.45 |
| 7.6.X4 | | 540.40 | | |
| 22.6.X4 | | 680.18 | | |
| 14.6.X4 | 200.37 | | | 29.84 |
| 4.7.X4 | | | 180.62 | |
| 12.7.X4 | | 235.68 | | |
| 12.7.X4 | 429.32 | | | 63.94 |
| 21.7.X4 | | | 460.37 | |
| 20.8.X4 | | | 390.12 | |
| 3.8.X4 | | 220.86 | | |
| 23.8.X4 | 350.38 | | | 52.18 |
| | 2,291.16 | 1,677.12 | 1,031.11 | 341.22 |

Total taxable turnover is £(2,291.16 - 341.22 + 1,677.12) = £3,627.06. Total turnover is £(3,627.06 + 1,031.11) = £4,658.17.

The output VAT in respect of fuel is £252.00 × 7/47 = £37.53, so total output VAT is £(341.22 + 37.53) = £378.75.

The scale charge net of VAT is £(252.00 - 37.53) = £214.47, so the Box 6 figure is £(4,658.17 + 214.47) = £4,872.64, rounded down to £4,872.

| *Date cash paid* | *Purchase* | *VAT at 7/47* |
|---|---|---|
| | £ | £ |
| 4.6.X4 | 521.44 | 77.66 |
| 3.6.X4 | 516.13 | 76.87 |
| 1.7.X4 | 737.48 | |
| 4.7.X4 | 414.68 | 61.76 |
| 12.7.X4 | 280.85 | |
| | 2,470.58 | 216.29 |

The purchases net of VAT (Box 7) are £(2,470.58 - 216.29) = £2,254.29, rounded down.

Input VAT attributable to exempt supplies is 1,031.11/4,872.64 = 21.16%, rounded to 21% (*exempt* percentage *down*) × £216.29 = £45.42. As this is not more than £625 a month on average and not more than half of all input VAT, all input VAT is recoverable.

**Value Added Tax Return**

For the period

01 06 X4 to 31 08 X4

| Registration number | Period |
|---|---|
| 483 8611 98 | 08 X4 |

You could be liable to a financial penalty if your completed return and all the VAT payable are not received by the due date.

MS S SMITH
32 CASE STREET
ZEDTOWN
ZY4 3JN

Due date: 30 09 X4

For official use

Your VAT Office telephone number is 0123-4567

Before you fill in this form please read the notes on the back and the VAT Leaflet *"Filling in your VAT return"*. Fill in all boxes clearly in ink, and write 'none' where necessary. Don't put a dash or leave any box blank. If there are no pence write "00" in the pence column. Do not enter more than one amount in any box.

For official use

| | Box | £ | p |
|---|---|---|---|
| VAT due in this period on sales and other outputs | 1 | 378 | 75 |
| VAT due in this period on acquisitions from other EC Member States | 2 | None | |
| Total VAT due (the sum of boxes 1 and 2) | 3 | 378 | 75 |
| VAT reclaimed in this period on purchases and other inputs (including acquisitions from the EC) | 4 | 216 | 29 |
| **Net VAT to be paid to Customs or reclaimed by you (Difference between boxes 3 and 4)** | 5 | 162 | 46 |
| Total value of sales and all other outputs excluding any VAT. Include your box 8 figure | 6 | 4,872 | 00 |
| Total value of purchases and all other inputs excluding any VAT. Include your box 9 figure | 7 | 2,254 | 00 |
| Total value of all supplies of goods and related services, excluding any VAT, to other EC Member States | 8 | None | 00 |
| Total value of all acquisitions of goods and related services, excluding any VAT, from other EC Member States | 9 | None | 00 |

**Retail schemes.** If you have used any ot the schemes in the period covered by this return, enter the relevant letter(s) in this box.

If you are enclosing a payment please tick this box. ✓

DECLARATION: You, or someone on your behalf, must sign below.

I, SUZANNE SMITH declare that the
(Full name of signatory in BLOCK LETTERS)
information given above is true and complete.

Signature *S Smith* Date 28 Sept 19 X4

**A false declaration can result in prosecution.**

## Solution to Exercise 4

*Tutorial note.* There must be an initial default before a surcharge liability period can start. However, once it has started it is extended by later defaults. In this case, there is a single surcharge liability period extending at least as far as 30 September 19X5. Because there is no break in the period, the percentage rate escalates right up to 15%.

| *Quarter ended* | *Working* | *Surcharge* | |
|---|---|---|---|
| | | £ | |
| 30.6.X3 | £5,000 × 2% = £100 | 0 | (under £200) |
| 30.9.X3 | £4,500 × 5% | 225 | |
| 31.3.X4 | £3,500 × 10% | 350 | |
| 30.6.X4 | £4,500 × 15% | 675 | |
| 30.9.X4 | £500 × 15% | 75 | (surcharges under £200 are collected when at 10% or 15%) |

# *Devolved assessments*

# Devolved assessment 1 Comma Ltd

## Performance criteria

The following performance criteria are covered in this Devolved Assessment.

### Element 7.1: Prepare periodic performance reports

1 Reports are prepared in a clear and intelligible form and presented to management within defined timescales

3 Cost and revenue data derived from different information systems within the organisation are correctly reconciled

4 An appropriate method allowing for changing price levels when comparing results over time is agreed and used

6 Ratios and performance indicators are accurately calculated in accordance with the agreed methodology

## Notes on completing the Assessment

This Assessment is designed to test your ability to prepare periodic performance reports.

You are provided with the information necessary to complete the tasks (a) to (c) on pages 134 and 135.

You are allowed 2 hours to complete your work.

A high level of accuracy is required. Check your work carefully.

Correcting fluid should not be used. Errors should be crossed out neatly and clearly. You should write in ink - not pencil.

A full solution to this Assessment is provided on page 163.

Do not turn to the suggested solution until you have completed all parts of the Assessment.

## DEVOLVED ASSESSMENT 1: COMMA LTD

### Background information

You work for Comma Ltd, the UK subsidiary of a Swedish parent company. The company has a 31 December year end.

### Tasks

Your manager, Don Waite, requires you to prepare information for presentation as a 'handout' at the monthly management meeting. He shows you a detailed income statement (page 135) which has been produced using a computer spreadsheet program, but feels that this is too detailed for the purposes of this meeting. Certain other information is also available (page 136).

The information which Don requires you to prepare is as follows.

(a) A simplified income statement showing the budgeted and actual results for the month of September 19X2, and the nine months to September 19X2, with both £million (rounded as considered appropriate but with no amount shown to more than three digits) and percentage columns (net sales = 100%; round to the nearest one per cent). The income statement should include the following lines.

Net sales
Less: Standard cost
Variances
Other costs
Inter-company contribution
Manufacturing margin
Selling expenses
Administrative expenses
Inter-company contribution
Operating income
Inter-company (net)
Income before tax
Tax
Net income

For the purposes of comparison, your statement should also incorporate the following previous year actual figures, rounded as appropriate and additionally showing the manufacturing margin and operating income expressed as a percentage of net sales.

*September 19X1*

| | £ |
|---|---|
| Net sales | 1,850,972 |
| Manufacturing margin | 611,227 |
| Operating income | 209,944 |

*9 months to September 19X2*

| | £ |
|---|---|
| Net sales | 22,402,106 |
| Manufacturing margin | 7,827,435 |
| Operating income | 2,210,810 |

(b) A pie chart comparing the split of the company's net sales between its major geographical markets in 19W6 and 19X1. The major geographical markets should be classified as follows.

UK
Exports: European Union
North America
Other

(c) A bar chart showing net sales per full-time employee (in 19X2 pounds) over the period 19W6 to 19X1. A part-time employee is to be treated as equivalent to one half of a full time employee for this purpose. The average Retail Prices Index figures below are to be used for the purpose of adjusting the relevant figures to 19X2 pounds.

| Year | RPI average |
|---|---|
| 19W6 | 128.2 |
| 19W7 | 132.7 |
| 19W8 | 139.5 |
| 19W9 | 146.2 |
| 19X0 | 150.7 |
| 19X1 | 157.8 |
| 19X2 | 164.9 |

You should add a brief commentary to each part (a), (b) and (c) of the information you present. These commentaries will be included in the handout to be presented at the meeting.

**Data**

## Comma Limited Income Statement

| | September 19X2 | | Year to date | |
|---|---|---|---|---|
| | Budget £ | Actual £ | Budget £ | Actual £ |
| Gross sales | 2,207,000 | 2,079,480 | 23,519,000 | 24,498,743 |
| Discounts | (64,000) | (60,510) | (684,000) | (703,871) |
| Net sales | 2,143,000 | 2,018,970 | 22,835,000 | 23,794,872 |
| Standard cost | 1,123,500 | 1,022,777 | 11,567,000 | 12,314,815 |
| Variances | 171,000 | 241,240 | 1,888,000 | 2,271,729 |
| Other costs | 187,400 | 227,004 | 2,734,000 | 1,911,008 |
| Inter-company contribution | (119,400) | (178,273) | (1,600,400) | (1,296,234) |
| Total cost of sales | 1,362,500 | 1,312,748 | 14,588,600 | 15,201,318 |
| Manufacturing margin | 780,500 | 706,222 | 8,246,400 | 8,593,554 |
| Direct sales | 70,000 | 57,271 | 682,000 | 672,827 |
| Promotion | 61,000 | 45,843 | 632,000 | 637,221 |
| Other marketing | 76,600 | 73,490 | 1,172,000 | 1,247,160 |
| General admin | 181,000 | 181,221 | 1,997,400 | 1,886,662 |
| Data processing | 68,000 | 70,147 | 721,000 | 713,072 |
| Loan interest | 62,000 | 65,014 | 710,000 | 702,942 |
| | 518,600 | 492,986 | 5,914,400 | 5,859,884 |
| Inter-company contribution | (40,000) | (20,102) | (490,000) | (189,722) |
| Total overheads | 478,600 | 472,884 | 5,424,400 | 5,670,162 |
| Operating income | 301,900 | 233,338 | 2,822,000 | 2,923,392 |
| Inter-company (net) | (19,000) | 21,270 | (210,000) | (22,972) |
| Income before taxes | 282,900 | 254,608 | 2,612,000 | 2,900,420 |
| Taxes on income | (151,000) | (103,700) | (1,397,000) | (1,411,670) |
| Net income | 131,900 | 150,908 | 1,215,000 | 1,488,750 |

NET SALES BY GEOGRAPHICAL MARKET

| | 19X1 | 19W6 |
|---|---|---|
| United Kingdom | 12,248,721 | 9,272,845 |
| Canada | 1,722,400 | 1,888,245 |
| Eire | 2,014,522 | - |
| Germany | 3,604,745 | 1,457,208 |
| France | 2,308,722 | 1,200,405 |
| Nigeria | 1,521,223 | 1,721,542 |
| Other EC | 2,418,717 | 894,281 |
| USA | 3,401,972 | 2,841,470 |
| Other non-EC | 1,182,718 | 1,141,722 |
| | 30,423,740 | 20,417,718 |

*Note.* Eire, Germany and France were all members of the European Union in both 19W6 and 19X1, as was the United Kingdom.

TOTAL NET SALES

| | £ |
|---|---|
| 19W6 | 20,417,718 |
| 19W7 | 22,084,165 |
| 19W8 | 23,782,722 |
| 19W9 | 25,621,481 |
| 19X0 | 28,088,390 |
| 19X1 | 30,423,740 |
| 19X2 Sept YTD | 23,794,872 |

Average number of employees

| | Full-time | Part-time |
|---|---|---|
| 19W6 | 694 | 38 |
| 19W7 | 721 | 37 |
| 19W8 | 742 | 44 |
| 19W9 | 765 | 48 |
| 19X0 | 870 | 53 |
| 19X1 | 852 | 57 |
| 19X2 Sept YTD | 842 | 61 |

# Devolved assessment
# 2 Consultancy Office

## Performance criteria

The following performance criteria are covered in this Devolved Assessment.

### Element 7.1: Prepare periodic performance reports

1 Reports are prepared in a clear and intelligible form and presented to management within defined timescales

2 Information about costs and revenues derived from different units of the organisation is consolidated in standard form

3 Cost and revenue data derived from different information systems within the organisation are correctly reconciled

4 An appropriate method allowing for changing price levels when comparing results over time is agreed and used

6 Ratios and performance indicators are accurately calculated in accordance with the agreed methodology

If a computer spreadsheet programme is used to complete this Assessment, parts of Unit 22: *Using spreadsheets* will also be covered.

## Notes on completing the Assessment

This Assessment is designed to test your ability to prepare periodic performance reports.

The example used in this Assessment is of a fictitious organisation in the public (government) sector. However, you do not need to have previous experience or knowledge of the public sector to complete it. If you have access to computer spreadsheet software, then you can use it for this Assignment. Alternatively the Assessment can be completed manually.

You are provided with background information and data which you must use to complete the task on page 138.

You are allowed 2 hours to complete your work.

A high level of accuracy is required. Check your work carefully.

Correcting fluid should not be used. Errors should be crossed out neatly and clearly. You should write in ink - not pencil.

A full solution to this Assessment is provided on page 166.

Do not turn to the suggested solution until you have completed all parts of the Assessment.

## DEVOLVED ASSESSMENT 2: CONSULTANCY OFFICE

### Data

You are employed in an executive agency called the Consultancy Office ('the Office'), which provides a grants consultancy service to individuals and small businesses.

You are involved in a project to construct unit cost and productivity indicators over a four year period ('Years 1 to 4').

The Office issues Consultancy Request Forms, usually immediately, whenever a form is requested by a client. A count is kept of the number of forms issued, ie the output of forms. The client completes the form, which is fairly detailed, to indicate the circumstances which give rise to the need for consultancy to be provided by the Office.

Having received the form duly completed by the client, the Office issues consultancy advice at a later date (which can be assumed to be one year later). The number of items of consultancy advice issued is accepted as a measure of output.

The Office additionally carries out a certain amount of research work whose output cannot practicably be measured.

Resources used by the department comprise labour (measured in hours), other running costs and capital. Resources used are attributed to the activities of forms, consultancy and research work respectively in the ratio 1: 2: 1.

### Task

You are required to prepare a table of variables covering the four year period in the form set out on page 139. The variables are to be calculated using the agreed methods set out on pages 140 - 141 and the additional data on page 141. Your form should be given a title.

The general price deflator index has been provided on the form, and your supervisor has completed line 2 for years 1 to 3 for to get you started.

| Variable | Year 1 | Year 2 | Year 3 | Year 4 |
|---|---|---|---|---|
| **INFLATION** | | | | |
| (1) General price deflator | 1.00 | 1.05 | 1.09 | 1.14 |
| **CAPITAL** | | | | |
| (2) Value of capital at start of year | £20,000 | £18,900 | £17,440 | |
| (3) Annual capital charge | | | | |
| (4) 'Physical' capital consumed | | | | |
| **LABOUR** | | | | |
| (5) Hours worked | | | | |
| (6) Labour costs | | | | |
| (7) Average wage rate | | | | |
| (8) Other running costs (cash) | | | | |
| (9) 'Physical' other running costs | | | | |
| **TOTALS** | | | | |
| (10) Total annual cost | | | | |
| (11) Total 'physical' running costs | | | | |
| (12) Total 'physical' resources consumed | | | | |
| **OUTPUTS** | | | | |
| (13) Forms issued | | | | |
| (14) Cases processed | | | | |
| **UNIT COSTS** | | | | |
| (15) Total costs: forms | | | | |
| (16) Unit cost of issuing forms | | | | |
| (17) Real unit cost of forms | | | | |
| (18) Total costs: consultancy | | | | |
| (19) Unit cost of consultancy | | | | |
| (20) Real unit cost of consultancy | | | | |
| **PRODUCTIVITY** | | | | |
| (21) 'Physical' output of forms and consultancy | | | | |
| (22) 'Physical' running costs: forms and consultancy | | | | |
| (23) Productivity of running costs: forms and consultancy | | | | |
| (24) Year-on-year increase in (23) | | | | |
| (25) Total physical resources consumed: forms and consultancy | | | | |
| (26) Productivity - all resources: forms and consultancy | | | | |
| (27) Year-on-year increase in (26) | | | | |

## Agreed methods

*Value of capital (2).* The value of capital is depreciated on a straight line basis over ten years; it is assumed to have no value after the ten years. The depreciated value is then adjusted for inflation, using the general price deflator, for which the base is Year 1.

*Examples:*

Value of capital at year 2 = £20,000 (value of capital at year 1) × 0.9 × 1.05
= £18,900 (This is the figure for the year 2 column, line 2)

Value of capital at year 3 = 20,000 × 0.8 × 1.09 = £17,440

*Annual capital charge (3).* This equals the amount of depreciation (inflated) plus an allowance for the cost of capital which is calculated as 6% of the mid-year value.

*Examples:* Year 1: $£20{,}000 \times \frac{1}{10} + 0.06 \times \frac{(20{,}000 + 18{,}900)}{2} = £3{,}167$

Year 2: $£18{,}900 \times \frac{1}{9} + 0.06 \times \frac{(18{,}900 + 17{,}440)}{2} = £3{,}190$

To calculate the capital charge for year 4, you need to know that the value of capital at the start of year 5 is £14,400 (since the general price deflator for year 5 is 1.20).

*'Physical' capital consumed* (4) is the annual charge (3) deflated by (1). (ie (3) ÷ (1)).

*'Physical' other running costs* (9) is other running costs (8) deflated by (1).

*Total annual cost* (10) is: Annual capital charge (3) + labour costs (6) + other running costs (8).

*Total 'physical' running costs* (11) are:

'Physical' other running costs (9) + 'physical' labour, where:
'physical' labour = hours worked weighted by the base year unit cost (7), ie:
Hours worked × Year 1 average wage rate (7).

*Total 'physical' resources consumed* (12) are: Total 'physical' running costs (11) + 'physical' capital consumed (4).

*Total costs: forms* (15) is defined as: Total annual cost (10) × ¼.

*Unit cost of issuing forms* (16) is: Total costs: forms (15) ÷ Forms issued (13).

*Real unit cost of forms* (17) is calculated by deflating the unit cost of issuing forms (16) using the general price deflator (1), (ie unit cost of issuing forms (16) ÷ general price deflator (1)).

*Total costs : consultancy* (18) is defined as Total annual cost (10) × ½.

*Unit cost of consultancy* (19). Consultancy advice is issued a year after the resources are input. Therefore, the unit cost is the previous year cost from (18), inflated by 6% cost of capital and by the general price deflator (1) relative to the previous year, divided by current year output.

*Example (Year 3)*
Unit cost of consultancy (19) = Total costs: consultancy, year 2 (18) × 1.06 × 1.09/1.05 ÷ current year output 4,000.

For year 1, the unit cost of consultancy is assumed to be £14.00.

*Real unit cost of consultancy* (20) is calculated by deflating the unit cost of consultancy (19) using the general price deflator (1).

*'Physical' output of forms and consultancy* (21). This is the sum of (13) and (14) weighted by their base-year unit cost (16) and (19) respectively, ie:

Forms issued in year (13) × Year 1 unit cost of issuing forms (16) + cases processed in year (14) × Year 1 unit cost of consultancy (19).

*'Physical' running costs: forms and consultancy* (22). As producing forms and consultancy uses three-quarters of resources, this is calculated as: Total 'physical' running costs (11) × $^3/_4$.

*Productivity of running costs: forms and consultancy* (23). This is:

'Physical' output of forms and consultancy (21) ÷ 'Physical' running costs: forms and consultancy (22).

*Total 'physical' resources consumed: forms and consultancy* (25). As producing forms and consultancy uses three-quarters of resources, this is:

Total 'physical' resources consumed (12) × $^3/_4$.

*Productivity - all resources: forms and consultancy* (26). This is:

'Physical' output of forms and consultancy (21) ÷ Total 'physical' resources consumed: forms and consultancy (25).

## Data

*Capital.* The capital was valued at £20,000 as at the start of Year 1.

*Hours worked* is assumed constant at 20,000 hours per year.

*Labour costs* were £100,000 in year 1. Year-on-year increases were as follows.

| | |
|---|---|
| Year 2 | 8% |
| Year 3 | 6% |
| Year 4 | 6% |

*Other running costs* are £2,000 per annum in years 1 and 2 and £1,800 per annum in years 3 and 4.

*Outputs* were as follows.

| | *Forms issued* | *Cases processed* |
|---|---|---|
| Year 1 | 8,000 | 3,900 |
| Year 2 | 8,200 | 3,960 |
| Year 3 | 8,450 | 4,000 |
| Year 4 | 8,550 | 4,020 |

# Devolved assessment
# 3 Harvey Hotel and Leisure
# Class assessment

## *Performance criteria*

The following performance criteria are covered in this Devolved Assessment.

### Element 7.1: Prepare periodic performance reports

2 Information about costs and revenues derived from different units of the organisation is consolidated in standard form

### Element 7.2: Prepare reports and returns for outside agencies

1 The conventions and definitions used by the external agency are correctly used in preparing the report or return

2 Relevant information is identified, collated and presented in accordance with the external agency's requirement

3 Calculations of ratios and performance indicators are accurate

### Notes on completing the Assessment

This Assessment is designed principally to test your ability to prepare reports and returns for outside agencies.

You are provided with background information which you must use to complete the task on page 145.

You are allowed 2 hours to complete your work.

A high level of accuracy is required. Check your work carefully.

Correcting fluid should not be used. Errors should be crossed out neatly and clearly. You should write in ink - not pencil.

## DEVOLVED ASSESSMENT 3: HARVEY HOTEL AND LEISURE

### Background information

Rita Jean Harvey is a sole trader, running a hotel and holiday business, trading as Harvey Hotel and Leisure. The main part of the business is the 12-bedroom Harvey Hotel, at 12 Drake Street, Ambleside, Cumbria CA4 7NR (Telephone 01693-742742), which Rita has owned and run for the past twelve years. Rita lives in a flat in the hotel.

Four years ago, Rita bought a small site twelve miles away called Ellwood Crag (at Ellwood, Ambleside CA5 7PX - no telephone), where she rents out three holiday chalets, each as a separate unit, on a weekly basis.

Rita's accounts are made up to 31 March each year. The following information is available.

| | *Hotel* | | *Holiday lettings* | |
|---|---|---|---|---|
| | *Year to 31.3.X4 Estimate* | *Year to 31.3.X5 Estimate* | *Year to 31.3.X4 Estimate* | *Year to 31.3.X5 Estimate* |
| | £ | £ | £ | £ |
| Turnover | 59,655 | 66,800 | 15,180 | 16,700 |
| Cost of sales | 12,840 | 14,400 | 2,994 | 3,100 |
| Fixed costs | 20,746 | 21,750 | 7,205 | 7,300 |
| Net profit | 26,069 | 30,650 | 4,981 | 6,300 |
| Staff wages and salaries* | | | | |
| Secretarial/reception | 2,560 | 2,600 | 600 | 600 |
| Catering | 10,074 | 10,200 | - | - |
| Cleaning | 3,940 | 4,000 | 2,080 | 2,100 |
| *Staff numbers (whole business)* | | | | |
| Secretarial/reception | 1 | | | |
| Catering | 2 | | | |
| Cleaning | 1 | | | |

*Included in the above cost figures

Staff wages and salaries and staff numbers exclude Joan Bright who will be the only Youth Training Scheme trainee working for Rita in the year to 31 March 19X5. Joan will be engaged in catering work.

A year-on-year increase in gross profit (in money terms, allowing for expected inflation) of 10% is expected in the year to 31 March 19X6.

Rita is dissatisfied with certain aspects of the insurance policy which she has held since she started the business. She has been seeking quotations for alternative annual policies as her current policy expires in 14 days' time, on 30 March 19X4. Rita has approached an insurance broker who has recommended a number of possibilities. A policy called Retailer Plus provided by Retail and General Insurance Ltd provides a satisfactory range of cover for a reasonable level of annual premium. (*Tutorial note*. This insurance company has been invented for the purpose of this Assessment.)

Although the level of cover required was outlined when a quotation was sought, the insurance company now requires a more detailed and formal return of information to be given on a standard insurance proposal form. Rita has stated a number of points about the cover she requires, as follows.

She is prepared to pay the insurance premium by direct debit, and wishes to spread the cost for as long a period as possible.

Rita wishes to be insured against business interruption losses arising from fire and burglary, but thinks that 'all risks' cover against such losses is too expensive. She considers that, following a fire or burglary, she would be able to return to normal trading within ten months at the most, allowing all necessary time for rebuilding etc. Rita does not wish the sum insured under the business interruption section to be any higher than is necessary.

Employer's liability insurance cover is to apply, and an indemnity limit of £1,000,000 is required for public and products liability cover.

Plant and machinery in the business should be covered on an 'unspecified' basis against the standard contingencies where available under the Retailer Plus policy.

The following information on plant and machinery has been extracted from the fixed asset register of the business as at 1 March 19X4.

| | *Year of purchase* | *At cost* | *Accum. dep'n* | *Net book value* |
|---|---|---|---|---|
| | | £ | £ | £ |
| Office equipment | 19X3 | 1,470 | 370 | 1,100 |
| Air conditioning system | 19X2 | 3,100 | 1,000 | 2,100 |
| Ovens | 19X1 | 1,840 | 578 | 1,262 |
| Refrigerators | 19X1 | 960 | 240 | 720 |

The following plant price index can be applied as appropriate to calculate estimated replacement values (ie the replacement costs) of plant and machinery in 19X4.

| | *Index* |
|---|---|
| 19X1 | 100.0 |
| 19X2 | 110.4 |
| 19X3 | 118.9 |
| 19X4 | 123.5 |

**Task**

Complete the extracts from the insurance proposal form set out on pages 146 to 149, using the information given.

The insurance is to cover both Harvey Hotel and Ellwood Crag.

Any assumptions which you need to make should be stated clearly in a separate note.

# Retailer Plus Insurance

Retail and General Insurance Ltd

**Important**
Please note that no cover is in force until confirmed by the Company in writing.
Please complete in BLOCK CAPITALS throughout.

---

**Full Name of Proposer**
If not a limited company show the full names (including forenames) of all principals or partners and the full trading name.
*Please show the names of all subsidiary and associated companies to be insured.*

RITA JEAN HARVEY
HARVEY HOTEL + LEISURE

Postal Address

12 DRAKE ST
AMBLESIDE, CUMBRIA

Tel. No. 01693 - 742742
Postcode CA4 7NR

Address(es) of Premises to be insured if different from above

| Address | Postcode | Tel. No. |
|---|---|---|
| ELLWOOD CRAG<br>ELLWOOD<br>AMBLESIDE | CA5 7PX | - |

Trade or Business

HOLIDAY LETTINGS

---

**Period of Insurance:**
One year commencing

| Day | Month | Year |
|---|---|---|
| 31 | 03 | 94 |

---

**Paying by Instalments**
Your premium may be paid by direct debit in five, seven or nine monthly instalments

Do you wish to pay your premium by instalments? Insert YES or NO ▶

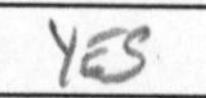
YES

---

**Index linking**
Index Linking applies to the following Sections unless you instruct or we advise otherwise.

- ★ Property Damage
- ★ Burglary
- ★ Goods in Transit
- Business Interruption

★ For these Sections this inflation protection is given free during the Period of Insurance

Sums insured are index-linked by adjusting them in line withthe following indices.

**Building sums insured**
The General Building Cost Index issued by the Building Cost Information Service of the Royal Institute of Chartered Surveyors

**All other sums insured**
The Producer Price Index for Home Sales of Manufactured Products issued by the Department of Trade and Industry

## SECTION 1: BUSINESS INTERRUPTION

**General notes**

The Business Interruption Section gives cover for loss due to:

*(a)* *a reduction in 'NET' profit*

*(b)* *payment of expenses which continue to be incurred despite a reductioin in income;*

*(c)* *the additional expense incurred in order to continue the business following damage by any of the contingencies covererd under this Section*

Gross Profit is defined as:

*Your turnover (net of discounts allowed) plus closing stock and work in progress*

*less*

*The amount of opening stock and work in progress, plus the cost of purchases (net of discounts received) and the amount of any other charges you specify which will vary in direct proportion to turnover*

---

1. Is cover required? Insert YES or NO ▶ [ YES ] If 'YES' complete this Section

---

2. Contingencies to be covered

   (a) EITHER Fire — Insert YES or NO ▶ [ YES ]

   OR All Risks (excluding Theft) — Insert YES or NO ▶ [ NO ]

   (b) Burglary — Insert YES or NO ▶ [ YES ]

---

3. Maximum Indemnity Period (tick appropriate box)

   12 months ▶ [✓] 18 months ▶ [ ] 24 months ▶ [ ] 36 months ▶ [ ]

   Other months (please specify) (not less than 12) ▶ [ ]

   *Note* This period commences at the date of the damage which affects your business and must be long enough for your business to return to normal. Allow sufficient time for rebuilding and refurbishing your premises and further time for a return to normal trading.

---

4. Amount Insured

   State here the Sum Insured £ 72600 Rate 10%

   *Note* The Sum Insured should represent not less than the Gross Profit of your business which you expect to obtain throughout the whole length of the Maximum Indemnity Period. Account must be taken of the possibility of a loss occurring towards the end of the period of insurance. This means that when calculating the sum insured full allowance should be made for growth and inflation during both the insurance period and the Maximum Indemnity Period so the sum insured represents the Gross Profit expected to be earned during the Maximum Indemnity Period from a date commencing at the very end of the insurance year.

   Our liability is limited to the sum insured and in the event that the sum insured proves inadequate claims become subject to a proportional reduction.

   If, when the actual Gross Profit becomes known the Sum Insured proves too high, a part of the premium is refundable.

---

5. Other information.

   Please give for the current financial year the estimated amount of Gross Profit. £ 59,001

---

## SECTION 2: EMPLOYER'S LIABILITY

### General notes

This section provides the cover required under the law relating to compulsory insurance for injury to employees. However, it goes further.

1 *The protection provided has no monetary limit.*

2 *Legal costs and expenses in defending prosecutions under the Health and Safety at Work etc Act 1974 are insured, as are legal costs and expenses arising in connection with the Health and Safety Inquiries (Procedure) Regulations 1975.*

3 *There is worldwide cover for employees normally resident in the UK who are temporarily working overseas.*

4 *If an employee is injured at work through the fault of a member of the public and despite a judgement in his favour is unable to obtain compensation, we shall settle the claim and seek to recover the compensation ourselves.*

'Employee' will include not only your own staff who work under a contract of service or apprenticeship but any self-employed person, labour only sub-contractor, youth training scheme employee or voluntary worker where work is under your supervision and control.

---

1 Is cover required? Insert YES or NO ▶ YES If 'YES' complete this Section

---

2. Estimated annual wages, salaries and other earnings for the coming year.

| Description of all Employees | | Estimate | No. of persons |
|---|---|---|---|
| Clerical and non-manual work | SECRETARIAL/RECEPTION | £ 3200 | 1 |
| Manual work (describe duties) | CATERING<br>CLEANING | £ 13200<br>£ 6100 | 3<br>1 |

*Note* The estimated wages should make allowance for all persons shown in the summary as 'Employees'. At least £7,500 must be allowed for each working director of a limited company and £3,000 for any person working under any youth training scheme. No deductions should be made for income tax, holiday with pay, contributory pensions or National Insurance.

---

3 How many certificates of insurance do you require? Insert number required ▶ 4

A certificate in the prescribed form must be displayed at each place of business and in such a position as to be clearly seen and read by every Employee.

---

## SECTION 3: PUBLIC AND PRODUCTS LIABILITY

### General notes

This section offers wide protection. For example the term 'Injury' will in addition to bodily injury include 'Personal' injury such as wrongful eviction and accusation of shoplifting.

In addition to 'Damage to Property' cover will apply to economic loss arising from obstruction, trespass, nuisance or interference with any right of way, air, light, water or other easement.

The Basic Cover also protects against liability for loss of or damage to premises hired or rented to you for your business, contingent liability arising from use of non-owned vehicles in the United Kingdom, injury or damage to property you may incur under the Defective Premises legislation and personal liability which may be incurred by employees and directors while they are overseas on your business.

Legal costs and expenses in defending prosecutions under the Health and Safety at Work etc Act 1974 are insured, as are legal costs and expenses arising in connection with the Health and Safety Inquiries (Procedure) Regulations 1975.

---

1 Is cover required? Insert YES or NO ▶ YES If 'YES' complete this Section

---

2 Indemnity limit required?
*(tick appropriate box)*

(a) £500,000 ▶ ☐ (b) £1,000,000 ▶ ☑ (c) Over £1,000,000 ▶ ☐ (d) If (c) show limit ▶ ☐

The limit of indemnity applies to each and every insured event for Public Liability and to all insured events occurring during

3 State estimated annual payments of wages, salaries and other earnings ▶ £ 30,000

This should be the figure declared under Employer's Liability plus an allowance of £7,500 per head for any Partners,

4 State estimated annual turnover for the coming year ▶ £ 66000

should be as defined in the Companies Acts, that is excluding trade discounts, VAT, excise duty and other sales taxes. Where there is any trading between your Companies show the total turnover after adding together the

## SECTION 4: ENGINEERING

### General notes

*Inspection*

An annnual inspection service (including an inspection service to satisfy your statutory requirements under the Health and

*Insurance*

The Standard Contingencies available under this section have been designed to provide the widest possible damage cover available in respect of your Plant and to provide you with the facility to tailor cover to suit your requirements.

In addition to plant requiring statutory inspections, Insurance cover is available for HEAT AND AIR CONDITIONING plant, BAKING OVENS, REFRIGERATING plant and other machinery and equipment used for your business.

The Plant covered can be on a specified basis where each item included is identified in detail on the Plant Schedule or an unspecified basis where only the general type and range of plant is described on the Plant Schedule.

Whether cover is arranged on a specified or unspecified basis the indemnity includes provision for Automatic Cover on all additional plant of a like type which is installed and ready for use during the period of insurance.

1 Is cover required? Insert YES or NO ▶ YES If 'YES' complete this Section

You are probably aware that, to comply with legislation, certain items of plant must be inspected by a competent engineer. These include steam boilers, air receivers, passenger lifts, fork lift trucks and other lifting plant. It is possible that safety regulations may be brought into force at any time calling for compulsory inspection of other equipment.

2 Location of Plant

| | Postcode |
|---|---|
| | Tel. No. |

It is only necessary to complete the Location box if the location of plant to be covered is different from the Address(es) of premises specified at the beginning of this form.

3 Is insurance cover required on an unspecified basis? Insert YES or NO ▶ YES

(a) If 'YES', please indicate the new replacement value of all Plant and Machinery at your premises. £ 6925

(b) If 'NO', please detail the individual items of Plant and Machinery on a separate sheet.

When calculating the new Replacement Value please exclude data processing equipment, accounting or office machinery, experimental or prototype plant and machinery, vehicles or self-propelled plant and machinery other than purpose built lifting and handling plant not insured for road use.

# Devolved assessment 4 Tonk plc

## Performance criteria

The following performance criteria are covered in this Devolved Assessment.

### Element 8.1: Prepare VAT returns

1 VAT returns are correctly completed from the appropriate sources and submitted within the statutory time limits

2 Relevant inputs and outputs are correctly identified and calculated

3 VAT documentation is correctly filed

4 Submissions are made in accordance with currently operative VAT laws and regulations

## Notes on completing the Assessment

This Assessment is designed to test your ability to prepare VAT returns.

You are provided with data (pages 152 to 155) which you must use to complete the tasks on page 155.

You are allowed 2 hours to complete your work.

A high level of accuracy is required. Check your work carefully.

Correcting fluid should not be used. Errors should be crossed out neatly and clearly. You should write in ink - not pencil.

A full solution to this Assessment is provided on page 170.

Do not turn to the suggested solution until you have completed all parts of the Assessment.

## DEVOLVED ASSESSMENT 4: TONK PLC

### Background information

As the accounts clerk at Tonk plc, you have been supplied with the following documents from which to prepare the company's VAT account and VAT return for the three months ended 30 November 19X7. Assume that no further documents will be issued in connection with any of these transactions. You are warned that some invoices contain errors (which you can detect).

TONK PLC
1 Plink Lane, Infertown. IN2 4DA
VAT reg no 154 9131 32

Invoice no. 572
Date: 4 September 19X7
Tax point: 4 September 19X7

To: Bar plc
32 Stoke Street
London NW12

| | *VAT rate* % | £ |
|---|---|---|
| Sales of goods | | |
| 3,000 small suitcases | 17.5 | 33,750.00 |
| 4,500 handbags | 17.5 | 15,840.00 |
| Total excluding VAT | | 49,590.00 |
| Total VAT at 17.5% | | 8,504.68 |
| Total payable within 30 days | | 58,094.68 |
| Less 2% discount if paid within 10 days | | 991.80 |
| Total payable within 10 days | | 57,102.88 |

TONK PLC
1 Plink Lane, Infertown. IN2 4DA
VAT reg no 154 9131 32

Invoice no. 573
Date: 12 September 19X7
Tax point: 12 September 19X7

To: Cormick Ltd
63 Saddle Road
Gulltown GL4 3CE

| | *VAT rate* % | £ |
|---|---|---|
| *Sales of goods* | | |
| 2,000 trunks | 17.5 | 38,000.00 |
| 7,000 shopping bags | 17.5 | 14,000.00 |
| Total excluding VAT | | 52,000.00 |
| Total VAT at 17.5% | | 10,400.00 |
| Total payable within 30 days, strictly net | | 62,400.00 |

TONK PLC
1 Plink Lane, Infertown. IN2 4DA
VAT reg no 154 9131 32

Invoice no. 574
Date: 3 October 19X7
Tax point: 3 October 19X7

To: Work plc
99 Mark Lane
Cartown CA1 9TP

| | *VAT rate* % | £ |
|---|---|---|
| Sales of goods | | |
| 7,200 large suitcases | 17.5 | 106,992.00 |
| 6,350 handbags | 17.5 | 22,352.00 |
| | | 129,344.00 |
| Less 5% quantity discount | | 6,467.20 |
| Total excluding VAT | | 122,876.80 |
| Total VAT at 17.5% | | 18,431.52 |
| Total payable within 30 days, strictly net | | 141,308.32 |

TONK PLC
1 Plink Lane, Infertown. IN2 4DA
VAT reg no 154 9131 32

Invoice no. 575
Date: 12 November 19X7
Tax point: 12 November 19X7

To: Monet plc
39 Giro Street
Bingotown BN6 2BC

| | *VAT rate* % | £ |
|---|---|---|
| *Sales of goods* | | |
| 7,000 small suitcases | 17.5 | 78,750.00 |
| 10,000 briefcases | 17.5 | 158,700.00 |
| Total excluding VAT | | 237,450.00 |
| Total VAT at 17.5% | | 40,722.67 |
| Total payable within 30 days | | 278,172.67 |
| Less 2% discount if paid within 10 days | | 4,749.00 |
| Total payable within 10 days | | 273,423.67 |

TONK PLC
1 Plink Lane, Infertown. IN2 4DA
VAT reg no 154 9131 32

Credit note no. 34
Date: 3 November 19X7
Tax point: 3 November 19X7

To: Sole plc
14 Power Street
Abbatown AB4 3BZ

Credit in respect of returned defective goods (invoice number 520; invoice date 1 July 19X7)

| | *VAT rate* % | £ |
|---|---|---|
| 125 handbags | 17.5 | 440.00 |
| VAT at 17.5% | | 77.00 |
| Total credit | | 517.00 |

TONK PLC
MEMORANDUM

To: Accounts clerk
From: Credit controller
Date: 2 October 19X7

Please write off the following two debts.

| *Debtor* | *Date payment due* | *Net* | *VAT* | *Gross* |
|---|---|---|---|---|
| | | £ | £ | £ |
| Off Ltd | 1.8.X7 | 2,000 | 350 | 2,350 |
| Trib Ltd | 14.1.X7 | 3,800 | 665 | 4,465 |

TONK PLC
MEMORANDUM

To: Accounts clerk
From: Finance director
Date: 4 November 19X7

Our auditors have found errors in our VAT accounting in a previous period. Output VAT was overstated by £2,500, and input VAT was overstated by £1,600. Please take the necessary corrective action.

TARSKI PLC
79 Reff Road
Selltown
SL2 9AT

VAT reg no 110 2511 35
Date: 12 October 19X7
Tax point: 12 October 19X7
Invoice no. 88577
To: Tonk plc
1 Plink Lane
Infertown IN2 4DA

| | *Net* | *VAT rate* | *VAT* |
|---|---|---|---|
| | £ | % | £ |
| *Sales of goods* | | | |
| 10,000 small suitcases | 60,000.00 | 17.5 | 10,500.00 |
| 10,000 large suitcases | 80,000.00 | 17.5 | 14,000.00 |
| 4,200 briefcases | 30,660.00 | 17.5 | 5,365.50 |
| Total excluding VAT | 170,660.00 | | 29,865.50 |
| Total VAT at 17.5% | 29,865.50 | | |
| Total payable within 30 days | 200,525.50 | | |

COURSE LTD
35 Work Street, Infertown. IN3 7ET
VAT reg no 624 0668 24

15 October 19X7

Sale of 2,000 steel corner brackets: £83.60 including VAT at 17.5%.

SILK LTD
74 Hull Street, Infertown IN1 5DD
VAT reg no 281 8238 13

This is a less detailed invoice for VAT purposes.

Sale of 3,500 brass clips: £270.25 including VAT at 17.5%.

TARSKI PLC
79 Reff Road
Selltown
SL2 9AT

VAT reg no 110 2511 35
Date: 5 November 19X7
Credit note no. 324
To: Tonk plc
1 Plink Lane
Infertown IN2 4DA

CREDIT NOTE
(Invoice no. 88577, date 12 October 19X7)

| | £ |
|---|---|
| 200 defective small suitcases returned | 1,200.00 |
| VAT at 17.5% | 210.00 |
| Gross credit | 1,410.00 |

TONK PLC
EXPENSES CLAIM

Name: A Spender — Three months ended: 30.11.X7

| | *Net* £ | *VAT* £ | *Gross* £ |
|---|---|---|---|
| Business entertaining (VAT invoice attached) | 300.00 | 52.50 | 352.50 |
| Call from public telephone* | 5.11 | 0.89 | 6.00 |
| Car park fee* | 15.32 | 2.68 | 18.00 |
| Car park fee* | 25.54 | 4.46 | 30.00 |
| | 345.97 | 60.53 | 406.50 |

* No invoice or receipt issued
Authorised: A Manager

## Tasks

(a) Prepare Tonk plc's VAT account and VAT return for the three months ended 30 November 19X7.

(b) State which of the documents given must be retained, and for how long.

A blank VAT return is provided below.

**Value Added Tax Return**
For the period
01 09 X7 to 30 11 X7

For Official Use

Registration number: 154 9131 32

Period: 11 X7

You could be liable to a financial penalty if your completed return and all the VAT payable are not received by the due date.

TONK PLC
1 PLINK LANE
INFERTOWN
IN2 4DA

Due date: 31 12 X7

For Official Use

Your VAT Office telephone number is 0123-4567

Before you fill in this form please read the notes on the back and the VAT Leaflet *"Filling in your VAT return"*. Fill in all boxes clearly in ink, and write 'none' where necessary. Don't put a dash or leave any box blank. If there are no pence write "00" in the pence column. Do not enter more than one amount in any box.

For official use

| | Box | £ | p |
|---|---|---|---|
| VAT due in this period on sales and other outputs | 1 | 78,096 | 27 |
| VAT due in this period on acquisitions from other EC Member States | 2 | NONE | |
| Total VAT due (the sum of boxes 1 and 2) | 3 | 78,096 | 27 |
| VAT reclaimed in this period on purchases and other inputs (including acquisitions from the EC) | 4 | 28,736 | 52 |
| Net VAT to be paid to Customs or reclaimed by you (Difference between boxes 3 and 4) | 5 | 49,359 | 75 |
| Total value of sales and all other outputs excluding any VAT. Include your box 8 figure | 6 | 458,862 | 00 |
| Total value of purchases and all other inputs excluding any VAT. Include your box 9 figure | 7 | 170,107 | 00 |
| Total value of all supplies of goods and related services, excluding any VAT, to other EC Member States | 8 | NONE | 00 |
| Total value of all acquisitions of goods and related services, excluding any VAT, from other EC Member States | 9 | NONE | 00 |

**Retail schemes.** If you have used any ot the schemes in the period covered by this return, enter the relevant letter(s) in this box.

If you are enclosing a payment please tick this box. ✓

DECLARATION: You, or someone on your behalf, must sign below.

I, A M INSLEY declare that the
(Full name of signatory in BLOCK LETTERS)
information given above is true and complete.

Signature A M Insley Date 24/10 19 97

**A false declaration can result in prosecution.**

# *Devolved assessment 5 Strode Ltd Class assessment*

## *Performance criteria*

The following performance criteria are covered in this Devolved Assessment.

### Element 8.1: Prepare VAT returns

1. VAT returns are correctly completed from the appropriate sources and submitted within the statutory time limits
2. Relevant inputs and outputs are correctly identified and calculated
4. Submissions are made in accordance with currently operative VAT laws and regulations
5. Discussions with VAT inspectors are conducted openly and constructively to promote the efficiency of the VAT accounting system

## Note on completing the Assessment

This Assessment is designed to test your ability to prepare VAT returns.

You are provided with data (pages 158 and 159) which you must use to complete the tasks on page 159.

You are allowed 2 hours to complete your work.

A high level of accuracy is required. Check your work carefully.

Correcting fluid should not be used. Errors should be crossed out neatly and clearly. You should write in ink - not pencil.

## DEVOLVED ASSESSMENT 5: STRODE LTD

### Background information

As the accountant of Strode Ltd, you are provided with the following documents to help you to prepare the company's VAT return for the three months ended 30 June 19X3. All transactions were with persons in the United Kingdom.

SUMMARY OF SUPPLIES MADE
(Some columns not shown)

| *Date* | *Item* | *VAT rate* | *Net amount* |
|---|---|---|---|
| | | % | £ |
| 2.4.X3 | Stockbroking services | Exempt | 62,000 |
| 12.4.X3 | Sale of books about finance | 0.0 | 27,000 |
| 21.4.X3 | Stockbroking services | Exempt | 35,250 |
| 30.4.X3 | Stockbroking services | Exempt | 24,870 |
| 2.5.X3 | Sale of books about finance | 0.0 | 33,500 |
| 12.5.X3 | Investment advice | 17.5 | 3,850 |
| 28.5.X3 | Trust administration services | 17.5 | 11,250 |
| 4.6.X3 | Insurance broking services for a Canadian company | 0.0 | 7,500 |
| 10.6.X3 | Investment advice | 17.5 | 8,500 |
| 17.6.X3 | Insurance broking services for a UK company | Exempt | 1,800 |
| 30.6.X3 | Stockbroking services | Exempt | 32,000 |

SUMMARY OF SUPPLIES RECEIVED
(Some columns not shown)

| *Date* | *Item* | *VAT rate* | *Net amount* |
|---|---|---|---|
| | | % | £ |
| 1.4.X3 | New car for managing director | 17.5 | 15,000 |
| 12.4.X3 | Petrol | 17.5 | 600 |
| 2.5.X3 | Office furniture | 17.5 | 5,400 |
| 3.6.X3 | Stationery | 17.5 | 7,400 |
| 15.6.X3 | Computer bureau services | 17.5 | 22,000 |
| 17.6.X3 | Materials to make own stationery | 17.5 | 3,000 |

MEMORANDUM

To: Accountant
From: Finance director
Date: 10 July 19X3
Subject: Your memo of 6 July 19X3

Thank you for your enquiries. I can reply as follows.

(a) The managing director was supplied with fuel free of charge for both business and private use. The car has a 1,800 cc petrol engine. The scale charge per quarter is £252.

(b) I agree that in the tax period ended 31 March 19X3 the company's output VAT was understated by £870.

MEMORANDUM

To: Accountant
From: Stationery department
Date: 7 July 19X3
Subject: Internal production of stationery

In June, in addition to our purchase of stationery, we produced our own stationery, at a cost (including materials (£3,000 before VAT), wages and production overhead) of £16,000. This is about the average quarterly cost of such production. All costs exclude any VAT.

MEMORANDUM

To: Accountant
From: Assistant accountant
Date: 18 July 19X3
Subject: Supplies received and supplies made

I have established that the only supply received which can be attributed to particular supplies made is the computer bureau services, which are entirely attributable to stockbroking. The stationery which we produced for our own use was not attributable to any particular supplies.

MEMORANDUM

To: Accountant
From: Credit controller
Date: 17 June 19X3
Subject: Bad debts

One of our clients, A Jones, to whom we have supplied only investment advice, now seems unlikely to pay his outstanding debts to us, so these debts should be written off. A complete list of supplies to this client is as follows.

| *Due date for payment of debt* | *Amount including VAT* |
|---|---|
| | £ |
| 1.3.X2 | 724 |
| 1.12.X2 | 830 |
| 1.3.X3 | 680 |
| 31.3.X3 | 520 |
| 10.6.X3 | 327 |

A Jones paid £1,000 on 15 December 19X2 and £200 on 1 January 19X3.

## Tasks

(a) Prepare Strode Ltd's VAT return for the period from 1 April to 30 June 19X3.

(b) State how you would justify your claim for bad debt relief if it were to be challenged by HM Customs & Excise.

A blank VAT return is provided below.

**Value Added Tax Return**
For the period
01 04 X3 to 30 06 X3

For Official Use

Registration number: 431 9824 79
Period: 06 X3

You could be liable to a financial penalty if your completed return and all the VAT payable are not received by the due date.

STRODE LTD
63 FIG STREET
TREETOWN
TR1 4NF

Due date: 31 07 X3

For Official Use

Your VAT Office telephone number is 0123-4567

Before you fill in this form please read the notes on the back and the VAT Leaflet *"Filling in your VAT return"*. Fill in all boxes clearly in ink, and write 'none' where necessary. Don't put a dash or leave any box blank. If there are no pence write "00" in the pence column. Do not enter more than one amount in any box.

For official use

| | Box | £ | p |
|---|---|---|---|
| VAT due in this period on sales and other outputs | 1 | | |
| VAT due in this period on acquisitions from other EC Member States | 2 | | |
| Total VAT due (the sum of boxes 1 and 2) | 3 | | |
| VAT reclaimed in this period on purchases and other inputs (including acquisitions from the EC) | 4 | | |
| Net VAT to be paid to Customs or reclaimed by you (Difference between boxes 3 and 4) | 5 | | |
| Total value of sales and all other outputs excluding any VAT. Include your box 8 figure | 6 | | 00 |
| Total value of purchases and all other inputs excluding any VAT. Include your box 9 figure | 7 | | 00 |
| Total value of all supplies of goods and related services, excluding any VAT, to other EC Member States | 8 | | 00 |
| Total value of all acquisitions of goods and related services, excluding any VAT, from other EC Member States | 9 | | 00 |

**Retail schemes.** If you have used any ot the schemes in the period covered by this return, enter the relevant letter(s) in this box.

If you are enclosing a payment please tick this box.

DECLARATION: You, or someone on your behalf, must sign below.

I, .................................................... declare that the
(Full name of signatory in BLOCK LETTERS)
information given above is true and complete.

Signature.................................................... Date .................. 19........

**A false declaration can result in prosecution.**

# *Solutions to devolved assessments*

## SOLUTION TO DEVOLVED ASSESSMENT 1: COMMA LTD

**Tutorial note.** Note that the commentaries you provide on the income statement and charts need to be brief, given their context as a meeting 'handout'. There is no need to comment on all of the data, as readers can see it for themselves. What is needed is to highlight the key points to which you wish to draw the readers' attention.

### Solution

(a) *Comma Limited*

*Income statement*

| | *September 19X2* | | | | *9 months to September 19X2* | | | |
|---|---|---|---|---|---|---|---|---|
| | *Budget* | | *Actual* | | *Budget* | | *Actual* | |
| | £m | % | £m | % | £m | % | £m | % |
| Net sales | 2.14 | 100 | 2.02 | 100 | 22.8 | 100 | 23.8 | 100 |
| Less: | | | | | | | | |
| Standard cost | 1.12 | 52 | 1.02 | 50 | 11.6 | 51 | 12.3 | 52 |
| Variances | 0.17 | 8 | 0.24 | 12 | 1.9 | 8 | 2.3 | 10 |
| Other costs | 0.19 | 9 | 0.23 | 11 | 2.7 | 12 | 1.9 | 8 |
| Inter-company contrib | (0.12) | (6) | (0.18) | (9) | (1.6) | (7) | (1.3) | (5) |
| Manufacturing margin | 0.78 | 36 | 0.71 | 35 | 8.2 | 36 | 8.6 | 36 |
| Selling expenses | 0.21 | 10 | 0.18 | 9 | 2.5 | 11 | 2.6 | 11 |
| Administrative expenses | 0.31 | 14 | 0.32 | 16 | 3.4 | 15 | 3.3 | 14 |
| Inter-company contrib | (0.04) | (2) | (0.02) | (1) | (0.5) | (2) | (0.2) | (1) |
| Operating income | 0.30 | 14 | 0.23 | 11 | 2.8 | 12 | 2.9 | 12 |
| Inter-company (net) | (0.02) | (1) | 0.02 | 1 | (0.2) | (1) | - | - |
| Income before tax | 0.28 | 13 | 0.25 | 12 | 2.6 | 11 | 2.9 | 12 |
| Tax | 0.15 | 7 | 0.10 | 5 | 1.4 | 6 | 1.4 | 6 |
| Net income | 0.13 | 6 | 0.15 | 7 | 1.2 | 5 | 1.5 | 6 |

| | *Last year* | | *Last year* | |
|---|---|---|---|---|
| Net sales | 1.85 | 100 | 22.4 | 100 |
| Manufacturing margin | 0.61 | 33 | 7.8 | 35 |
| Operating income | 0.21 | 11 | 2.2 | 10 |

*Comment*

Sales were 6% down on budget in September. Manufacturing margin was down slightly, and operating income was 23% down on budget. Over the nine months to September, sales were 4% up on budget and 6% up on the same period last year. Manufacturing margin was also 4% up on budget and was 10% up on last year. Overheads (before inter-company contribution) were held at 1% below budget, with operating income 4% up on budget and 32% up on last year.

(b) *Net sales by geographical market 19W6 and 19X1*

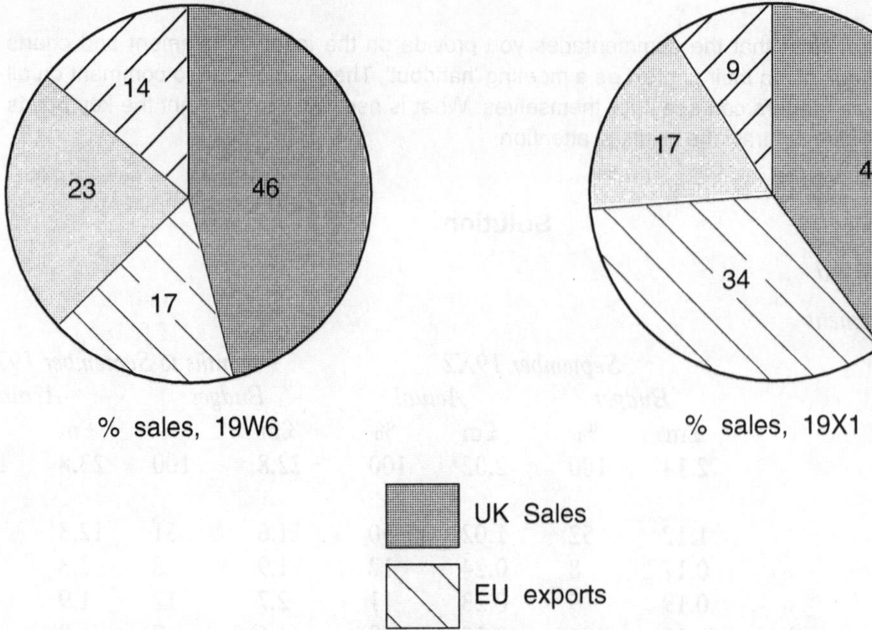

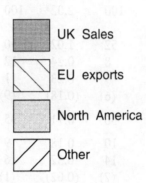

(c) *Average net sales per employee (19X2 thousands of pounds)*

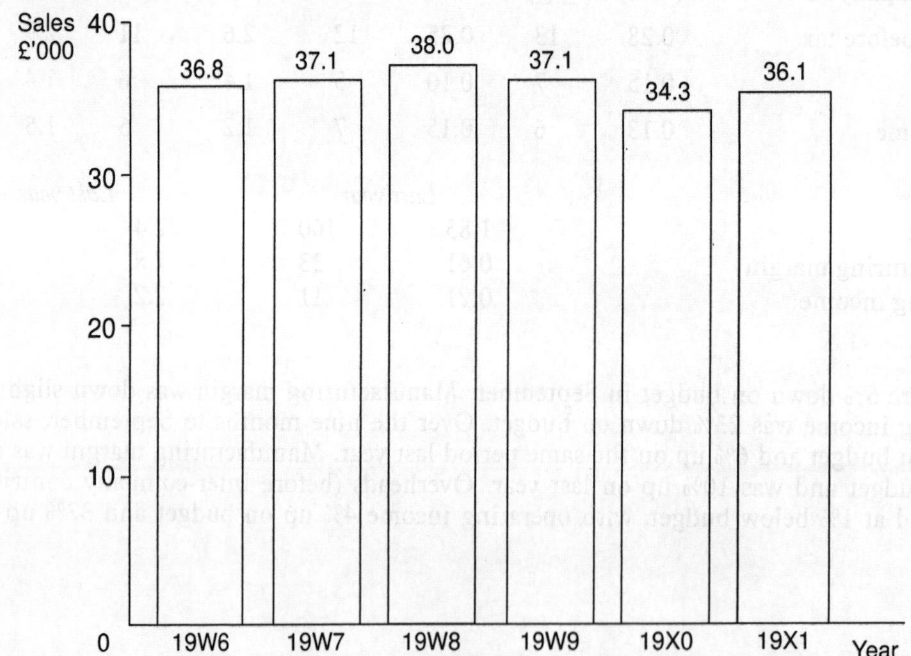


*Comments*

*Net sales by geographical market (b)*

Sales increased by 21% between 19W6 and 19X1 in real terms. Home sales declined significantly over the period, with their share of total sales declining from 46% to 40%. The growth was in sales within the EU, particularly in Eire, Germany and France. Sales to North America declined in real terms, with most of this decline being attributable to sales in Canada. The share of sales to other countries declined from 14% to 9%: Nigeria makes up the majority of these sales, although its share has declined over the period.

*Average net sales per employee (c)*

Over the period 19W6 to 19X0 increases in the real value of sales were accompanied by increases in employee numbers. Sales per employee rose year by year over the period 19W6 to 19W7 but declined in the three following years. The largest increase in employee numbers was in 19X0 (15% up on 19W9). This was also the year in which sales per employee fell by 7.5%. Small cutbacks in staff numbers accompanied a further rise in the real value of sales in 19X1, and average net sales per employee rose by 5% in that year.

*Workings*

(b)

| | | *19X1* | | | *19W6* | |
|---|---|---|---|---|---|---|
| | £'000 | £'000 | % | £'000 | £'000 | % |
| Home sales | | 12,249 | 40 | | 9,273 | 46 |
| Eire | 2,015 | | | - | | |
| Germany | 3,605 | | | 1,457 | | |
| France | 2,309 | | | 1,200 | | |
| Other EU | 2,419 | | | 894 | | |
| EU exports total | | 10,348 | 34 | | 3,551 | 17 |
| Canada | 1,722 | | | 1,888 | | |
| USA | 3,402 | | | 2,841 | | |
| North America | | 5,124 | 17 | | 4,729 | 23 |
| Nigeria | 1,521 | | | 1,722 | | |
| Other non-EU | 1,182 | | | 1,142 | | |
| Other total | | 2,703 | 9 | | 2,864 | 14 |
| | | 30,424 | 100 | | 20,417 | 100 |

(c) *Total net sales*

| | £'000 | | | *Current value 19X2* £'000 | *Average e'ees* | *Sales per e'ee* £'000 |
|---|---|---|---|---|---|---|
| 19W6 | 20,418 | × 164.9/128.2 | = | 26,263 | 713 | 36.8 |
| 19W7 | 22,084 | × 164.9/132.7 | = | 27,443 | 739.5 | 37.1 |
| 19W8 | 23,783 | × 164.9/139.5 | = | 28,113 | 764 | 36.8 |
| 19W9 | 25,621 | × 164.9/146.2 | = | 28,898 | 789 | 36.6 |
| 19X0 | 28,088 | × 164.9/150.7 | = | 30,735 | 896.5 | 34.3 |
| 19X1 | 30,424 | × 164.9/157.8 | = | 31,793 | 880.5 | 36.1 |

## SOLUTION TO DEVOLVED ASSESSMENT 2: CONSULTANCY OFFICE

**Tutorial note.** The agreed methods used in this Assessment follow examples set out by HM Treasury in *Executive agencies: a guide to setting targets and measuring performance* (HMSO, 1992).

If you have completed the Assessment without the help of a computer, your workings will be similar to those we set out below. If you have used a computer spreadsheet, there will be no need to set out full workings like this. However, it will be helpful if you show the formulae you have used to construct the spreadsheet. If your spreadsheet has produced different figures to those in our solution, check carefully each of the formulae you have used.

### Solution

The table of *Productivity and unit cost measures* is set out on page 169.

*Workings*

(2) *Value of capital (worked out by the supervisor)*

| | | |
|---|---|---|
| Year 1: | (given in Data) | £20,000 |
| Year 2: | £20,000 × 0.9 × 1.05 = | £18,900 |
| Year 3: | £20,000 × 0.8 × 1.09 = | £17,440 |
| Year 4: | £20,000 × 0.7 × 1.14 = | £15,960 |

(3) *Annual capital charge*

Year 3: $£17{,}440 \times \frac{1}{8} + 0.06 \times \frac{(17{,}440 + 15{,}960)}{2} = £3{,}182$

Year 4: $£15{,}960 \times \frac{1}{7} + 0.06 \times \frac{(15{,}960 + 14{,}440)}{2} = £3{,}191$

(6) *Labour costs*

| | |
|---|---|
| Year 1: | £100,000 |
| Year 2: | £100,000 × 1.08 = £108,000 |
| Year 3: | £108,000 × 1.06 = £114,480 |
| Year 4: | £114,480 × 1.06 = £121,439 |

(7) *Average wage rate* = (6) ÷ (5)

(9) *'Physical' other running costs*

Year 1: £2,000 ÷ 1.00 = £2,000
Year 2: £2,000 ÷ 1.05 = £1,905
Year 3: £1,800 ÷1.09 = £1,651
Year 4: £1,800 ÷ 1.14 = £1,579

(10) *Total annual cost*

Year 1: £(3,167 + 100,000 + 2,000) = £105,167
Year 2: £(3,190 + 108,000 + 2,000) = £113,190
Year 3: £(3,182 + 114,480 + 1,800) = £119,462
Year 4: £(3,191 + 121,349 + 1,800) = £126,340

(11) *Total 'physical' running costs*

Year 1: £(2,000 + 20,000 × 5) = £102,000
Year 2: £(1,905 + 20,000 × 5) = £101,905
Year 3: £(1,651 + 20,000 × 5) = £101,651
Year 4: £(1,579 + 20,000 × 5) = £101,579

(12) *Total physical resources consumed*

Year 1: £(102,000 + 3,167) = £105,167
Year 2: £(101,905 + 3,038) = £104,943
Year 3: £(101,651 + 2,919) = £104,570
Year 4: £(101,579 + 2,799) = £104,378

(15) *Total costs: forms*

Year 1: £105,167 × ¼ = £26,292
Year 2: £113,190 × ¼ = £28,298
Year 3: £119,462 × ¼ = £29,866
Year 4: £126,340 × ¼ = £31,585

(16) *Unit cost of issuing forms*

Year 1: £26,292 ÷ 8,000 = £3.29
Year 2: £28,298 ÷ 8,200 = £3.45
Year 3: £29,866 ÷ 8,450 = £3.53
Year 4: £31,585 ÷ 8,550 = £3.69

(17) *Real unit cost of forms*

Year 1: £3.29 ÷ 1.00 = £3.29
Year 2: £3.45 ÷ 1.05 = £3.29
Year 3: £3.53 ÷ 1.09 = £3.24
Year 4: £3.69 ÷ 1.14 = £3.24

(18) *Total costs: consultancy*

Year 1: £105,167 × ½ = £52,584
Year 2: £113,190 × ½ = £56,595
Year 3: £119,462 × ½ = £59,731
Year 4: £126,340 × ½ = £63,170

(19) *Unit cost of consultancy*

Year 2: £52,584 × 1.06 × 1.05 ÷ 3,960 = £14.78
Year 3: £56,595 × 1.06 × 1.09/1.05 ÷ 4,000 = £15.57
Year 4: £59,731 × 1.06 × 1.14/1.09 ÷ 4,020 = £16.47

(20) *Real unit cost of consultancy*

Year 1: £14.00 ÷ 1.00 = £14.00
Year 2: £14.78 ÷ 1.05 = £14.08
Year 3: £15.57 ÷ 1.09 = £14.28
Year 4: £16.47 ÷ 1.14 = £14.45

(21) *'Physical' output of forms and consultancy*

Year 1: (8,000 × £3.29) + (3,900 × £14.00) = £80,920
Year 2: (8,200 × £3.29) + (3,960 × £14.00) = £82,418
Year 3: (8,450 × £3.29) + (4,000 × £14.00) = £83,801
Year 4: (8,550 × £3.29) + (4,020 × £14.00) = £84,410

(22) *Physical running costs: forms and consultancy*

Year 1: £102,000 × 0.75 = £76,500
Year 2: £101,905 × 0.75 = £76,429
Year 3: £101,651 × 0.75 = £76,238
Year 4: £101,579 × 0.75 = £76,184

(23) *Productivity of running costs: forms and consultancy*

Year 1: £80,920 ÷ £76,500 = 1.058
Year 2: £82,418 ÷ £76,429 = 1.078
Year 3: £83,801 ÷ £76,238 = 1.099
Year 4: £84,410 ÷ £76,184 = 1.108

(25) *Total physical resources consumed: forms and consultancy*

Year 1: £105,167 × 0.75 = £78,875
Year 2: £104,943 × 0.75 = £78,707
Year 3: £104,570 × 0.75 = £78,428
Year 4: £104,378 × 0.75 = £78,284

(26) *Productivity - all resources: forms and consultancy*

| | |
|---|---|
| Year 1: | £80,920 ÷ £78,875 = 1.026 |
| Year 2: | £82,418 ÷ £78,707 = 1.047 |
| Year 3: | £83,801 ÷ £78,428 = 1.069 |
| Year 4: | £84,410 ÷ £78,284 = 1.078 |

## The Consultancy Office: Productivity and unit cost measures

| Variable | Year 1 | Year 2 | Year 3 | Year 4 |
|---|---|---|---|---|
| **INFLATION** | | | | |
| (1) General price deflator | 1.00 | 1.05 | 1.09 | 1.14 |
| **CAPITAL** | | | | |
| (2) Value of capital at start of year | £20,000 | £18,900 | £17,440 | £15,960 |
| (3) Annual capital charge | £3,167 | £3,190 | £3,182 | £3,191 |
| (4) `Physical' capital consumed | £3,167 | £3,038 | £2,919 | £2,799 |
| **LABOUR** | | | | |
| (5) Hours worked | 20,000 | 20,000 | 20,000 | 20,000 |
| (6) Labour costs | £100,000 | £108,000 | £114,480 | £121,349 |
| (7) Average wage rate | £5.00 | £5.40 | £5.72 | £6.07 |
| (8) Other running costs (cash) | £2,000 | £2,000 | £1,800 | £1,800 |
| (9) `Physical' other running costs | £2,000 | £1,905 | £1,651 | £1,579 |
| **TOTALS** | | | | |
| (10) Total annual cost | £105,167 | £113,190 | £119,462 | £126,340 |
| (11) Total `physical' running costs | £102,000 | £101,905 | £101,651 | £101,579 |
| (12) Total `physical' resources consumed | £105,167 | £104,943 | £104,570 | £104,378 |
| **OUTPUTS** | | | | |
| (13) Forms issued | 8,000 | 8,200 | 8,450 | 8,550 |
| (14) Cases processed | 3,900 | 3,960 | 4,000 | 4,020 |
| **UNIT COSTS** | | | | |
| (15) Total costs: forms | £26,292 | £28,298 | £29,866 | £31,585 |
| (16) Unit cost of issuing forms | £3.29 | £3.45 | £3.53 | £3.69 |
| (17) Real unit cost of forms | £3.29 | £3.29 | £3.24 | £3.24 |
| (18) Total costs: consultancy | £52,584 | £56,595 | £59,731 | £63,170 |
| (19) Unit cost of consultancy | £14.00 | £14.78 | £15.57 | £16.47 |
| (20) Real unit cost of consultancy | £14.00 | £14.08 | £14.28 | £14.45 |
| **PRODUCTIVITY** | | | | |
| (21) `Physical' output of forms and consultancy | £80,920 | £82,418 | £83,801 | £84,410 |
| (22) `Physical' running costs: forms and consultancy | £76,500 | £76,429 | £76,238 | £76,184 |
| (23) Productivity of running costs: forms and consultancy | 1.058 | 1.078 | 1.099 | 1.108 |
| (24) Year-on-year increase in (23) | - | 1.89% | 1.95% | 0.82% |
| (25) Total physical resources consumed: forms and consultancy | £78,875 | £78,707 | £78,428 | £78,284 |
| (26) Productivity - all resources: forms and consultancy | 1.026 | 1.047 | 1.069 | 1.078 |
| (27) Year-on-year increase in (26) | - | 2.05% | 2.01% | 0.84% |

## SOLUTION TO DEVOLVED ASSESSMENT 4: TONK PLC

**Tutorial note.** In this Assessment, it was important not to take all the documents on trust. For example the invoice to Cormick Ltd charged too much VAT, while that to Work plc charged too little VAT. The invoice from Silk Ltd cannot qualify as a less detailed invoice, because it is for over £100 including VAT. VAT on business entertaining cannot be recovered. VAT on amounts over £25 and for which no tax invoice is held cannot be recovered, even if they are for telephone calls or car park fees or are inserted into cash operated machines.

### Solution

(a) Output VAT is as follows.

| | £ |
|---|---|
| Invoice to Bar plc | 8,504.68 |
| Invoice to Cormick Ltd (full amount shown) | 10,400.00 |
| Invoice to Work plc £141,308.32 × 7/47 | 21,045.92 |
| Invoice to Monet plc | 40,722.67 |
| | 80,673.27 |
| Less credit note to Sole plc | 77.00 |
| | 80,596.27 |
| Less error in previous period | 2,500.00 |
| | 78,096.27 |

Input VAT is as follows.

| | £ |
|---|---|
| Invoice from Tarski plc | 29,865.50 |
| Invoice from Course Ltd: £83.60 × 7/47 | 12.45 |
| Invoice from Silk Ltd: no valid VAT invoice | 0.00 |
| Call from public telephone | 0.89 |
| Car park fee | 2.68 |
| | 29,881.52 |
| Less credit note from Tarski plc | 210.00 |
| | 29,671.52 |
| Bad debt relief on debt from Trib Ltd (over six months old) | 665.00 |
| | 30,336.52 |
| Less error in previous period | 1,600.00 |
| | 28,736.52 |

The net error is £(2,500 - 1,600) = £900, which is not over £2,000 so it may be corrected on the return.

The total net turnover is as follows.

| | £ |
|---|---|
| Invoice to Bar plc | 49,590.00 |
| Invoice to Cormick Ltd | 52,000.00 |
| Invoice to Work plc £(141,308.32 - 21,045.92) | 120,262.40 |
| Invoice to Monet plc | 237,450.00 |
| | 459,302.40 |
| Less credit note to Sole plc | 440.00 |
| | 458,862.40 |

Total net purchases are as follows.

| | £ |
|---|---|
| Invoice from Tarski plc | 170,660.00 |
| Invoice from Course Ltd £83.60 × 40/47 | 71.15 |
| Invoice from Silk Ltd £270.25 × 40/47 | 230.00 |
| Expenses | 345.97 |
| | 171,307.12 |
| Less credit note from Tarski plc | 1,200.00 |
| | 170,107.12 |

TONK PLC

VAT ACCOUNT FOR THE VAT PERIOD FROM SEPTEMBER TO NOVEMBER 19X7

| *VAT allowable* | £ | *VAT payable* | £ |
|---|---|---|---|
| Input VAT allowable | | Output VAT due | 80,673.27 |
| £(29,881.52 - 210.00) | 29,671.52 | Adjustment for credit | |
| Correction of error | (1,600.00) | allowed | (77.00) |
| Refunds for bad debts | 665.00 | Correction of error | (2,500.00) |
| | 28,736.52 | | |
| Cash (payment to HM | | | 78,096.27 |
| Customs & Excise) | 49,359.75 | | |
| | 78,096.27 | | 78,096.27 |

(b) All the documents shown should be retained, including the memoranda and the expenses claim. They must be kept for six years unless HM Customs & Excise allow a shorter period.

## Value Added Tax Return

For the period
01 09 X7 to 30 11 X7

For Official Use

Registration number: 154 9131 32

Period: 11 X7

You could be liable to a financial penalty if your completed return and all the VAT payable are not received by the due date.

TONK PLC
1 PLINK LANE
INFERTOWN
IN2 4DA

Due date: 31 12 X7

For Official Use

Your VAT Office telephone number is 0123-4567

Before you fill in this form please read the notes on the back and the VAT Leaflet *"Filling in your VAT return"*. Fill in all boxes clearly in ink, and write 'none' where necessary. Don't put a dash or leave any box blank. If there are no pence write "00" in the pence column. Do not enter more than one amount in any box.

For official use

| | Box | £ | p |
|---|---|---|---|
| VAT due in this period on sales and other outputs | 1 | 78,096 | 27 |
| VAT due in this period on acquisitions from other EC Member States | 2 | NONE | |
| Total VAT due (the sum of boxes 1 and 2) | 3 | 78,096 | 27 |
| VAT reclaimed in this period on purchases and other inputs (including acquisitions from the EC) | 4 | 28,736 | 52 |
| **Net VAT to be paid to Customs or reclaimed by you (Difference between boxes 3 and 4)** | 5 | 49,359 | 75 |
| Total value of sales and all other outputs excluding any VAT. Include your box 8 figure | 6 | 458,862 | 00 |
| Total value of purchases and all other inputs excluding any VAT. Include your box 9 figure | 7 | 170,107 | 00 |
| Total value of all supplies of goods and related services, excluding any VAT, to other EC Member States | 8 | NONE | 00 |
| Total value of all acquisitions of goods and related services, excluding any VAT, from other EC Member States | 9 | NONE | 00 |

**Retail schemes.** If you have used any ot the schemes in the period covered by this return, enter the relevant letter(s) in this box.

If you are enclosing a payment please tick this box. ✓

DECLARATION: You, or someone on your behalf, must sign below.

I, PETRA SMITH declare that the
(Full name of signatory in BLOCK LETTERS)
information given above is true and complete.

Signature P Smith Date 15/12 19 X7

**A false declaration can result in prosecution.**

# TRIAL RUN DEVOLVED ASSESSMENT

## INTERMEDIATE STAGE - NVQ/SVQ3

## Unit 7

## Preparing reports and returns

## Data and tasks

The purpose of this Trial Run Devolved Assessment is to give you an idea of what a Unit 7 Devolved Assessment looks like. It is not intended as a definitive guide to the tasks you may be required to perform.

The suggested time allowance for this Assessment is 2½ hours. Up to 30 minutes extra time may be permitted in an AAT simulation. Breaks in assessment will be allowed in the AAT simulation, but it must normally be completed in one day.

Calculators may be used but no reference material is permitted.

**DO NOT OPEN THIS PAPER UNTIL YOU ARE READY TO START UNDER TIMED CONDITIONS**

## DATA, TASKS AND ANSWER BOOKLET

### INSTRUCTIONS

This Assessment is designed to test your ability to prepare periodic performance reports and to prepare returns for outside agencies.

You are provided with background information and data which you must use to complete the tasks listed.

You are allowed 2½ hours to complete your work.

A high level of accuracy is required. Check your work carefully.

Correcting fluid should not be used. Errors should be crossed out neatly and clearly. You should write in black ink - not pencil.

You are advised to read through the whole of the simulation before commencing as all of the information may be of value and is not necessarily supplied in the sequence in which you might wish to deal with it.

Do not use any additional notes or books during this Trial Run Devolved Assessment.

## THE SITUATION

You are employed on a temporary assignment at Grady's Tutorial College. The College was set up in 19W8 and provides training courses, particularly for those wishing to return to work after a career break. Since 19X0, the college has also operated a small bookshop which sells mainly to course registrants but also to members of the public.

It is 12 April 19X4. Kim Harvey, the Financial Controller, hands to you some Office for National Statistics forms (see pages 178 to 183) which she received some time ago. At 5.30pm today, Kim, who needs to review and sign the form, is leaving to go on a 10-day holiday. She asks if you would make sure that the forms are available for her to sign on her return from holiday.

Kim's telephone number at the college is 0171-711 4240 (Fax: 0171-711 4200).

The business has two divisions, called College Division (courses) and Bookshop (book sales). The accounting year end is 31 March.

The following table shows 'year-to-date' (YTD) figures for the business as at the end of each quarter in the year ending 31 March 19X4. These figures have been extracted from management accounts.

| | *30 June 19X3* *YTD* £ | *30 Sept 19X3* *YTD* £ | *31 Dec 19X3* *YTD* £ | *31 March 19X4* *YTD* £ |
|---|---|---|---|---|
| *College Division* | | | | |
| Turnover | 124,694 | 269,818 | 422,629 | 583,636 |
| Direct costs | 64,128 | 130,813 | 199,207 | 270,010 |
| Other operating costs | 22,031 | 43,498 | 72,882 | 97,509 |
| *Bookshop* | | | | |
| Turnover | 12,721 | 28,223 | 46,931 | 71,094 |
| Cost of sales | 8,081 | 17,710 | 29,614 | 44,829 |
| Staff costs | 4,211 | 8,321 | 12,600 | 17,014 |
| Other operating costs | 2,412 | 4,401 | 6,589 | 9,420 |

Bookshop turnover includes books removed from the shop by members of College Division for their own use in course teaching. These books are invoiced at the full cover price to College Division, which has included them in 'other operating costs'. The average mark-up on the cost of books is 35%. The amounts of such interdivisional sales were as follows in the year to March 19X4.

*Interdivisional book sales (at cover price): Year to March 19X4*

| *Month* | £ | *Month* | £ |
|---|---|---|---|
| Apr | 205 | Oct | 234 |
| May | 110 | Nov | 121 |
| Jun | 20 | Dec | 333 |
| Jul | 312 | Jan | 394 |
| Aug | 333 | Feb | 481 |
| Sep | 214 | Mar | 192 |

*Staff*

College Division has employed 10 full-time members of staff (6 women and 4 men) and 1 part-time male member of staff throughout the whole of the year to 31 March 19X4. In the same year, the bookshop has employed 1 full-time male staff member and 1 part-time female staff member, who started her job at the beginning of July 19X3.

*Fixed assets*

The following information has been extracted from the fixed asset register of Grady's Tutorial College.

| | Land and buildings £ | Plant and machinery £ | Motor vehicles £ | Office equipment £ | Total £ |
|---|---|---|---|---|---|
| *Cost* | | | | | |
| At 1 January 19X4 | 154,500 | 9,840 | 27,900 | 10,240 | 202,480 |
| Additions | 56,250 | 2,840 | 9,890 | 1,280 | 70,260 |
| Disposals | - | (4,465) | (14,700) | (2,980) | (22,145) |
| At 31 March 19X4 | 210,750 | 8,215 | 23,090 | 8,540 | 250,595 |
| *Depreciation* | | | | | |
| At 1 January 19X4 | - | 6,720 | 19,220 | 5,745 | 31,685 |
| Charge for quarter | - | 355 | 1,720 | 540 | 2,615 |
| Disposals | - | (3,465) | (10,200) | (940) | (14,605) |
| At 31 March 19X4 | - | 3,610 | 10,740 | 5,345 | 19,695 |

Of the additions to land and buildings shown above, £32,150 was spent in buying a small building adjacent to the college. The remainder of these additions was in respect of improvements to the building in order to convert it to lecture room accommodation.

Certain fixed assets were sold, all for cash, in the quarter to 31 March 19X4. The debit entries in the cash book in respect of these sales are summarised below.

| | £ |
|---|---|
| Land and buildings | - |
| Plant and machinery | 1,400 |
| Motor vehicles | 5,200 |
| Office equipment | 1,655 |

## TASKS TO BE COMPLETED

(a) Complete the Office for National Statistics forms in accordance with the accompanying notes (see pages 178 to 183).

(b) State how much time is available for the ONS forms to be completed. State what action you would take to ensure that the forms are submitted on time.

(c) Kim also requires you to set out in a table various items of information specified below for the following four periods.

(i) Quarter ending 30 June 19X3
(ii) Quarter ending 30 September 19X3
(iii) Quarter ending 31 December 19X3
(iv) Quarter ending 31 March 19X4

The information required is as follows. (Design your table with care before you begin this task.)

*College Division*
Turnover*
Direct costs*
Other operating costs*
Contribution*
Direct costs as % of turnover
Other operating costs as % of turnover
Contribution as % of turnover

* in £'000 to one decimal place

*Notes.* Contribution = Turnover – (Direct costs + Other operating costs)

*Bookshop*
Turnover (including sales to College Division)
Cost of sales*
Staff costs*
Other operating costs*
Gross profit*
Contribution*
Gross profit percentage (ie as % of turnover)
Sales per staff member
Contribution as % of turnover

* in £'000 to one decimal place

*Notes.* Gross profit = Turnover – Cost of sales
Contribution = Gross profit – (Staff costs + Other operating costs)

For the purpose of calculating numbers of staff members in this task, a part-time staff member is treated as equivalent to one half of a full-time member of staff.

(d) Present the following ratios and percentages for each of the four quarters to 31 March 19X4, as calculated in Task (c) above, in an appropriate graphical format.

(i) College Division:
Direct costs as % of turnover
Other operating costs as % of turnover
Contribution as % of turnover

(ii) Bookshop:
Gross profit percentage
Sales per staff member

(e) An issue raised at a management meeting has been that of whether it is possible to measure the productivity of the teaching staff at Grady's Tutorial College. This has proved to be a contentious matter. You have been invited to attend the next management meeting to make a contribution to this discussion.

In preparation for the meeting, outline briefly different ways in which the productivity of the teaching staff might be measured, indicating the records which you consider would be necessary if such measurement is to be possible.

*All calculations are to be displayed to two places of decimals.*

*Tutorial note.* The fictitious letter below (pages 178 to 180) includes a Notice under Section 1 of the Statistics of Trade Act 1947 of a type sent out by the Office for National Statistics (ONS).

A compulsory inquiry conducted by
the Government Statistical Service

## *Office for National Statistics*

**IN CONFIDENCE**

Office for National Statistics
Newport, Gwent NP9 1XG
Our ref T16/770424000072/112
***Please give this reference number if you contact us***

GRADY'S TUTORIAL COLLEGE
ATTN KIM HARVEY
GRADY HOUSE
249 EDGERTON ROAD
LONDON
NW5 7XR

*Please correct any errors in name, address or postcode*

**26 March 19X4**

### Quarterly inquiries into turnover of the distributive and service trades

EDUCATIONAL SERVICES
FIRST QUARTER 19X4 (1 JAN 19X4 TO 31 MAR 19X4)

**Notice under Section 1 of the Statistics of Trade Act 1947**

Dear Contributor

Every quarter we send out this inquiry to obtain up-to-date statistics about the distributive and services trades. All larger businesses and a sample of smaller ones are included. Your business has been included in the inquiry.

Your figures will be used with those from other businesses to provide government with information about developments in the distributive and services trades and in the economy. Together with other information, this is an essential part of economic forecasting and policy making.

The inquiry results contribute to quarterly estimates of Gross Domestic Product which are published in a ONS press notice and in other ONS publications.

Because of the importance of the information, this is a statutory inquiry. *Under the Act of 1947, it is compulsory for you to provide the information. This should be returned within three weeks of the end of the period which it covers.* The information you provide will be treated as strictly confidential as required by the Act. I can assure you that it will not be revealed in published statistics in a way which would allow anybody to identify your business or be given to any unauthorised person without your permission.

To save you time, we have made the form as short as possible. There are notes to help you but if you have any difficulties or need more information, my staff on the telephone number shown above will be pleased to assist. If exact figures are not available, informed estimates will do. If you need additional copies of the form, please let us know.

Please accept my thanks for your co-operation. Without this we could not provide a good service to government.

Yours sincerely,

Business Statistics Division

| Official use only | |
|---|---|
| Rec only | |
| Receipted | |
| Data pre T/O | |
| On line T/O | |
| P/A | |

| | FV | | | |
|---|---|---|---|---|
| | T16/770424000072/112 | | | |

## IMPORTANT

Please read the notes before you fill in this form. Give the best estimates you can if you do not have exact figures.

## 1. Details of business

Your business is classified as being in the industry described briefly on the front of this form. If you think this is wrong, please give a full description of your business. If you are involved in two or more activities, please describe the main one.

## 2. Period

Period for which you have filled in the form

| | Day | | Month | | Year | |
|---|---|---|---|---|---|---|
| from | 1 | / | 11 | / | 94 | 11 |
| to | 31 | / | 3 | / | 94 | 12 |

## 3. Turnover to the nearest £thousand (not including VAT)

Total turnover (including fees receivable) | 184,170 | 40

## 4. Employees

Number of persons employed by the business at the end of the period covered by this return.

| | | | |
|---|---|---|---|
| 4.1 | Total employees | 13 | 50 |
| **of which:-** | | | |
| 4.2 | Full-time male | 5 | 51 |
| 4.3 | Part-time male | 1 | 52 |
| 4.4 | Full-time female | 6 | 53 |
| 4.5 | Part-time female | 1 | 54 |

## 5. Other businesses included in this form

The form should be completed for the business named overleaf. If exceptionally, you are unable to limit your return to the activities of this business, please list below the names and VAT Registration numbers of the other businesses included.

Name of business ........................................ VAT registration number ........................................

........................................ ........................................

(Please continue on a separate sheet if necessary)

REMARKS: If you have given any information which is significantly different from the last quarter, please explain.

..................................................................................................................

..................................................................................................................

PLEASE USE BLOCK CAPITALS

Name of person we should contact if necessary

Position in business | Date

Telephone no/ext | Fax/Telex

# NOTES ON FILLING IN THIS FORM

**Quarterly inquiries into turnover of the distributive and service trades**

## Period

Your return should cover the three months shown on the front of the form. If you do not have figures for that period, the return may be made for the nearest period of a similar length as long as it relates mainly to the one specified. It is important that there are no gaps or overlaps with this period and the period covered by any previous returns that you have made to this inquiry.

## Turnover

Give the total amount receivable by the business for services provided or goods sold during the period covered by the form. These amounts should not include VAT. Do not include any amounts receivable from selling or transferring capital assets. The figure given should be for services or goods which you have invoiced rather than cash which you have received, unless a figure for invoiced amounts is not readily available. It is important that the figure is given on a consistent basis from quarter to quarter. Show it to the nearest £ thousand. For example, £27,025 should be shown as 27.

## Scope of the inquiry

Your turnover should include any business activities carried out within the United Kingdom, (that is, England, Scotland, Wales and Northern Ireland). This should include work done in connection with overseas contracts or activities for which invoices are issued by you in the United Kingdom.

## Employees

Include full-time and part-time employees (part-time means those who normally work 30 hours a week or less); temporary and casual workers; those off sick, on holiday or on short-term; youth training scheme trainees who have a contract of employment and employment training trainees on continuation training; employees who work away from the workplace such as sales reps and lorry drivers.

Exclude those employed by outside contractors or agencies; working proprietors, partners, self-employed, directors not on contract; youth training scheme or employment training trainees without a contract of employment; home workers on piecework rates; former employees still on payroll as pensioners; those who normally work at another establishment such as temporary transfers and secondments.

*Tutorial note.* Like the letter on pages 178 to 180, this fictitious letter (pages 181 to 183) includes an official Notice the same as one used by the ONS. The notes on page 183 do not include all of the notes which the ONS includes with its inquiry form.

# Office for National Statistics

A compulsory inquiry conducted by
the Government Statistical Service

**IN CONFIDENCE**

NEWPORT Gwent NP9 1XG

Ref: QC/17/8100/7104420000/721

GRADY'S TUTORIAL COLLEGE
GRADY HOUSE
249 EDGERTON ROAD
LONDON
NW5 7XR

17 March 19X4

Please correct any errors in name or address

**QUARTERLY INQUIRY INTO CAPITAL EXPENDITURE**

FIRST QUARTER 19X4 (1 Jan 19X4 to 31 Mar 19X4)

Dear Contributor

**Notice under Section 1 of the Statistics of Trade Act 1947**

We conduct this inquiry to obtain up to date information on capital expenditure. The results provide government with essential information for the national accounts and make an important contribution to monitoring the economy. The number of forms is kept to the minimum required to produce reliable results.

Under the above Act, it is necessary for you to provide us with the information requested overleaf. This will be treated as strictly confidential as required by the Act. It will not be revealed in published statistics in a way which would enable your company to be identified, or disclosed to any unauthorised person without your consent.

**Please return your completed form by the date shown on the next page of this letter. If exact figures are not readily available, informed estimates are acceptable.**

I enclose notes to help you complete the form. In particular, please see the note dealing with the scope of the inquiry. If you have any difficulties in providing data, or on any other point, please contact A ........ L ..... on 0123 45678.

Thank you for your co-operation.

Yours sincerely

Business Statistics Division
Production Census and Capital Expenditure Branch

PLEASE COMPLETE AND RETURN THIS FORM BY 14 April 19X4

| FV | 93 | Q1 |
|---|---|---|
| 8100/7104420000 | | |

**IMPORTANT** Please read the enclosed notes before completing this form. If you do not have precise figures available give the best estimates you can. All values should be shown to the nearest £ thousand.

## 1. PERIOD (see note 1)

Period covered by the return

| | | Day | Month | Year |
|---|---|---|---|---|
| from | 08 | / | / | |
| to | 09 | / | / | |

## 2. LAND AND BUILDINGS (see note 2)

**£ thousand**

| | | | |
|---|---|---|---|
| 2.1 | New building work or other constructional work of a capital nature (excluding the cost of land and of new dwellings) | 10 | |
| 2.2 | Acquisition of land and of existing buildings | 20 | |
| 2.3 | Proceeds of land and buildings disposed of | 30 | |

## 3. VEHICLES (see note 3)

| | | | |
|---|---|---|---|
| 3.1 | New and second-hand acquisitions | 40 | |
| 3.2 | Proceeds of vehicles disposed of | 50 | |

## 4. PLANT, MACHINERY etc. (see note 4)

| | | | |
|---|---|---|---|
| 4.1 | New and second-hand acquisitions | 60 | |
| 4.2 | Proceeds of plant, machinery etc. disposed of | 70 | |

## 5. TOTAL

| | | | |
|---|---|---|---|
| 5.1 | Total acquisitions (2.1 + 2.2 + 3.1 + 4.1) | 90 | |
| 5.2 | Total disposals (2.3 + 3.2 + 4.2) | 100 | |

## 6. FINANCE LEASING

| | | | |
|---|---|---|---|
| 6.1 | Total amount included in acquisitions at 2.1, 3.1 and 4.1 for assets leased under finance leasing arrangements. | 80 | |

## 7. COMMENTS ON UNUSUAL FLUCTUATIONS IN FIGURES WOULD BE APPRECIATED

..............................................................................................................................

Name of person to be contacted if necessary..........................................................................
BLOCK CAPITALS PLEASE

Position in company........................................ Signature..................................................

Telephone No/Ext.................................. Fax.................................. Date..........................

# Office for National Statistics

NEWPORT Gwent NP9 1XG

**QUARTERLY INQUIRY INTO CAPITAL EXPENDITURE**

**PLEASE READ THESE NOTES BEFORE COMPLETING YOUR RETURN**

**SCOPE OF THE INQUIRY**

This inquiry covers businesses which operate in the United Kingdom. The business is the individual company, partnership, sole proprietorship etc., to which the form has been sent. Figures for subsidiaries of the business addressed should be excluded. In particular, where the business addressed is a holding company figures are required only in respect of the holding company and not for the group as a whole.

**NOTES ON INDIVIDUAL QUESTIONS**

**1. PERIOD**

You should enter the start and end dates of the period covered by your return. This should be the calendar quarter specified on the front of the form, or the nearest period of similar length for which figures are available. Where the period is not the calendar quarter, the start date should be no earlier than 20 November 19X3. The total length of the period should not be less than 12 weeks nor more than 16 weeks.

**CAPITAL EXPENDITURE**

The amounts entered should generally reflect all acquisitions and disposals charged to capital account during the period, together with any other amounts which are regarded as capital items for taxation purposes.

All figures should exclude value added tax, except that the non-deductible value added tax and Customs and Excise tax paid on passenger cars should be included. Do not deduct any amounts received in grants and/or allowances from government sources, statutory bodies or local authorities.

Expenditure indirectly associated with the acquisition of capital goods, such as the cost of arranging bank loans and servicing them, should be excluded.

If the capital expenditure of the business is nil or very small, a form should be completed to this effect.

**2. LAND AND BUILDINGS**

**New building work (2.1)**

Include expenditure on the construction of new building works (other than dwellings) contracted by you, whether directly with the constructors or arranged via property developers. Also covered here is expenditure on the associated architects' and surveyors' fees and any legal charges, stamp duties, agents' commissions, etc. Any expenditure undertaken by you when acting as a property developer contracted to carry out the building work by a third party should be excluded.

New building work covers the construction of new buildings, and extensions and improvements to old buildings (including fixtures such as lifts, heating and ventilation systems). The cost of site preparation and other civil engineering work should be included but the cost of land should be recorded against question 2.2

**Land and existing buildings (2.2 and 2.3)**

Against question 2.2 include all expenditure on land and existing buildings. Land purchased in connection with new building work should also be recorded here and should be estimated where precise figures are not known.

Amounts shown should include the capital cost of freeholds and leaseholds purchased and any leasehold premiums paid. Also covered are architects' and surveyors' fees and any legal charges, stamp duties, agents' commissions, etc. associated with these transactions.

**Under disposals of land and existing buildings (question 2.3) enter the net amount received after deduction of all transfer costs.**

**3. VEHICLES (3.1 and 3.2)**

These questions cover motor vehicles, ships, aircraft, and railway rolling stock etc.

**4. PLANT, MACHINERY AND OTHER CAPITAL EQUIPMENT (4.1 and 4.2)**

These questions cover plant, machinery and all other capital equipment (e.g. computer equipment, office machinery, furniture, mechanical handling equipment and mobile powered equipment such as earth movers, excavators, levellers, mobile cranes.)

# SOLUTIONS TO UNIT 7 TRIAL RUN DEVOLVED ASSESSMENT

**DO NOT TURN THIS PAGE UNTIL YOU HAVE COMPLETED THE TRIAL RUN DEVOLVED ASSESSMENT**

**Tutorial note.** Not many figures need to be entered on the ONS forms. However, the forms have quite lengthy accompanying notes. This highlights an important skill when completing reports and returns: to be able to review the information available in full and to select the information which is relevant to the task.

## Solutions

(a) See the completed forms on pages 187 and 188.

*Working*

Total turnover is calculated as follows.

| | £ | £ |
|---|---|---|
| *College Division* | | |
| YTD 31.3.X4 | 583,636 | |
| YTD 31.12.X3 | (422,629) | |
| | | 161,007 |
| *Bookshop* | | |
| YTD 31.3.X4 | 71,094 | |
| YTD 31.12.X3 | (46,931) | |
| | | 24,163 |
| Interdivisional (394 + 481 + 192) | | (1,067) |
| | | 184,103 |

(b) The return for the *Quarterly inquiry into turnover*, as stated in the ONS letter, should be returned within three weeks of the end of the period to which it relates. This period ends on 31 March 19X4 and so the form should be returned by 21 April 19X4.

The return for the *Quarterly inquiry into capital expenditure* should be returned by 14 April 19X4, as stated at the top of the form.

In view of these dates, neither form can wait for Kim's return from holiday and I would therefore take the following action.

(i) Remind Kim of the dates by which the returns must be made and request that she be available to sign them before she leaves at 5.30 pm this evening.

(ii) Make arrangements to complete the forms for signature today. The forms should be drafted by 4 pm at the latest, in case any changes are necessary following Kim's review of them.

*Quarterly inquiry into turnover*

| FV | | | |
|---|---|---|---|
| T16/770424000072/112 | | | |

**IMPORTANT**

Please read the notes before you fill in this form. Give the best estimates you can if you do not have exact figures.

## 1. Details of business

Your business is classified as being in the industry described briefly on the front of this form. If you think this is wrong, please give a full description of your business. If you are involved in two or more activities, please describe the main one.

## 2. Period

Period for which you have filled in the form

| | Day | Month | Year | |
|---|---|---|---|---|
| from | 01/ | 01 / | X4 | 11 |
| to | 31 / | 03/ | X4 | 12 |

## 3. Turnover to the nearest £thousand (not including VAT)

Total turnover (including fees receivable)

| 184 | 40 |
|---|---|

## 4. Employees

Number of persons employed by the business at the end of the period covered by this return.

| | | | |
|---|---|---|---|
| 4.1 | Total employees | 13 | 50 |
| **of which:-** | | | |
| 4.2 | Full-time male | 5 | 51 |
| 4.3 | Part-time male | 1 | 52 |
| 4.4 | Full-time female | 6 | 53 |
| 4.5 | Part-time female | 1 | 54 |

## 5. Other businesses included in this form

The form should be completed for the business named overleaf. If exceptionally, you are unable to limit your return to the activities of this business, please list below the names and VAT Registration numbers of the other businesses included.

Name of business ........................................ VAT registration number ........................................

........................................ ........................................

**(Please continue on a separate sheet if necessary)**

REMARKS: If you have given any information which is significantly different from the last quarter, please explain.

....................................................................................................

....................................................................................................

PLEASE USE BLOCK CAPITALS

Name of person we should contact if necessary: KIM HARVEY

Position in business: FINANCIAL CONTROLLER

Date: 8 APRIL 19X4

Telephone no/ext: 0171 711 4240

Fax/Telex: 0171 711 4200

*Quarterly inquiry into capital expenditure*

PLEASE COMPLETE AND RETURN THIS FORM BY 14 April 19X4

| FV | 93 | Q1 |
|---|---|---|
| 8100/7104420000 | | |

**IMPORTANT** Please read the enclosed notes before completing this form. If you do not have precise figures available give the best estimates you can. All values should be shown to the nearest £ thousand.

## 1. PERIOD (see note 1)

| | | | Day | Month | Year |
|---|---|---|---|---|---|
| Period covered by the return | from | 08 | 01/ | 01/ | X4 |
| | to | 09 | 31/ | 03/ | X4 |

## 2. LAND AND BUILDINGS (see note 2)

| | | | £ thousand |
|---|---|---|---|
| 2.1 | New building work or other constructional work of a capital nature (excluding the cost of land and of new dwellings) | 10 | 24 |
| 2.2 | Acquisition of land and of existing buildings | 20 | 32 |
| 2.3 | Proceeds of land and buildings disposed of | 30 | NIL |

## 3. VEHICLES (see note 3)

| | | | |
|---|---|---|---|
| 3.1 | New and second-hand acquisitions | 40 | 10 |
| 3.2 | Proceeds of vehicles disposed of | 50 | 5 |

## 4. PLANT, MACHINERY etc. (see note 4)

| | | | |
|---|---|---|---|
| 4.1 | New and second-hand acquisitions | 60 | 4 |
| 4.2 | Proceeds of plant, machinery etc. disposed of | 70 | 3 |

## 5. TOTAL

| | | | |
|---|---|---|---|
| 5.1 | Total acquisitions (2.1 + 2.2 + 3.1 + 4.1) | 90 | 70 |
| 5.2 | Total disposals (2.3 + 3.2 + 4.2) | 100 | 8 |

## 6. FINANCE LEASING

| | | | |
|---|---|---|---|
| 6.1 | Total amount included in acquisitions at 2.1, 3.1 and 4.1 for assets leased under finance leasing arrangements. | 80 | NIL |

## 7. COMMENTS ON UNUSUAL FLUCTUATIONS IN FIGURES WOULD BE APPRECIATED

.................................................................................................................................

Name of person to be contacted if necessary............KIM HARVEY............................................................
**BLOCK CAPITALS PLEASE**

Position in company..FINANCIAL CONTROLLER.. Signature..........................................................................

Telephone No/Ext.....0171 711 4240 Fax...0171 711 4200 Date....8 APRIL 19X4............

(c)

| *Quarter to* | *31 Mar 19X4* | | *31 Dec 19X3* | | *30 Sept 19X3* | | *30 June 19X3* | |
|---|---|---|---|---|---|---|---|---|
| *College Division* | £'000 | % | £'000 | % | £'000 | % | £'000 | % |
| Turnover | 161.0 | 100.0 | 152.8 | 100.0 | 145.1 | 100.0 | 124.7 | 100.0 |
| Direct costs | (70.8) | (44.0) | (68.4) | (44.8) | (66.7) | (46.0) | (64.1) | (51.4) |
| Other operating costs | (24.6) | (15.3) | (29.4) | (19.2) | (21.5) | (14.8) | (22.0) | (17.6) |
| Contribution | 65.6 | 40.7 | 55.0 | 36.0 | 56.9 | 39.2 | 38.6 | 31.0 |
| *Bookshop* | | | | | | | | |
| Turnover | 24.2 | 100.0 | 18.7 | 100.0 | 15.5 | 100.0 | 12.7 | 100.0 |
| Cost of sales | (15.2) | | (11.9) | | (9.6) | | (8.1) | |
| Gross profit | 9.0 | 37.2 | 6.8 | 36.4 | 5.9 | 38.1 | 4.6 | 36.2 |
| Staff costs | (4.4) | | (4.3) | | (4.1) | | (4.2) | |
| Other operating costs | (2.8) | | (2.2) | | (2.0) | | (2.4) | |
| Contribution | 1.8 | 7.4 | 0.3 | 1.6 | (0.2) | (1.3) | (2.0) | (15.7) |
| Bookshop staff nos. | 1.5 | | 1.5 | | 1.5 | | 1.0 | |
| Sales per staff member (£'000) | 16.1 | | 12.5 | | 10.3 | | 12.7 | |

(d) (i) *College Division*

Percentage of turnover

| *Quarter to* | *31 Mar 19X4* | *31 Dec 19X3* | *30 Sept 19X3* | *30 June 19X3* |
|---|---|---|---|---|
| Direct costs | 44.0 | 44.8 | 46.0 | 51.4 |
| Other operating costs | 15.3 | 19.2 | 14.8 | 17.6 |
| Contribution | 40.7 | 36.0 | 39.2 | 31.0 |

(ii) *Bookshop*

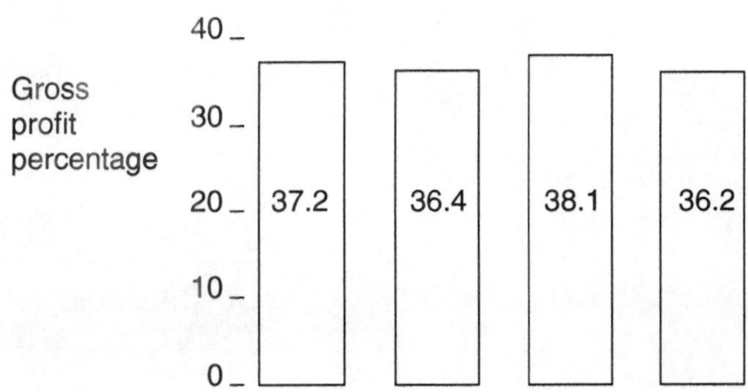

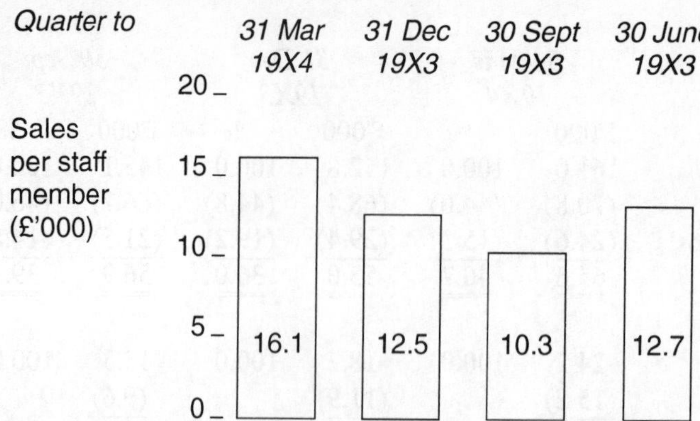


(e) The measurement of the productivity of the teaching staff requires the establishment of an appropriate unit to measure the output of teachers.

If records are kept of the number of hours of contact between students and staff, productivity could be measured as lecture hours per teacher or student contact hours per teacher, where student contact hours equals the number of students in a lecture multiplied by the length of the lecture. Such measures might be applied to the teaching staff overall or to individual teachers.

If we want to measure the quality of teachers' work more closely, we might use records of the grades obtained by students and weight the output of teachers according to the grades of their students, thus awarding different teachers scores according to the performance of their students. This measure will require records on student grades to be maintained, and it may be seen as unfair if different student groups have different ability ranges.

# TRIAL RUN DEVOLVED ASSESSMENT

## INTERMEDIATE STAGE - NVQ/SVQ3

## Unit 8

## Preparing VAT returns

The purpose of this Trial Run Devolved Assessment is to give you an idea of what a Unit 8 Devolved Assessment looks like. It is not intended as a definitive guide to the tasks you may be required to perform.

The suggested time allowance for this Assessment is two hours.

Calculators may be used but no reference material is permitted apart from the VAT Guide (Notice 700) published by HM Customs & Excise.

**DO NOT OPEN THIS PAPER UNTIL YOU ARE READY TO START UNDER TIMED CONDITIONS**

## NOTES ON COMPLETING THE ASSESSMENT

This Assessment is designed to test your ability to prepare VAT returns.

You are provided with data (pages 193 to 195) which you must use to complete the tasks listed on page 195.

You are allowed two hours to complete your work.

A high level of accuracy is required. Check your work carefully.

Correcting fluid should not be used. Errors should be crossed out neatly and clearly. You should write in ink - not pencil.

A full solution to this Assessment is provided on page 198 to 201.

Do not turn to the suggested solution until you have completed all parts of the Assessment.

## BACKGROUND INFORMATION

You are the recently appointed accountant at Iris Ltd. You are about to prepare the company's VAT return for the three months ended 31 December 19X5. You have the following documents to help you.

### SALES REPORT

| *Month* | *Sales* £ | *VAT* £ |
|---|---|---|
| October 19X5 | 327,190.00 | 40,545.75 |
| November 19X5 | 458,429.00 | 63,486.50 |
| December 19X5 | 259,361.00 | 31,608.50 |

### PURCHASES REPORT

| *Month* | *Purchases* £ | *VAT* £ |
|---|---|---|
| October 19X5 | 210,630.00 | 22,863.40 |
| November 19X5 | 296,539.00 | 32,805.85 |
| December 19X5 | 137,784.00 | 16,894.15 |

### MEMORANDUM

To: Accountant
From: Sales Director
Date: 7 January 19X6
Subject: VAT returns

I can provide my usual confirmation that we have done no business (sales or purchases) outside the UK in the quarter just ended, and that we have had no dealings in zero rated goods or services. All our exempt sales were of services. All exempt purchases were attributable to exempt sales. 20% of standard rated purchases were attributable to exempt sales, and 45% to standard rated sales.

### MEMORANDUM

To: Accountant
From: Warehouse Manager
Date: 13 January 19X6
Subject: Invoicing

I have noticed that in the past month, your department has been working a bit too fast. Goods worth £16,000 (plus VAT) were invoiced before the end of the year, even though they were still in the warehouse when we did our stockcount on 2 January. Won't the customers object to being billed so early? I suppose it's still better for us than the incident three months ago, when goods worth £24,600 (plus VAT) were delivered to the customer on 29 September but not invoiced until 10 October.

MEMORANDUM

To: Accountant
From: Data Processing Manager
Date: 20 January 19X6
Subject: Sales and purchases reports

You telephoned my secretary yesterday and asked a couple of questions about the reports produced by our computerised accounting system. The answers are as follows.

(a) Sales and purchases are shown net of VAT.

(b) Any sale of goods is recorded in the system on the day the goods leave the warehouse. This is because we work from the despatch notes. I know that for VAT purposes you always use the date of invoicing, but your predecessor (who left in November) said that she made adjustments on the rare occasions when the invoice did not go out on the same day. We never adjusted our figures to take her adjustments into account. Any sale of services is recorded on the day of invoicing.

MEMORANDUM

To: Accountant
From: Managing Director
Date: 23 January 19X6
Subject: The basement storeroom

Your staff keep on filling up our storage space with files, but we could do with that space for cleaning materials and other things which actually help to run the business. When I found one of your clerks putting another ten files in there yesterday, and asked what the point of it was, all he could say was "VAT rules". What records do we really *need* to keep, and for how long?

MEMORANDUM

To: Accountant
From: Credit Controller
Date: 23 January 19X6
Subject: Bad debts

In March 19X5, we made sales of goods to a customer of £7,600 plus VAT. Payment for the goods was due by 30 April 19X5. We received a cheque for £3,000 in August, but the customer went into liquidation in October. I have now heard that creditors will be paid 40p for every pound they are owed. I have written off the balance of the debt, which will not be paid.

MEMORANDUM

To: Accountant
From: Finance Director
Date: 28 January 19X6
Subject: Mistakes in VAT returns

A friend of mine runs a small business, and he has a query about his VAT. I wouldn't normally trouble you with things which don't concern Iris Ltd directly, but it's probably very simple so I hope you won't mind answering it. He isn't very good at accounts, and is very concerned that he might put the wrong figures on his VAT returns. He wants to know:

(a) can he just put right any underpayment or overpayment on a later return;
(b) could he be made to pay a penalty if he makes a mistake?

MEMORANDUM

To: Accountant
From: Data Processing Manager
Date: 28 January 19X6
Subject: New accounting software

We may soon be changing our software. One issue which has come up is that of rounding. The computer could work out amounts of VAT to the nearest hundredth of a penny, but all our invoices will of course have to be in whole pounds and pennies. So that our software is correctly designed, could you remind me of the rules on rounding amounts of VAT?

## TASKS

(a) Complete Iris Ltd's VAT return for the period.
(b) Reply to the managing director's memorandum.
(c) Reply to the finance director's memorandum.
(d) Reply to the second memorandum from the data processing manager.

A blank VAT return is provided below.

## Value Added Tax Return

For the period
01 10 X5 to 31 12 X5

For Official Use

| Registration number | Period |
|---|---|
| 653 5306 77 | 12 X5 |

You could be liable to a financial penalty if your completed return and all the VAT payable are not received by the due date.

IRIS LTD
1 FLOWER STREET
BLOOMTOWN
BL1 4LN

Due date: 31 01 X6

For Official Use

Your VAT Office telephone number is 0123-4567

Before you fill in this form please read the notes on the back and the VAT Leaflet *"Filling in your VAT return"*. Fill in all boxes clearly in ink, and write 'none' where necessary. Don't put a dash or leave any box blank. If there are no pence write "00" in the pence column. Do not enter more than one amount in any box.

For official use

| | Box | £ | p |
|---|---|---|---|
| VAT due in this period on sales and other outputs | 1 | | |
| VAT due in this period on acquisitions from other EC Member States | 2 | | |
| Total VAT due (the sum of boxes 1 and 2) | 3 | | |
| VAT reclaimed in this period on purchases and other inputs (including acquisitions from the EC) | 4 | | |
| **Net VAT to be paid to Customs or reclaimed by you (Difference between boxes 3 and 4)** | 5 | | |
| Total value of sales and all other outputs excluding any VAT. Include your box 8 figure | 6 | | 00 |
| Total value of purchases and all other inputs excluding any VAT. Include your box 9 figure | 7 | | 00 |
| Total value of all supplies of goods and related services, excluding any VAT, to other EC Member States | 8 | | 00 |
| Total value of all acquisitions of goods and related services, excluding any VAT, from other EC Member States | 9 | | 00 |

**Retail schemes.** If you have used any ot the schemes in the period covered by this return, enter the relevant letter(s) in this box.

If you are enclosing a payment please tick this box.

DECLARATION: You, or someone on your behalf, must sign below.

I, .............................................................................................. declare that the
(Full name of signatory in BLOCK LETTERS)
information given above is true and complete.

Signature.............................................................. Date .................... 19 ........

**A false declaration can result in prosecution.**

# SOLUTIONS TO UNIT 8 TRIAL RUN DEVOLVED ASSESSMENT

**DO NOT TURN THIS PAGE UNTIL YOU HAVE COMPLETED THE TRIAL RUN DEVOLVED ASSESSMENT**

## Solutions

(a) *Information from the sales report*

Total sales, excluding VAT, are £1,044,980, and total VAT is £135,640.75.

The standard rated sales are £135,640.75/0.175 = £775,090.

The exempt sales are £(1,044,980 – 775,090) = £269,890.

*Adjustments to the sales report figures*

The sales of £16,000 invoiced in December but delivered in January must be added to the total of standard rated sales, and the sales of £24,600 delivered in September but invoiced in October must also be added. The adjusted figures are as follows.

Total sales: £(1,044,980 + 16,000 + 24,600) = £1,085,580

Standard rated sales: £(775,090 + 16,000 + 24,600) = £815,690

Output VAT: £815,690 × 17.5% = £142,745.75

Exempt sales: £269,890

Recoverable percentage of unattributed input VAT: £815,690/£1,085,580 = 75.1%, rounded up to 76%.

*Purchases*

Total purchases are £644,953, and the total VAT is £72,563.40.

*Bad debt relief*

The total amount owed by the customer in liquidation, including VAT, was £7,600 × 1.175 = £8,930. Of this, £5,930 is still owing.

The bad debt, including VAT, is £5,930 × 60% = £3,558.

The VAT in this amount is £3,558 × 7/47 = £529.91.

*Recoverable input VAT*

| | £ |
|---|---|
| Attributable to taxable supplies £72,563.40 × 45% | 32,653.53 |
| Unattributable £72,563.40 × 35% × 76% | 19,301.86 |
| | 51,955.39 |
| Bad debt relief | 529.91 |
| | 52,485.30 |

The '£625 a month on average' limit for exempt input VAT is clearly exceeded, so not all input VAT is recoverable.

The VAT return can now be completed.

## Value Added Tax Return

For the period
01 10 X5 to 31 12 X5

For Official Use

Registration number: 653 5306 77

Period: 12 X5

You could be liable to a financial penalty if your completed return and all the VAT payable are not received by the due date.

IRIS LTD
1 FLOWER STREET
BLOOMTOWN
BL1 4LN

Due date: 31 01 X6

For Official Use

Your VAT Office telephone number is 0123-4567

Before you fill in this form please read the notes on the back and the VAT Leaflet *"Filling in your VAT return"*. Fill in all boxes clearly in ink, and write 'none' where necessary. Don't put a dash or leave any box blank. If there are no pence write "00" in the pence column. Do not enter more than one amount in any box.

| For official use | | Box | £ | p |
|---|---|---|---|---|
| | VAT due in this period on sales and other outputs | 1 | 142,745 | 75 |
| | VAT due in this period on acquisitions from other EC Member States | 2 | NONE | |
| | Total VAT due (the sum of boxes 1 and 2) | 3 | 142,745 | 75 |
| | VAT reclaimed in this period on purchases and other inputs (including acquisitions from the EC) | 4 | 52,485 | 30 |
| | **Net VAT to be paid to Customs or reclaimed by you (Difference between boxes 3 and 4)** | 5 | 90,260 | 45 |
| | Total value of sales and all other outputs excluding any VAT. Include your box 8 figure | 6 | 1,085,580 | 00 |
| | Total value of purchases and all other inputs excluding any VAT. Include your box 9 figure | 7 | 644,953 | 00 |
| | Total value of all supplies of goods and related services, excluding any VAT, to other EC Member States | 8 | NONE | 00 |
| | Total value of all acquisitions of goods and related services, excluding any VAT, from other EC Member States | 9 | NONE | 00 |
| | **Retail schemes.** If you have used any ot the schemes in the period covered by this return, enter the relevant letter(s) in this box. | | | |

If you are enclosing a payment please tick this box. ✓

DECLARATION: You, or someone on your behalf, must sign below.

I, ANDREW TECH declare that the
(Full name of signatory in BLOCK LETTERS)
information given above is true and complete.

Signature A Tech Date 30/01 19 X6

**A false declaration can result in prosecution.**

(b)

MEMORANDUM

To: Managing Director
From: Accountant
Date: 29 January 19X6
Subject: The basement storeroom and VAT records

Thank you for your memorandum dated 23 January. I appreciate that the bulk of records kept may seem excessive, but unfortunately we are bound by VAT law to keep certain records for six years. If we did not keep the required records for this long, we could be made to pay penalties. The required records are as follows.

(i) Copies of VAT invoices, credit notes and debit notes issued

(ii) VAT invoices, credit notes and debit notes received

(iii) Records of goods received from and sent to other European Union member states

(iv) Documents relating to imports from and exports to outside the European Union

(v) Order and delivery notes, correspondence, appointment books, job books, purchases and sales books, cash books, account books, records of takings (such as till rolls), bank paying-in slips, bank statements and annual accounts

(vi) Records of zero rated and exempt supplies, gifts or loans of goods, taxable self-supplies and any goods taken for non-business use

(vii) Summaries of supplies made and received

(viii) A VAT account

We could save some space by using microfilm, microfiche or computer records.

(c)

MEMORANDUM

To: Finance Director
From: Accountant
Date: 29 January 19X6
Subject: Mistakes in VAT returns

Thank you for your memorandum dated 28 January.

(i) If your friend makes errors on a VAT return, he can simply correct the error on a later return so long as the net error (error in output VAT net of error in input VAT) does not exceed £2,000. He should simply increase or reduce the figure in box 1, box 2 or box 4 as appropriate. If a figure becomes negative because of this, it should be shown in brackets.

Errors exceeding £2,000 net must be separately notified to the local VAT office.

(ii) There are two penalties for understatements of the amount of VAT due. They are the misdeclaration penalty for very large errors and the misdeclaration penalty for repeated errors.

The former penalty applies when the VAT which would have been lost is at least £1m or is at least 30% of the sum of the correct input VAT and the correct output VAT.

The latter penalty applies when there is a series of material inaccuracies, meaning errors when the VAT which would have been lost is at least £500,000 or is at least 10% of the sum of the correct input VAT and the correct output VAT. The first material inaccuracy leads to a penalty period of eight VAT return periods starting. Any material inaccuracies in that period, apart from the first one, incur the penalty.

In both cases, the penalty is 15% of the VAT which would have been lost. If the penalty for very large errors applies to an error, the penalty for repeated errors cannot also apply but the error can lead to the start of a penalty period.

(d)

MEMORANDUM

To: Data Processing Manager
From: Accountant
Date: 29 January 19X6
Subject: New accounting software - rounding of VAT.

Thank you for your memorandum of 28 January. The rules on the rounding of amounts of VAT are as follows.

(a) If amounts of VAT are calculated for individual lines on an invoice, they must be:

  (i) rounded down to the nearest 0.1p, so 86.76p would be shown as 86.7p; or

  (ii) rounded to the nearest 0.5p, so 86.76p would be shown as 87p and 86.26p would be shown as 86.5p

(b) If amounts of VAT are calculated from an amount of VAT per unit or article, the amount of VAT should be:

  (i) calculated to the nearest 0.01p and then rounded to the nearest 0.1p, so 0.24p would be rounded to 0.2p; or

  (ii) rounded to the nearest 0.5p, but with a minimum of 0.5p for any standard rated item, so 0.24p would be rounded to 0.5p rather than to 0p.

(c) The total VAT shown on an invoice should be rounded down to the nearest 1p, so £32.439 would be shown as £32.43.

# *Unit 7 Central assessments*

# Unit 7 R & R Central assessments

The following exercises are provided as practice for the Unit 7 Central Assessment, now known as R & R. They comprise case studies which have been included in AAT Central Assessments from December 1993 to December 1994, plus others of the same standard.

The format of the Central Assessment for Unit 7 changed from June 1995, so that a single Central Assessment covers Unit 7 rather than Unit 6 and 7 being combined in one Central Assessment as previously. The June 1995 Central Assessment is included as the first Trial Run Central Assessment in this Workbook, followed by the December 1995 and June 1996 Central Assessments: you should have a go at these after you have attempted the case studies listed on this page.

Those exercises which are taken from past AAT assessments are indicated by dates. The exercise entitled Sports Supermarkets was included in a Sample Central Assessment produced by the AAT. Solutions to the Class exercise Midwich General Hospital are provided in the Lecturers' Pack for this Unit.

**Case studies**

## CASE STUDIES

### 1 Ajay

#### *Data*

Ajay Ltd operates two launderettes, A and J. Turnover in pounds for each launderette in the two years 19X6 and 19X8 was as follows.

| | *19X6* | | *19X8* | |
|---|---|---|---|---|
| | *Launderette* | | *Launderette* | |
| | *A* | *J* | *A* | *J* |
| Washers | 3,750 | 3,920 | 4,970 | 4,770 |
| Dryers | 2,110 | 2,340 | 2,970 | 2,870 |
| Dry cleaning | 1,990 | 2,870 | 2,020 | 2,170 |
| Total | 7,850 | 9,130 | 9,960 | 9,810 |

#### *Task 1*

Present these data in a component bar chart.

#### *Task 2*

Present these data in a percentage component bar chart.

#### *Task 3*

Report to Ajay Ltd upon the trends indicated in these data and the comparison of the two launderettes' performances.

*Notes*

A component bar chart shows actual figures.

A percentage component bar chart shows percentages of total figures. In a percentage component bar chart, all the bars are the same height.

*Note.* The suggested time allocation for the case study above is 50 minutes.

### 2 Sports Supermarkets (Sample CA)

#### *Data*

Sports Supermarkets Ltd started trading three years ago in three out-of-town locations in Manchester, Birmingham and Newcastle. The premises are all leased and there had been a significant increase in rents in year 3. The marketing concept was to offer a range of medium-price sports equipment and sportswear for a wide variety of indoor and outdoor sporting activities. It was hoped to attract young people with above-average disposable income who would buy higher value items on the strength of offering good value for money, a wide choice and specialist advice from the sales staff.

Table 1 sets out some basic information about the progress of the firm in the first three years of its operation. The directors of the company are considering the business's future and as a first step they have asked the management accountant for an analysis of performance over the period. They are particularly interested in trends in profitability, margins, turnover and the effectiveness of their marketing policies.

The management accountant has asked you to do some preparatory work on this report in two parts.

### *Task 1*

Draft a short report calculating for each year and commenting on:

(a) gross profit as a percentage of purchases (mark-up);
(b) net profit as a percentage of turnover;
(c) net profit as a percentage of average staff costs;
(d) turnover at year 1 prices.

### *Task 2*

Write a short report to John Bright on the efficiency and effectiveness of the sales staff and the firm's marketing effort in general on the basis of the information which is available. What information would be required to compare the marketing effectiveness of the three branches of Sports Supermarkets Ltd?

*Sports Supermarkets Ltd*

| | *Year 1* | *Year 2* | *Year 3* |
|---|---|---|---|
| Turnover (£) | 3,850,000 | 4,630,000 | 5,280,000 |
| Number of customers | 298,000 | 353,000 | 396,000 |
| Purchases (£) | 1,680,000 | 2,270,000 | 2,850,000 |
| Standing charges (£) | 650,000 | 720,000 | 830,000 |
| Staff costs (£) | 810,000 | 950,000 | 910,000 |
| Number of staff (full-time equivalents) | 60 | 65 | 59 |
| Other operating costs (£) | 290,000 | 300,000 | 310,000 |
| Retail Prices Index | 100 | 106 | 110 |
| UK unemployment (as percentage of working population) | 5.1% | 6.1% | 8.3% |

*Note.* The suggested time allocation for the case study above is 1 hour.

## 3 Toy Manufacturers' Trade Association (December 1993)

### *Data*

The Toy Manufacturers' Trade Association was established several years ago to assist its member companies with legal/administrative matters and to provide an advisory service. You are employed by the Trade Association and are mainly involved with the advisory service. One of the services offered is an inter-firm comparison which involves collecting quarterly information from its member companies. After analysis, the best and average results are supplied to all participating firms but no company names are revealed. It is up to each company to compare their own results with the figures provided and to decide what action needs to be taken. NTL plc, a new company to this service, asks for your help as it does not understand what calculations it needs to do or what conclusions to draw. The most recent figures for NTL plc are as follows.

TRADING AND PROFIT AND LOSS ACCOUNT
FOR THE QUARTER TO 30 SEPTEMBER 19X3

| | £ | £ |
|---|---|---|
| Sales | | 653,000 |
| Materials | 361,109 | |
| Labour | 80,319 | |
| Production overheads | 108,398 | |
| Production cost | | 549,826 |
| Distribution and marketing | | 18,937 |
| Administration | | 44,404 |
| Total cost | | 613,167 |
| Net profit | | 39,833 |

BALANCE SHEET AS AT 30 SEPTEMBER 19X3

| | £ | £ |
|---|---|---|
| Fixed assets | | 185,729 |
| Current assets | | |
| Stock | 92,046 | |
| Debtors | 56,192 | |
| | 148,238 | |
| Current liabilities | | |
| Creditors | 48,075 | |
| Overdraft | 40,009 | |
| | 88,084 | |
| Working capital | | 60,154 |
| Capital employed | | 245,883 |

*Task 1*

**Complete the form below by calculating the inter-firm ratios for NTL plc and inserting them in the space provided. (Calculations to one decimal place.)**

| TOY MANUFACTURERS' TRADE ASSOCIATION | | | |
|---|---|---|---|
| INTER-FIRM COMPARISON REPORT, QUARTER TO 30 SEPTEMBER 19X3 | | | |
| | *Most profitable* | *Average* | *NTL plc* |
| Direct materials as a percentage of sales | 46.9 | 52.6 | |
| Direct labour as a percentage of sales | 10.4 | 10.1 | |
| Production overheads as a percentage of sales | 14.0 | 16.9 | |
| Production cost as a percentage of sales | 71.3 | 79.6 | |
| Distribution and marketing as a percentage of sales | 4.9 | 3.8 | |
| Administration as a percentage of sales | 5.6 | 5.7 | |
| Net profit as a percentage of sales | 18.2 | 10.9 | |
| Net profit as a percentage of capital employed | 40.4 | 22.6 | |
| Current ratio (current assets to current liabilities) | 2.2:1 | 1.9:1 | |
| Quick ratio (debtors to current liabilities) | 1.1:1 | 0.9:1 | |

*Task 2*

**Write a report to the Managing Director of NTL plc explaining the main differences revealed in Task 1. Comment on both the profitability and the financial position of the company suggesting areas for further investigation and possible corrective action.**

*Task 3*

**The managing director is under pressure from the other managers to spend £20,000 on an advertising campaign, which it is believed would increase sales by 10%. An investigation into production overheads has shown that £32,658 was variable and £75,740 was fixed. To test out the proposed advertising campaign you are asked to:**

**(a) Recalculate the trading and profit and loss account to 30 September 19X3 using the form below. Assume that material, labour and variable production overheads increase at the same rate as sales (calculations to the nearest pound).**

RE-WORKED TRADING AND PROFIT AND LOSS ACCOUNT
FOR THE QUARTER TO 30 SEPTEMBER 19X3

| | £ |
|---|---|
| Sales | |
| Materials | |
| Labour | |
| Variable production overheads | |
| Fixed production overheads | |
| Production cost | |
| Distribution and marketing (fixed) | |
| Advertising campaign (fixed) | |
| Administration (fixed) | |
| Total cost | |
| Net profit | |

(b) Write a brief report to the Managing Director explaining whether or not the advertising campaign is justified.

*Note.* The suggested time allocation for the case study above is 1 hour.

## 4 BTC (June 1994)

### *Data*

Until three years ago BTC, an accountancy training organisation, ran its own fleet of vans and delivered manuals to retailers and colleges. The decision was taken to concentrate on core activities and so several organisations were carefully considered before RD plc was selected to take on the responsibility for storing and delivering the manuals. It was agreed that RD would purchase the manuals from BTC at the recommended selling price, less an agreed discount. This ensures that RD would automatically benefit from future increases in the selling price of the manuals. The arrangement has worked well for both organisations and a good relationship has been established.

The managing director of RD has been satisfied with the profits that have been earned, but he is concerned with the efficiency of the transport operation. You, as the assistant accountant, have been asked to provide regular information to the general manager, who is responsible for all aspects of transportation. The general manager has always controlled this area by observing what he calls 'key ratios' which he sees as delivery costs and drivers' wages as a percentage of sales, sales per van and the number of deliveries. He believes that if these ratios are improving then the transport operation is working well. He is also a great believer that graphs help to clarify the statistics in any report.

### *Task 1*

Using the figures from Appendix 1 below, draw a multiple bar chart (sometimes called a compound bar chart) showing for each year:

(a) the sales value of the manuals sold;
(b) the van expenses;
(c) the drivers' wages.

A squared rectangle for the chart is provided below the Appendix.

| Appendix 1 | | | |
|---|---|---|---|
| *Years* | *1* | *2* | *3* |
| Sales £s | 200,000 | 222,200 | 272,630 |
| Van expenses £s | 14,000 | 15,000 | 18,000 |
| As % of sales | 7 | 6.7 | 6.6 |
| Drivers' wages £s | 52,000 | 56,600 | 68,150 |
| As % of sales | 26 | 25.5 | 25 |
| Number of vans | 3 | 3 | 4 |
| Sales per van £s | 66,667 | 74,067 | 68,158 |
| Number of deliveries | 1,000 | 1,100 | 2,000 |

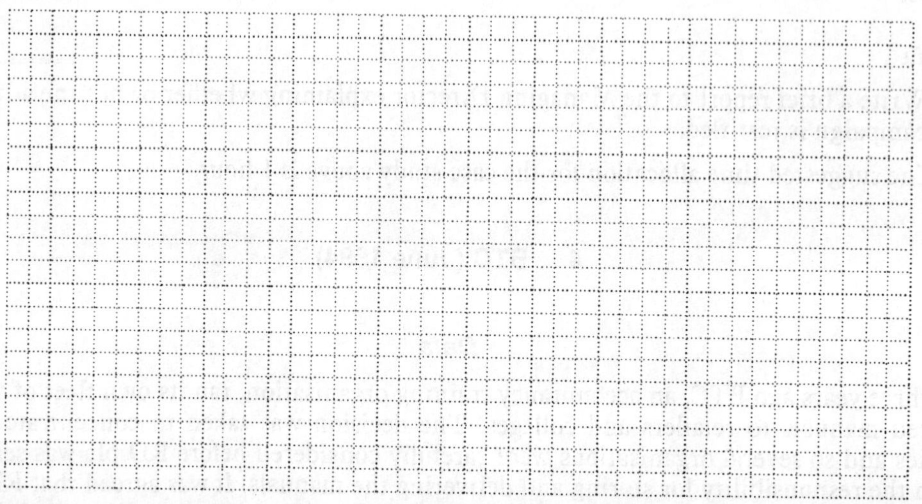

The accountant, although very interested in performance measures, is worried about the information in Appendix 1. His main concern is that the selling prices of the manuals have increased dramatically over the last two years. This was due to BTC's policy of initially pricing below the normal market price and then, once the manuals had been accepted by the market, increasing prices quite sharply. The accountant wants to remove these specific price rises from the figures before calculating the 'key ratios' and has produced the following index numbers of price changes based on Year 1.

| *Years* | *1* | *2* | *3* |
|---|---|---|---|
| Sales | 100 | 110 | 137 |
| Van expenses | 100 | 104 | 106 |

Drivers' wages have shown very little change during these years and can remain as per Appendix 1.

*Task 2*

Complete Appendix 2 below by:

(a) converting the actual figures for Years 2 and 3 (from Appendix 1) to Year 1 prices by using the price index given (calculations to the nearest pound);

(b) calculating the 'key ratios' including a new one of sales per delivery in pounds (percentage calculations to 1 decimal place; calculations in £s to the nearest pound).

| Appendix 2 | | | |
|---|---|---|---|
| *Years* | *1* | *2* | *3* |
| Sales £s | 200,000 | | |
| Van expenses £s | 14,000 | | |
| As % of sales | 7 | | |
| Drivers' wages £s | 52,000 | 56,600 | 68,150 |
| As % of sales | 26 | | |
| Number of vans | 3 | 3 | 4 |
| Sales per van £s | 66,667 | | |
| Number of deliveries | 1,000 | 1,100 | 2,000 |
| Sales per delivery £s | 200 | | |

### *Task 3*

Write a report to the general manager commenting upon the performance of the transport operation. The report should be in three sections.

*Section 1:* should explain whether the 'key ratios' in Appendix 1 support the general manager's opinion.

*Section 2:* should explain whether the 'key ratios' in Appendix 2 indicate an efficient operation.

*Section 3:* (a) should state whether you consider that the transport operation is efficient and whether Appendix 1 or Appendix 2 should be the basis of future reports, giving reasons for your decisions;

(b) should also suggest one other 'key ratio' that should be observed (no calculation is required) and say how often this type of information should be presented.

*Note.* The suggested time allocation for the case study above is 1 hour.

## 5 WMSC (December 1994)

### *Data*

The WMSC owns three ships which it offers for charter to three different markets. The first ship, the BB, is used for oil transportation; the second ship, the SS, is hired out to transport general cargo and the third ship, the TT, is used mainly for passenger transportation. The shipping industry has declined in recent years due to a surplus of ships and a fall in user demand. The world fleet has now fallen and there is evidence that the demand for charter ships is increasing.

### *Task 1*

Complete the following Annual Operating Statement by calculating:

(a) the hire charges for TT as a percentage of the total hire charge;
(b) the four ratios for the total column.

Calculations should be to the nearest whole number.

ANNUAL OPERATING STATEMENT - WMSC - 19X4

| | Total £'000 | % | BB £'000 | % | SS £'000 | % | TT £'000 |
|---|---|---|---|---|---|---|---|
| Hire charges (revenue) | 8,263 | | 4,512 | | 2,429 | | 1,322 |
| As a % of total hire charge | | | | 55 | | 29 | |
| Voyage & operating costs | 4,358 | | 2,566 | | 1,263 | | 529 |
| Gross profit | 3,905 | | 1,946 | | 1,166 | | 793 |
| As a % of hire charges | | 43 | | 48 | | 60 | |
| General expenses | 2,720 | | 1,378 | | 903 | | 439 |
| Net profit | 1,185 | | 568 | | 263 | | 354 |
| As a % of hire charges | | 13 | | 11 | | 27 | |
| Capital employed | 3,385 | | 1,517 | | 1,282 | | 586 |
| ROCE (net profit to capital employed) | | 37 | | 21 | | 60 | |
| Budgeted hire charges | 10,200 | | 5,000 | | 4,000 | | 1,200 |
| Utilisation % (Hire charges / Budgeted hire charges) | | 90 | | 61 | | 110 | |

*Task 2*

Write a report to the General Manager of WMSC commenting on:

(a) the overall performance of the company (using the figures and the ratios in the 'total' column only). Shipping industry averages for last year were: ROCE 24%, gross profit to hire charges 40% and net profit to hire charges 15%;

(b) the individual performance of each ship, stressing the good points revealed and those points that require investigation.

Funds are available for new investment and in the final section of the report you are asked to:

(c) comment on a proposal to buy a second 'SS' to carry more general cargo;

(d) suggest one non-financial factor that needs to be considered before another ship is purchased.

*Task 3*

The administration manager of WMSC receives regular information on the analysis of the general expenses in the form of pie charts. He is having some difficulty in understanding the charts and, to make matters worse, when last month's charts were sent out the 'key' was not completed. You are asked to:

(a) use the figures provided to complete the key to the pie charts by identifying which segment (labelled A to E) represents which expense. (Eg if you think A = Depreciation, then write A opposite Depreciation in the letter column.)

| | *November 19X4* £'000 | *November 19X3* £'000 |
|---|---|---|
| Wages and salaries | 69 | 53 |
| Building occupation costs | 46 | 52 |
| Agent's commission | 58 | 42 |
| General administration expenses | 23 | 31 |
| Depreciation | 34 | 32 |
| | 230 | 210 |

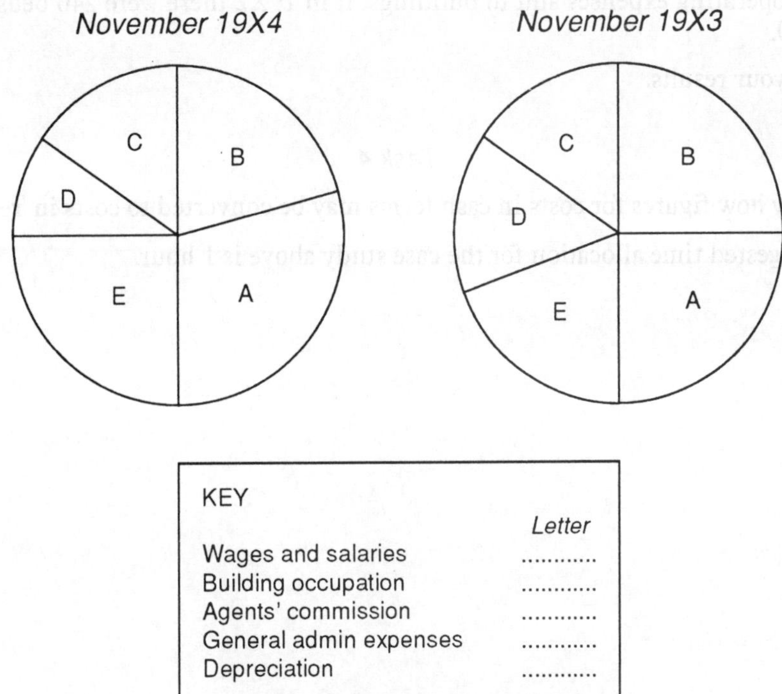


(b) write a short report to the Administration Manager:

(i) explaining the main points that are revealed by a comparison of the pie charts;

(ii) suggesting an explanation for the changes in the agent's commission and the general administration expenses.

*Note.* The suggested time allocation for the case study above is 1 hour.

## Class Exercise: Midwich General Hospital

The Midwich General Hospital operates its own laundry for washing bed linen, uniforms, doctor's coats etc. In 19X2, the expenditure on wages related to the Personnel section was £52,188 for administration, £28,340 for supervisors and £111,786 for laundry staff; the expenditure related to operating expenses was £17,188 on soap powder, £6,485 on water softeners and £3,335 on starch. The expenditure on buildings in 19X2 amounted to £16,427 on maintenance, £31,990 on fuel and £47,468 on equipment and furniture. Similar expenditure in 19X7 was £27,010 on maintenance, £38,460 on fuel and £22,875 on equipment and furniture. Personnel expenditure in 19X7 was £61,342 on administration wages, £24,050 on supervisors' wages and £125,670 on laundry staff wages; operating expenses were £19,676 on soap powder, £10,004 on water softeners and £4,460 on starch.

*Task 1*

The hospital's Financial Director requires that these data be collated in a good presentational form for the next meeting of the Expenditure Committee.

Represent the data in a single, clearly labelled table.

*Task 2*

Create a second, similar table to show percentage expenditures for each year, and comment upon the trends indicated.

*Task 3*

In 19X2, the hospital bed occupancy rate averaged 82%; in 19X7, this rate was 93%.

Calculate, for both 19X2 and 19X7, the average laundry cost per occupied bed attributable to personnel, to operating expenses and to buildings, if in 19X2 there were 240 beds but in 19X7 there were 220.

Comment on your results.

*Task 4*

Explain briefly how figures for costs in cash terms may be converted to costs in 'real' terms.

Note. The suggested time allocation for the case study above is 1 hour.

# *Solutions to Unit 7 central assessments*

# SOLUTIONS TO CASE STUDIES

## 1 Ajay

### *Task 1*

A component bar chart shows actual figures.

| | *19X6* | | | | *19X8* | | | |
|---|---|---|---|---|---|---|---|---|
| | *A* | *Cumul A* | *J* | *Cumul J* | *A* | *Cumul A* | *J* | *Cumul J* |
| Washers | 3,750 | 7,850 | 3,920 | 9,130 | 4,970 | 9,960 | 4,770 | 9,810 |
| Dryers | 2,110 | 4,100 | 2,340 | 5,210 | 2,970 | 4,990 | 2,870 | 5,040 |
| D/C | 1,990 | 1,990 | 2,870 | 2,870 | 2,020 | 2,020 | 2,170 | 2,170 |

*Note.* D/C = Dry cleaning

*Component bar chart*

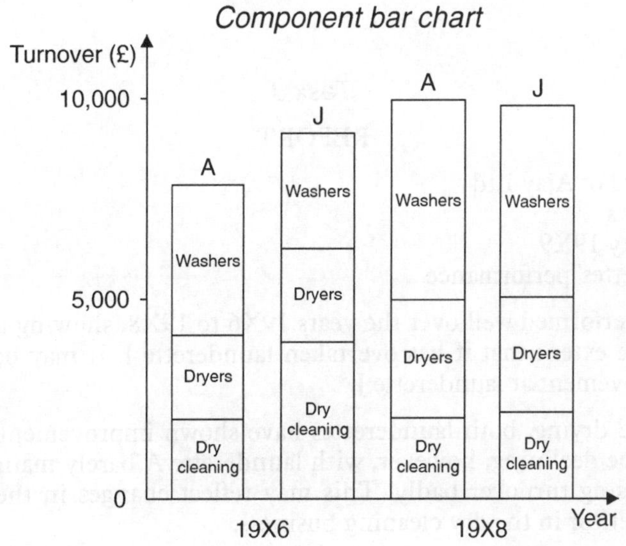


### *Task 2*

A percentage component bar chart shows percentages of total figures.

| | *19X6* | | | | *19X8* | | | |
|---|---|---|---|---|---|---|---|---|
| | *Cumul A* | *Cumul %A* | *Cumul J* | *Cumul %J* | *Cumul A* | *Cumul %A* | *Cumul J* | *Cumul %J* |
| Washers | 7,850 | 100.0 | 9,130 | 100.0 | 9,960 | 100.0 | 9,810 | 100.0 |
| Dryers | 4,100 | 52.2 | 5,210 | 57.1 | 4,990 | 50.1 | 5,040 | 51.4 |
| D/C | 1,990 | 25.4 | 2,870 | 31.4 | 2,020 | 20.3 | 2,170 | 22.1 |

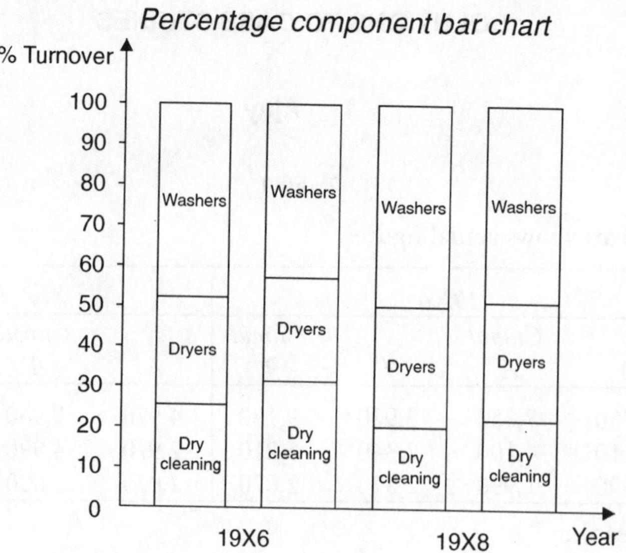


*Task 3*

REPORT

To: The Board of Ajay Ltd
From: A A Tonks
Date: 1 February 19X9
Subject: Launderettes' performance

Launderette A has performed well over the years 19X6 to 19X8, showing a marked increase in total turnover, to the extent that it has overtaken launderette J. It may be that there is scope for significant improvement at launderette J.

In both washing and drying, both launderettes have shown improvements. The dry cleaning business appears to be declining, however, with launderette A barely maintaining its turnover and launderette J losing turnover badly. This may reflect changes in the clothes market, or perhaps a new competitor in the dry cleaning business.

## 2 Sports Supermarkets

*Task 1*

REPORT

To: The Directors
From: A Technician
Date: XX March 19X4
Subject: Report on company performance years 1 to 3

1 Results and key ratios are set out below.

| | Year 1 | Year 2 | Year 3 |
|---|---|---|---|
| | £'000 | £'000 | £'000 |
| Turnover | 3,850 | 4,630 | 5,280 |
| Purchases | 1,680 | 2,270 | 2,850 |
| Gross profit | 2,170 | 2,360 | 2,430 |
| Standing charges | 650 | 720 | 830 |
| Staff costs | 810 | 950 | 910 |
| Other operating costs | 290 | 300 | 310 |
| | 1,750 | 1,970 | 2,050 |
| Net profit | 420 | 390 | 380 |
| Gross profit as percentage of purchases | 129% | 104% | 85% |
| Net profit as percentage of turnover | 10.9% | 8.4% | 7.2% |
| Average staff costs | £13,500 | £14,615 | £15,424 |
| Turnover at year 1 prices | £3,850,000 | £4,368,000 | £4,800,000 |
| UK unemployment rate | 5.1% | 6.1% | 8.3% |
| Net profit as percentage of average staff costs | 3,111 | 2,668 | 2,464 |

*Notes*

(1) Average staff costs are staff costs per employee.

(2) Turnover is adjusted by the Retail Prices Index to arrive at turnover at year 1 prices.

2 The main reason for the fall in profitability can be seen in the gross profit figures. The average mark up (gross profit as a percentage of purchases) has declined from 129% in year 1 to 85% in year 3. This could result from both increases in price competition which depress selling prices and an inability to pass on increased purchase prices to customers in higher prices.

3 There has been real growth in turnover of 25% between year 1 and year 3. Such growth in turnover is to be expected in the early years of a new business, and perhaps would have been higher if there had not been recessionary conditions (as indicated by the rise in the unemployment rate over the period).

4 Staff costs per employee (average staff costs) rose by more than the rate of inflation in year 2 (8.3%) and in year 3 (5.5%). The fall in total staff costs in year 3 reflects the decrease in staff numbers from 65 to 59. The rising average staff costs together with the falling net profit led to a decline in net profit as a percentage of average staff costs over the period.

5 Standing charges rose by 10.8% in year 2 and by 15.3% in year 3. The year 3 rise reflects the increase in rents in that year.

6 The decline in profitability from 10.9% to 7.2% results from different factors which have already been highlighted above. There have been reductions in profit margins and increases in operating costs.

## *Task 2*

## REPORT

To: John Bright
From: A Technician
Date: XX March 19X4
Subject: Efficiency and effectiveness of sales staff and marketing

1 Some key ratios are set out below.

| | Year 1 | Year 2 | Year 3 |
|---|---|---|---|
| Turnover per customer | £12.92 | £13.12 | £13.33 |
| Turnover per staff member | £64,167 | £71,231 | £89,492 |
| Turnover per staff member at Year 1 prices | £64,167 | £67,199 | £81,356 |
| Average staff costs | £13,500 | £14,615 | £15,424 |

2 Measured in terms of turnover per staff member in real terms (Year 1 prices), the effectiveness of staff has increased over the period, rising by 4.7% in year 2 and by a

further 21.1% in year 3, when the total number of staff fell from 65 to 59. However, there were also increases in staff costs above the rate of inflation in year 2 and year 3.

3 Sales per customer have changed little over the period, and indeed have declined in real terms. This may be because of customers' tendency to hold back on larger purchases during a recessionary period. Customer numbers have increased substantially, but there is no indication that the marketing policy of attracting purchases of higher-price items has been successful.

4 The following additional information would enable a comparison to be made of the three branches.

(1) Turnover, customer numbers, staff costs and staff numbers for each branch.

(2) Market research information about the proportions of different age groups and income groups in the three market areas.

(3) Regional statistics for economic trends in the three market areas: economic recession might affect one branch more than another.

## 3 Toy Manufacturers' Trade Association

### *Task 1*

*Tutorial note.* A space was provided on the answer paper below the table, for you to show your workings.

| TOY MANUFACTURERS' TRADE ASSOCIATION | | | | |
|---|---|---|---|---|
| INTER-FIRM COMPARISON REPORT, QUARTER TO 30 SEPTEMBER 19X3 | | | | |
| | *Most profitable* | *Average* | *NTL plc* | |
| Direct materials as a percentage of sales | 46.9 | 52.6 | 55.3 | W1 |
| Direct labour as a percentage of sales | 10.4 | 10.1 | 12.3 | W2 |
| Production overheads as a percentage of sales | 14.0 | 16.9 | 16.6 | W3 |
| Production cost as a percentage of sales | 71.3 | 79.6 | 84.2 | W4 |
| Distribution and marketing as a percentage of sales | 4.9 | 3.8 | 2.9 | W5 |
| Administration as a percentage of sales | 5.6 | 5.7 | 6.8 | W6 |
| Net profit as a percentage of sales | 18.2 | 10.9 | 6.1 | W7 |
| Net profit as a percentage of capital employed | 40.4 | 22.6 | 16.2 | W8 |
| Current ratio (current assets to current liabilities) | 2.2:1 | 1.9:1 | 1.7:1 | W9 |
| Quick ratio (debtors to current liabilities) | 1.1:1 | 0.9:1 | 0.6:1 | W10 |

*Workings*

W1 361,109 ÷ 653,000 × 100 = 55.3
W2 80,319 ÷ 653,000 × 100 = 12.3
W3 103,398 ÷ 653,000 × 100 = 16.6
W4 549,826 ÷ 653,000 × 100 = 84.2
W5 18,937 ÷ 653,000 × 100 = 2.9
W6 44,404 ÷ 653,000 × 100 = 6.8
W7 39,833 ÷ 653,000 × 100 = 6.1
W8 39,833 ÷ 245,883 × 100 = 16.2
W9 148,238 ÷ 88,084 = 1.7
W10 56,192 ÷ 88,084 = 0.6

*Task 2*

REPORT

To: Managing Director, NTL plc
From: A Technician, Toy Manufacturers' Trade Association
Date: 14 December 19X3
Subject: Inter-firm comparison, quarter to 30 September 19X3

1 The purpose of this report is to indicate the main differences revealed by the attached inter-firm comparison report.

2 The overall return on capital employed (ROCE) for NTL plc is well below that of the most profitable company and is also below the average for all companies.

3 Net profit is low as a percentage of sales. Production cost is the most significant cost factor, making up 90% of total cost. Both direct materials and direct labour costs are higher than average relative to sales. This may indicate poor materials buying policies. These policies should be studied along with materials scrap rates. The grade of labour employed and the level of labour efficiency should also be examined.

4 The ratios for total production cost and administration overheads could improve if sales can be increased, possibly following an examination of the company's pricing policy. Some overheads costs will be fixed or semi-fixed and will thus not increase in line with levels of activity.

5 NTL has a significantly lower ratio than the average for distribution and marketing costs. This area deserves further investigation as it could indicate that more resources need to be devoted to marketing.

6 The financial (working capital) ratios for NTL are currently unfavourable. The relatively low current ratio suggests that there could be problems in financing working capital in the near future. The low quick ratio is a cause for concern because the company has an overdraft and can only now pay its short-term debts by increasing the overdraft. Whether the company's bankers are prepared to allow the overdraft to increase needs to be ascertained.

7 If the overdraft cannot be increased, an alternative source of finance will need to be found. Within working capital, the level of stocks might be reduced. However, the scope for this could be limited, since stocks currently represent only 0.5 months' cost of sales (92,046/(549,826 ÷ 3)).

*Task 3*

(a) REWORKED TRADING AND PROFIT AND LOSS ACCOUNT FOR THE QUARTER TO 30 SEPTEMBER 19X3

| | £ | £ | £ |
|---|---|---|---|
| Sales | | | 718,300 |
| Materials | | 397,220 | |
| Labour | | 88,351 | |
| Variable production overheads | 35,924 | | |
| Fixed production overheads | 75,740 | | |
| | | 111,664 | |
| Production cost | | | 597,235 |
| Distribution and marketing | | | 18,937 |
| Advertising campaign | | | 20,000 |
| Administration | | | 44,404 |
| Total cost | | | 680,576 |
| Net profit | | | 37,724 |

*Workings*

| | |
|---|---|
| Sales | 653,000 × 110/100 = 718,300 |
| Materials | 361,109 × 110/100 = 397,220 |
| Labour | 80,319 × 110/100 = 88,351 |
| Variable production overheads | 32,658 × 110/100 = 35,924 |

(b)

REPORT

To: Managing Director, NTL plc
From: A Technician
Date: XX December 19X3
Subject: Proposed advertising campaign

1 I mentioned in my earlier report that marketing expenditure might be too low. The proposal of an advertising campaign is therefore a positive development.

2 It is believed that the campaign will increase sales by 10%. The attached re-worked trading and profit and loss account for the quarter shows the expected effect of the campaign if it had been in operation for the quarter to 30 September 19X3.

3 The reworked accounts show that the net profit would probably fall as a result of the campaign.

4 The campaign should be reconsidered as it is clearly not justified in its present proposed form. Any alternative proposals being considered should be adopted only if it is believed that profits will increase.

5 Particularly in light of the financial state of the company, it is important to ensure that steps are taken to make funds available for a campaign before it is begun.

## 4 BTC

*Task 1*

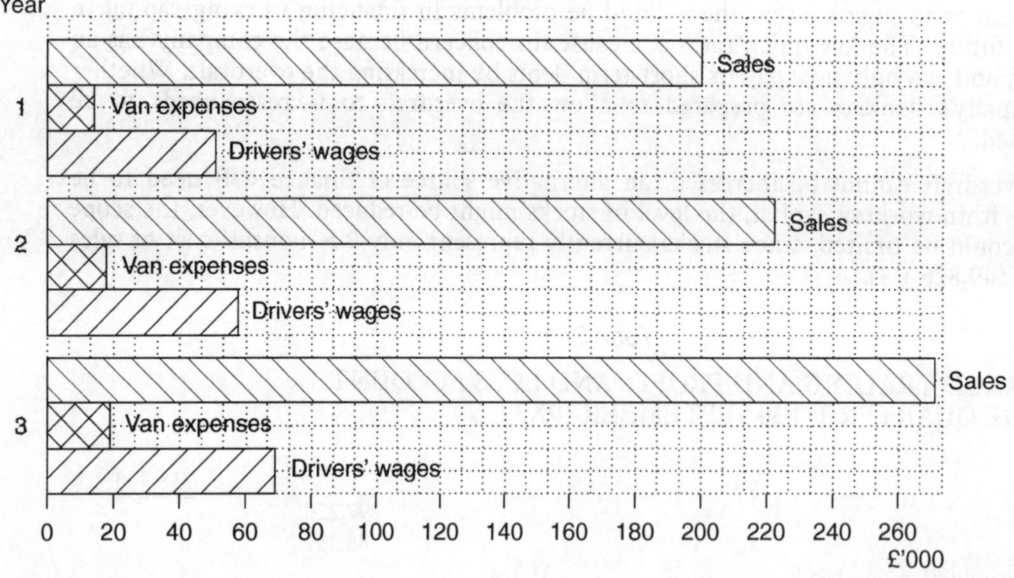


*Task 2*

| **Appendix 2** | | | |
|---|---|---|---|
| *Years* | *1* | *2* | *3* |
| Sales £s | 200,000 | 202,000 | 199,000 |
| Van expenses £s | 14,000 | 14,423 | 16,981 |
| As % of sales | 7 | 7.1 | 8.5 |
| Drivers' wages £s | 52,000 | 56,600 | 68,150 |
| As % of sales | 26.0 | 28.0 | 34.2 |
| Number of vans | 3 | 3 | 4 |
| Sales per van £s | 66,667 | 67,333 | 49,750 |
| Number of deliveries | 1,000 | 1,100 | 2,000 |
| Sales per delivery £s | 200 | 184 | 100 |

*Workings*

*Sales*

Year 2: 222,200 × 100/110 = 202,000
Year 3: 272,630 × 100/137 = 199,000

*Van expenses*

Year 2: 15,000 × 100/104 = 14,423
Year 3: 18,000 × 100/106 = 16,981

*Task 3*

REPORT

To: The General Manager, RD
From: Assistant Accountant
Date: XX June 19X4
Subject: Performance of the transport operation

*Section 1: Appendix 1 ratios*

1.1 The ratio of van expenses as a percentage of sales has fallen over the period of years 1 to 3. However, this ratio, like the others in Appendix 1, is calculated using figures in money terms, unadjusted for inflation. The ratio masks the fact that van expenses rose by 28% between years 1 and 3.

1.2 Similarly, the ratio of drivers' wages as a percentage of sales also shows a decline over the period. However, drivers' wages rose by 31% between year 1 and year 3. As with van expenses, the ratio may seem to show a positive trend because the rise in the money value of sales is greater (36% increase between year 1 and year 3).

1.3 Three vans were generated in year 1 and year 2, with a fourth being added in year 4. The money value of sales per van is slightly higher in year 3 compared with year 1. However, that is not to say that the *volume* of goods delivered by each van has risen, as no account is taken of the effect of increased selling prices for the goods delivered.

1.4 The number of deliveries has broadly followed the number of vans operated, with approximately 350 deliveries being made by each van. To assess whether delivery performance is satisfactory, we would need to have information on the volume of goods carried in each delivery as well as the number of deliveries.

*Section 2: Appendix 2 ratios*

2.1 The sales and van expenses figures used in calculating the ratios in Appendix 2 have been adjusted using index numbers reflecting specific price rises. Drivers' wage rates have not increased significantly over the period and so have not been adjusted.

2.2 Both van expenses and drivers' wages have risen as a percentage of sales in real terms. This means that it is costing more to deliver a given volume of sales and so indicates declining efficiency in the transport operation. Van and drivers' costs have both risen in real terms over a period in which sales volumes have not changed significantly, staying around £200,000 as expressed in year 1 prices.

2.3 The real value of sales per van was similar in years 1 and 2, but then dropped by 26% when the fourth van was added in year 3. This raises the question of whether the fourth van is necessary.

2.4 As already noted, the number of deliveries has certainly risen over the period, but the sales per delivery, measured in real terms, has fallen to only half its year 1 level by year 3. There are many more deliveries, but on average much less is being delivered each time. This may be because of, for example, a drop in the quantities included in each order, or an increase in the number of part-orders being delivered. To improve efficiency, the reasons should be investigated, with a view to increasing the average sales value for each delivery made.

*Section 3: Overall appraisal*

3.1 The rising real costs of delivery and drivers' wages as a percentage of sales and the declining real value of goods delivered per van and per delivery indicate declining efficiency in the transport operation. This can be seen from the Appendix 2 ratios. As is clear from Section 1 of this report, the Appendix 1 ratios appear to give a favourable impression of the performance of the transport operation.

3.2 The Appendix 2 ratios should be used as the basis of future reports because they are based on figures which have been adjusted for price inflation over the period. This means that they reflect the real volume of sales per van and per delivery, and the real level of costs relative to sales. The 'money terms' ratios of Appendix 1, on the other hand, are distorted by price changes in the variables used to calculate them.

3.3 In order to monitor performance effectively in future, the key ratios should be calculated on a more regular basis, for example quarterly, so that corrective action can be taken more quickly and the effect of improvements made can be monitored sooner.

3.4 An additional 'key ratio' which should be calculated is that of the number of deliveries per van. The fourth van added in Year 3 is probably unnecessary; improved route planning for deliveries may enable each van to achieve more deliveries in a given time period.

## 5 WMSC

*Tutorial note.* In Task 1, percentages need to be rounded to the nearest whole number, as specified in the question.

In Task 2, alternative non-financial factors you might mention include safety, market growth, strength of competition and innovation in ship design.

For part (b)(ii) of Task 3, alternative plausible explanations would also be acceptable.

### *Task 1*

TT hire charges as % of total hire charge $\frac{1,322}{8,263} \times 100\% = 16\%$

Total gross profit as % of hire charges $\frac{3,905}{8,263} \times 100\% = 47\%$

Total net profit as % of hire charges $\frac{1,185}{8,263} \times 100\% = 14\%$

Total net profit/capital employed $\frac{1,185}{3,385} \times 100\% = 35\%$

Total utilisation $\frac{8,263}{10,200} \times 100\% = 81\%$

### *Task 2*

REPORT

To: General Manager
From Assistant Accountant
Date: 6 December 19X4
Subject: Annual operating statement

*Company performance*

1 The company achieved a higher ROCE (35%) than the industry average of 24%. This reflects the higher gross profit to hire charges percentage and the fairly high utilisation of capacity which was achieved.

2 At 14%, the net profit as a percentage of hire charges is lower than the 15% industry average. This suggests that general expenses should be examined further.

*Ships*

3 BB accounts for more than half of total hire charges and is therefore very important for the company. ROCE for BB is good at 37%. General expenses as a percentage of hire charges are the lowest of all the ships at 31%, and the level of utilisation is fairly high at 90%.

4 The level of general expenses is high for SS, which provides 29% of the total hire charges. The gross profit percentage is good. However, the level of utilisation is low at 61% and an increase in revenue volume is required.

5 The revenue of TT, which provides just 16% of total hire charges, has exceeded expectations by 10%. The gross profit and net profit percentages are the highest, and the ROCE achieved is 60%.

*Proposed investment*

6 Given the relatively low utilisation of SS, the proposal to buy a second SS is questionable. The ROCE of SS is the lowest of the three ships. The proposed investment is thus not supported by the operating statements. The company should consider whether other investments would be more worthwhile.

7 The availability of suitably skilled labour should be considered before a decision is made on what investment to make.

*Working*

*General expenses as % of hire charges*

| | |
|---|---|
| BB | (1,378 ÷ 4,512) × 100% = 31% |
| SS | (903 ÷ 2,429) × 100% = 37% |
| TT | (439 ÷ 1,322) × 100% = 33% |
| Total | (2,720 ÷ 8,263) × 100% = 33% |

*Task 3*

| | *Letter* | *Nov 'X4* | *Nov 'X3* |
|---|---|---|---|
| | | % | % |
| Wages and salaries | A | 30 | 25 |
| Building occupation costs | B | 20 | 25 |
| Agents' commission | E | 25 | 20 |
| General administration expenses | D | 10 | 15 |
| Depreciation | C | 15 | 15 |
| | | 100 | 100 |

REPORT

To: Administration Manager
From: Assistant Accountant
Date: 6 December 19X4
Subject: November 19X4/19X3 pie charts

1 The pie charts enable us to compare the relative sizes, rather than the absolute amounts, of the different categories of expenses.

2 Categories A and B make up 50% of total expenses in both years. However, the proportion of each has changed between the two years, with A increasing and B reducing.

3 The level of depreciation expense C has remained the same proportion in each year.

4 The proportion of agents' commission (category E) has increased from 20% to 25%, while the proportion of D has reduced, from 15% to 10%.

5 Agents' commission (E) may have increased as a result of an increased volume of sales. General administration expenses (D) may have reduced because of more work which was previously contracted out to external bureaux (eg computing) being carried out in-house. This could also explain the increase in wages and salaries.

# *Unit 7*
# *Trial run central assessments*

# UNIT 7 TRIAL RUN CENTRAL ASSESSMENT 1

## INTERMEDIATE STAGE - NVQ/SVQ3

## PREPARING REPORTS AND RETURNS (R & R)

## June 1995

The Central Assessment is in two sections.

You should complete all tasks.

Time allowed - 2 hours.

You are advised to spend approximately 1 hour on each section.

The purpose of this Trial Run Central Assessment is to give you an idea of what a Central Assessment looks like. It is not intended as a guide to the topics which are likely to be assessed. The time allocations indicated above will give you an idea of how long you should spend on each task, but you should not expect to be under time pressure.

**DO NOT OPEN THIS PAPER UNTIL YOU ARE READY TO START UNDER TIMED CONDITIONS**

## SECTION 1

### Data

The National Stores Group consists of four national chains of stores:

(a) *Brighter Homes* are large department stores selling clothes, furniture and other household products.

(b) *Happy Life* sell high quality furniture and other decorative items.

(c) *Kidsfair* sells children's and babies' clothes and other baby equipment.

(d) *Roberts* stores sell smart, but affordable, clothes for women.

Results for the group for the financial years 19X3 and 19X4 were as follows.

| | *Brighter Homes* | *Happy Life* | *Kidsfair* | *Roberts* |
|---|---|---|---|---|
| *19X3* | | | | |
| Number of stores | 143 | 38 | 282 | 241 |
| Total selling area ('000 $m^2$) | 390 | 172 | 118 | 49 |
| Turnover (excluding VAT) (£m) | 623.4 | 207.4 | 237.9 | 94.3 |
| Net profit (£m) | 22.4 | (12.7) | 7.4 | 1.6 |
| *19X4* | | | | |
| Number of stores | 135 | 37 | 283 | 241 |
| Total selling area ('000 $m^2$) | 385 | 164 | 119 | 50 |
| Turnover (excluding VAT) (£m) | 638.4 | 198.7 | 235.2 | 98.4 |
| Net profit (£m) | 26.4 | (9.2) | (3.7) | 0.8 |

*Note.* There was a negligible rise in the UK RPI between 19X3 and 19X4.

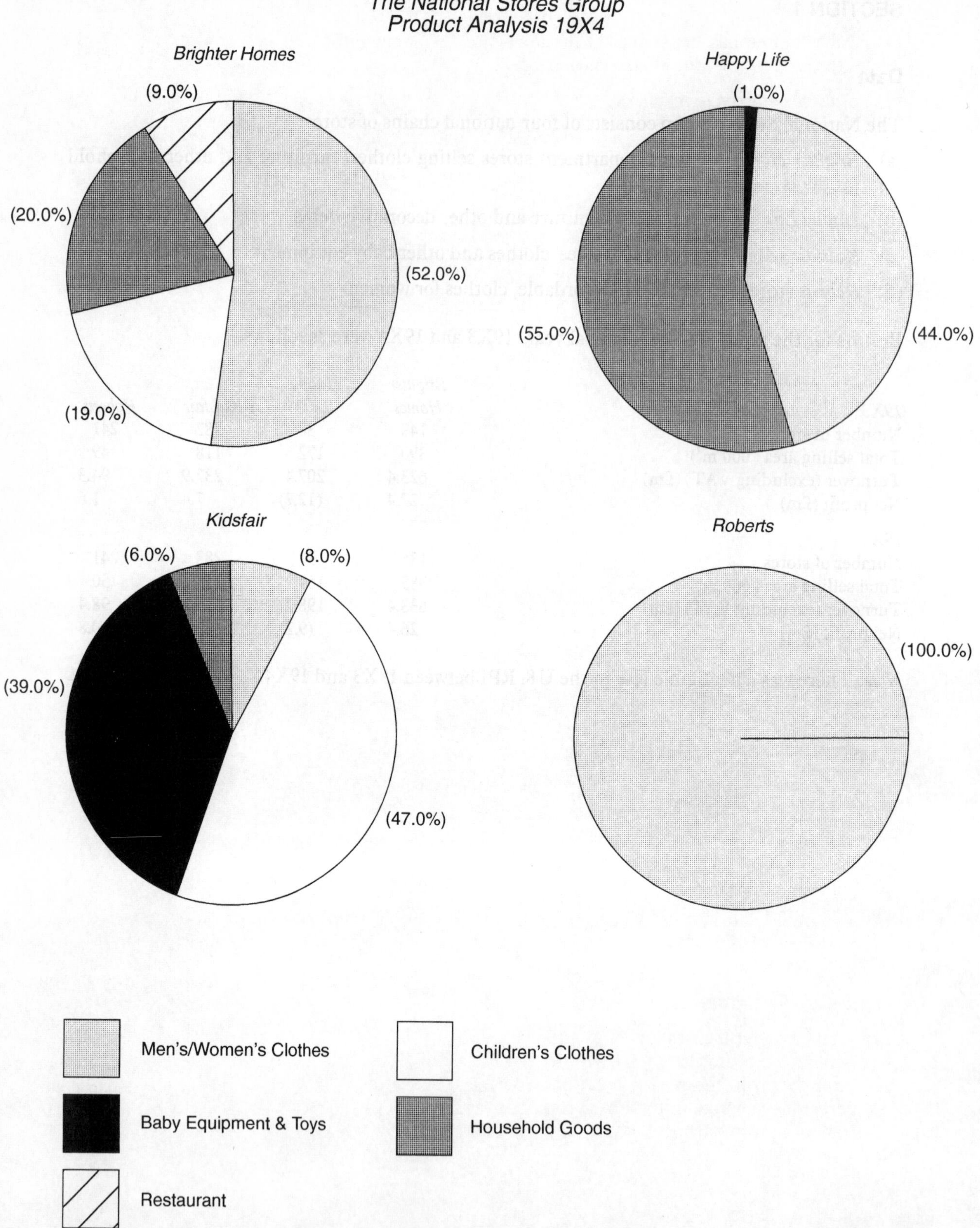
The National Stores Group
Product Analysis 19X4
Brighter Homes
(9.0%)
(20.0%)
(52.0%)
(19.0%)
Happy Life
(1.0%)
(55.0%)
(44.0%)
Kidsfair
(6.0%)
(8.0%)
(39.0%)
(47.0%)
Roberts
(100.0%)
Men's/Women's Clothes
Children's Clothes
Baby Equipment & Toys
Household Goods
Restaurant

**Task 1**

The table below has been devised to show the following information relating to 19X3 and 19X4 for each of the four chains in the group.

(i) Average store size in '000 $m^2$.
(ii) Average turnover per store.
(iii) Turnover per $m^2$.
(iv) Net profit/turnover ratio.
(v) Net profit per $m^2$.

This table has been completed below for 19X3 and for Brighter Homes, Happy Life and Roberts for 19X4.

*Required*

Complete the 19X4 table for Kidsfair.

*National Stores Group*
*Profitability analysis 19X3*

| | *Brighter Homes* | *Happy Life* | *Kidsfair* | *Roberts* |
|---|---|---|---|---|
| Average size of store ('000 $m^2$) | 2.73 | 4.53 | 0.42 | 0.20 |
| Turnover per store (£m) | 4.36 | 5.46 | 0.84 | 0.39 |
| Turnover per $m^2$ | £1,598.4 | £1,205.8 | £2,016.1 | £1,924.4 |
| Net profit/turnover | 3.59% | (6.12%) | 3.11% | 1.70% |
| Net profit per $m^2$ | £57.44 | (£73.84) | £62.71 | £32.65 |

*National Stores Group*
*Profitability analysis 19X4*

| | *Brighter Homes* | *Happy Life* | *Kidsfair* | *Roberts* |
|---|---|---|---|---|
| Average size of store ('000 $m^2$) | 2.85 | 4.43 | | 0.21 |
| Turnover per store (£m) | 4.73 | 5.37 | | 0.41 |
| Turnover per $m^2$ | £1,658.1 | £1,211.5 | | £1,968 |
| Net profit/turnover | 4.14% | (4.63%) | | 0.81% |
| Net profit per $m^2$ | £68.57 | (£56.10) | | £16.00 |

**Task 2**

Calculate for the group as a whole:

(a) total turnover figures for 19X3 and 19X4
(b) percentage change in total turnover from 19X3 to 19X4
(c) total net profit figures for 19X3 and 19X4
(d) percentage change in total net profit from 19X3 to 19X4
(e) total net profit/turnover ratios for 19X3 and 19X4

Present your answer, in the form of a table, below.

**Task 3**

The management accountant of the group is concerned about the fall in profitability from 19X3 to 19X4. As a project, which she thinks will be helpful to your AAT studies, she has asked you to carry out some analysis of the data and prepare a detailed report for her.

*Required*

Write a detailed report explaining the fall in profitability between 19X3 and 19X4 and identifying possible causes of that fall in profitability.

The report should communicate differences between the chains in the group and should make reference to the analysis of the different product categories sold by the chains as shown in the Product Analysis for 19X4 above. This analysis was little changed from 19X3.

Suggestions for improvements in profitability should also be included.

## SECTION 2

### Data

Your company is planning to make a small investment in a company which manufactures soft drinks. You have been asked to help analyse the most recent set of accounts for the soft drinks company.

### Task 1

In the most recent set of published accounts for International Cola Limited, the managing director stated that he was proud of the fact that both sales and trading profit had been rising considerably for each of the last four years and that consequently the company was becoming ever more profitable.

*International Cola Limited*
*Four year performance data*

| | *19X1* | *19X2* | *19X3* | *19X4* |
|---|---|---|---|---|
| | £'000 | £'000 | £'000 | £'000 |
| Sales | 51,980 | 58,524 | 68,137 | 72,904 |
| Trading profit | 5,393 | 6,865 | 8,030 | 8,189 |
| Trading profit/sales | 10.4% | 11.7% | 11.8% | 11.2% |
| *Additional data and calculations* | | | | |
| UK Retail Prices Index (19W7 = 100) | 130.2 | 135.6 | 137.7 | 143.2 |
| Sales (at 19X4 prices) | | | | |
| Trading profit (at 19X4 prices) | | | | |

*Required*

(a) Complete the table above, converting both the sales and trading profit figures to 19X4 prices.

(b) Use graph paper to show sales and trading profit at both original and adjusted prices for the period 19X1 - 19X4.

(c) Write a brief memorandum to your chief accountant, using the format set out below. In this memorandum you should express your opinion of the managing director's statement, clearly explaining the reasons for your opinion.

**MEMORANDUM**

| | |
|---|---|
| To: | Chief Accountant |
| From: | Accounting Technician |
| Date: | 20 June 19X5 |
| Subject: | Profitability of International Cola Ltd |

## Task 2

The following data is taken from the 19X4 set of published accounts of International Cola Limited.

| | £'000 |
|---|---|
| Sales | 72,904 |
| Gross profit | 33,800 |
| Selling and distribution overheads | 18,115 |
| Administration overheads | 7,496 |
| Trading profit | 8,189 |

*Note.* Gross profit has been calculated after deducting raw materials, production labour and production overheads.

Industrial averages have been obtained by the management accountant showing key profitability and expense ratios.

| | *Industrial average* | *International Cola Limited* |
|---|---|---|
| Gross profit/Sales | 49.6% | |
| Selling and distribution overheads/Sales | 25.4% | |
| Administration overheads/Sales | 8.6% | |
| Trading profit/Sales | 15.6% | 11.2% |

There is concern that International Cola Limited's net profit/sales ratio is less than that for the industry.

In order to address this concern, you have been asked to:

(a) complete the table above to calculate the gross profit/sales ratio and expense ratios for International Cola Limited;

(b) write a short report for the chief accountant which explains why the net profit/sales ratio is less than that for the industry and the steps which International Cola Limited might take to improve its profitability.

# UNIT 7 TRIAL RUN CENTRAL ASSESSMENT 2

## INTERMEDIATE STAGE - NVQ/SVQ3

## PREPARING REPORTS AND RETURNS (R & R)

## December 1995

The Central Assessment is in two sections.

You should complete all tasks.

Time allowed - 2 hours.

The purpose of this Trial Run Central Assessment is to give you an idea of what a Central Assessment looks like. It is not intended as a guide to the topics which are likely to be assessed. Time allocations are shown at beginning of each section, but you should not expect to be under time pressure.

**DO NOT OPEN THIS PAPER UNTIL YOU ARE READY TO START UNDER TIMED CONDITIONS**

## SECTION 1

**You are advised to spend approximately 45 minutes on this section.**

### Data

The Snowy Ski Company manufacture skis and related equipment. Charles O'Hagan is manager of the main factory based in South Wales. There is a second factory in Yorkshire, England. The production department is made up of the following sections.

1 Moulding
2 Assembly
3 Finishing

Mr O'Hagan has become concerned about the performance of his workforce compared with the factory in Yorkshire. He has collected performance data from the two factories and produced a spreadsheet model to analyse the data. The results of this analysis are given below.

You are an accounting technician, assisting Mr O'Hagan in the South Wales factory.

THE SNOWY SKI COMPANY PERFORMANCE ANALYSIS

| *Ski units completed* | *Week 1* | *Week 2* | *Week 3* | *Week 4* |
|---|---|---|---|---|
| South Wales | 1,200 | 1,350 | 1,400 | 1,300 |
| Yorkshire | 1,000 | 1,050 | 1,150 | 1,100 |
| *Budgeted labour hours per ski unit* | | | | |
| (the same for each factory) | | | | |
| Moulding | 3.4 | | | |
| Assembly | 4.3 | | | |
| Finishing | 6.4 | | | |
| *Actual hours worked* | *Week 1* | *Week 2* | *Week 3* | *Week 4* |
| *South Wales:* | | | | |
| Moulding | 4,200 | 4,320 | 4,760 | 4,940 |
| Assembly | 4,950 | 5,795 | 5,995 | 5,724 |
| Finishing | 7,432 | 8,745 | 9,315 | 8,562 |
| *Yorkshire:* | | | | |
| Moulding | 3,600 | 3,570 | 4,025 | 3,810 |
| Assembly | 4,213 | 4,530 | 5,120 | 4,875 |
| Finishing | 6,457 | 7,021 | 7,765 | 6,912 |
| *Standard hours produced* | | | | |
| (Ski units completed × budgeted hours per ski unit) | | | | |
| *South Wales:* | | | | |
| Moulding | 4,080 | 4,590 | 4,760 | 4,420 |
| Assembly | 5,160 | 5,805 | 6,020 | 5,590 |
| Finishing | 7,680 | 8,640 | 8,960 | 8,320 |
| *Yorkshire:* | | | | |
| Moulding | 3,400 | 3,570 | 3,910 | 3,740 |
| Assembly | 4,300 | 4,515 | 4,945 | 4,730 |
| Finishing | 6,400 | 6,720 | 7,360 | 7,040 |
| *Variance (hours worked)* | | | | |
| *South Wales:* | | | | |
| Moulding | (120) | 270 | 0 | (520) |
| Assembly | 210 | 10 | 25 | (134) |
| Finishing | 248 | (105) | (355) | (242) |
| *Total* | 338 | 175 | (330) | (896) |
| *Yorkshire:* | | | | |
| Moulding | (200) | 0 | (115) | (70) |
| Assembly | 87 | (15) | (175) | (145) |
| Finishing | (57) | (301) | (405) | 128 |
| *Total* | (170) | (316) | (695) | (87) |

## Task 1

Calculate the total actual hours worked in each factory and the actual hours per ski unit produced (to one decimal place). Present your results in the table below.

| | Week 1 | Week 2 | Week 3 | Week 4 |
|---|---|---|---|---|
| *Total actual hours:* | | | | |
| South Wales | 16582 | 18860 | 20070 | 19226 |
| Yorkshire | 14270 | 15121 | 16910 | 15597 |
| *Ski units completed:* | | | | |
| South Wales | 1,200 | 1,350 | 1,400 | 1,300 |
| Yorkshire | 1,000 | 1,050 | 1,150 | 1,100 |
| *Hours per unit:* | | | | |
| South Wales | 13·82 | 13·97 | 14·34 | 14·79 |
| Yorkshire | 14·27 | 14·40 | 14·70 | 14·18 |

## Task 2

Write a report for Mr O'Hagan which compares the efficiency of the two factories and highlights any problem areas. The report should also consider the limitations of the analysis carried out and possible reasons for the differences in performance.

Introduction

I have analysed the performance results of S Wales compared to Yorkshire over weeks 1 to 4.

Findings

In weeks 1 to 3, performance in S Wales is approx 3% better than Yorkshire. However in week 4, Yorkshire is 4% better than S Wales. Yorkshire produces stable results over the 4-week period, which are close to the budgeted standard hours of 14·1. S-Wales' performance is, in fact, deteriorating with week 4 taking 1 hour per unit longer than week 1.

Analysis of variances shows that S Wales is moving from a positive overall favourable variance in week 1 to a large adverse variance in all depts in week 4.

In contrast, Yorkshire is moving towards a more favourable total variance

## SECTION 2

**You are advised to spend approximately 1 hour 15 minutes on this section**

### Data

You are an accounting technician employed by an area health authority. As part of your current job you are assessing the performance of different hospitals.

The information below concerns two hospitals in the area, Eastbridge General Hospital and Westhampton Hospital.

Eastbridge General has large surgical and medical wards. Surgical wards are concerned with operating on patients whereas medical wards care for patients who do not require surgery.

Westhampton Hospital carries out some surgical and medical work, but also has a number of wards for the needs of the elderly and those recovering from serious operations. Such patients need some medication and general care. Some Eastbridge patients are sent to Westhampton to recover once the treatment or operation has been completed.

Both hospitals deal with both in-patients and out-patients. Out-patients attend either the out-patients' department or the day case unit for treatment and recovery taking less than one day. Any patient admitted for more than one day becomes an in-patient.

*Information for the year ended 31 March 19X5*

| | *Eastbridge* | | *Westhampton* | |
|---|---|---|---|---|
| | *In-patients* | *Out-patients* | *In-patients* | *Out-patients* |
| *Cost of services* | £ | £ | £ | £ |
| Direct patient care (eg nurses) | 12,643,200 | 1,824,600 | 7,426,800 | 321,200 |
| *Medical support services* | | | | |
| X-ray | 728,600 | 518,700 | 78,600 | 88,400 |
| Pathology (diseases) | 1,246,200 | 794,200 | 363,400 | 148,500 |
| Pharmacy (medicines) | 2,321,700 | 823,100 | 2,034,100 | 45,200 |
| *Non-medical support services* | | | | |
| Laundry | 216,700 | 18,900 | 172,000 | 9,600 |
| Catering | 364,000 | 8,600 | 296,000 | 2,740 |
| Administration | 3,147,500 | 846,700 | 2,863,100 | 616,200 |

| *Other data* | *Eastbridge* | *Westhampton* |
|---|---|---|
| Number of in-patients | 15,800 | 850 |
| Average stay per in-patient | 8 days | 132 days |
| Number of available beds | 620 | 370 |
| Average number of beds occupied | 462 | 345 |
| Number of out-patient attendances | 162,800 | 12,450 |

**Task 1**

Complete the following return, summarising the financial and non-financial data for the year ending 31 March 19X5 for Westhampton Hospital. The figures for Eastbridge General Hospital have already been completed.

| *Performance return* | | | |
|---|---|---|---|
| | *Eastbridge* | *Westhampton* | *Significance* |
| Number of in-patient days | 126,400 | 112,200 | |
| Bed occupancy rate | 74.5% | 93.2% | |
| *In-patient cost analysis*<br>*Cost per in-patient day:* | | | |
| | £ | £ | |
| Direct patient care | 100.0 | 66.2 | * |
| X-ray | 5.8 | 0.7 | * |
| Pathology | 9.9 | 3.2 | * |
| Pharmacy | 18.4 | 18.1 | |
| Laundry | 1.7 | 1.5 | * |
| Catering | 2.9 | 2.6 | * |
| Administration | 24.9 | 25.5 | |
| *Outpatient cost analysis*<br>*Cost per out-patient attendance:* | | | |
| | £ | £ | |
| Direct patient care | 11.2 | 25.8 | * |
| X-ray | 3.2 | 7.1 | * |
| Pathology | 4.9 | 11.9 | * |
| Pharmacy | 5.1 | 3.6 | * |
| Laundry | 0.1 | 0.8 | * |
| Catering | 0.1 | 0.2 | * |
| Administration | 5.2 | 49.5 | * |
| In the significance column, enter * where the difference is greater than 10% of the lower figure. | | | |

**Task 2**

Write a report for the chief accountant which explains the difference in efficiency of the two hospitals.

The report should concentrate on explanations for the significant differences in performance between the two hospitals, referring to the different nature of the two hospitals.

**Task 3**

Some concern has been expressed about the growth in administration costs. For the last five years these have been as follows.

| | 19X1 | 19X2 | 19X3 | 19X4 | 19X5 |
|---|---|---|---|---|---|
| Eastbridge (£) | 2,614,900 | 2,862,400 | 3,263,200 | 3,648,000 | 3,994,200 |
| Westhampton (£) | 1,612,300 | 1,982,900 | 2,416,600 | 2,862,700 | 3,479,300 |
| UK Retail Price Index (19W7 = 100) | 130.2 | 135.6 | 137.7 | 143.2 | 146.7 |
| *Administration costs at 19X5 prices:* | | | | | |
| Eastbridge (£) | 2,946,281 | 3,096,711 | 3,476,481 | 3,737,162 | 3,994,200 |
| Westhampton (£) | ………… | ………… | ………… | ………… | ………… |

*Required*

(a) Complete the table above, converting the administration costs to 19X5 prices for Westhampton Hospital.

(b) Use graph paper to show the administration costs for both hospitals at both original and adjusted prices for the period 19X1-19X5.

(c) Write a few *brief* notes to the chief accountant, to explain the findings from your graph. You should mention any assumptions you have made in your analysis.

# UNIT 7 TRIAL RUN CENTRAL ASSESSMENT 3

## INTERMEDIATE STAGE - NVQ/SVQ3

## PREPARING REPORTS AND RETURNS (R & R)

## June 1996

The Central Assessment is in two sections. You must complete EVERY task in EACH section.

Time allowed - 2 hours.

The purpose of this Trial Run Central Assessment is to give you an idea of what a Central Assessment looks like. It is not intended as a guide to the topics which are likely to be assessed. Time allocations are shown at beginning of each section, but you should not expect to be under time pressure.

**DO NOT OPEN THIS PAPER UNTIL YOU ARE READY TO START UNDER TIMED CONDITIONS**

## SECTION 1

**You are advised to spend approximately 45 minutes on this section.**

### Data

Business Computers Ltd is a computer company specialising in the manufacture of hardware, software and the provision of related consultancy services. The company is split into three divisions:

Hardware - commercial
Hardware - government
Software services and consultancy services

The company has traditionally traded in the hardware market, selling computers to business and government organisations. However, in recent years an increasing amount of business is being done in software services for the company's own products and related consultancy provision.

The company is now reviewing its products, services and markets. The commercial hardware market is likely to become more competitive with development costs rising. The government hardware market will be restricted by government spending limits over the next three years. However, the long-term projection is that more government departments and organisations will adopt more commercial practices and demand products the company produces. The software services and consultancy division work originated from government contracts, and most of the company's work comes from this source.

You work in the finance department of the company as an Accounting Technician and you have been given a number of tasks by the Financial Accountant in order to provide information for the review.

Results for the 19X4/19X5 financial years were as follows.

| *Year* | | *Hardware - commercial* | *Hardware - government* | *Software and consultancy* |
|---|---|---|---|---|
| | | £ | £ | £ |
| 19X5 | Sales | 15,957,000 | 24,768,000 | 11,368,000 |
| 19X5 | Development costs | 6,376,000 | 7,832,000 | 2,134,000 |
| 19X5 | Other costs | 7,215,000 | 8,150,000 | 3,716,000 |
| 19X5 | Number of employees | 831 | 607 | 423 |
| 19X4 | Sales | 17,643,000 | 25,974,000 | 9,276,000 |

*Note.* It is company policy to write off development costs in the year of expenditure because of the pace of technological change within the industry.

### Task 1

Complete the following table of ratios for 19X5. The ratios for 19X4 are given.

**Business Computers Ltd**
**Table of ratios**

| *Division* | *Ratio* | 19X4 | 19X5 |
|---|---|---|---|
| Hardware - commercial | Net profit/sales | 17.5% | |
| | Development costs/sales | 34.7% | |
| | Sales per employee | £22,107 | |
| Hardware - government | Net profit/sales | 36.6% | |
| | Development costs/sales | 30.9% | |
| | Sales per employee | £41,200 | |
| Software and consultancy | Net profit/sales | 39.4% | |
| | Development costs/sales | 21.7% | |
| | Sales per employee | £23,614 | |

**Task 2**

Write a DETAILED report to the Financial Accountant using the report form below comparing divisional performance between 19X4 and 19X5 and giving recommendations for the company's future direction.

**BUSINESS COMPUTERS LTD**

**REPORT ON DIVISIONAL PERFORMANCE**

To: The Financial Accountant

From: A N Insley

Date: 21.5.95

INTRODUCTION

I have completed the required ratios relating to performance in 1995 for the purpose of comparison with 1994.

FINDINGS

The net profit/sales ratio shows a decline in the Commercial Hardware and Government hardware since 1994. However, the Software Services division shows a marked increase in net profit/sales. This is compatible with a slight increase in the development costs/sales ratios in both the Hardware divisions, whilst the Software Services shows a decrease in this ratio. The Software Services division is the most profitable in terms of sales per employee, which has substantially increased over the last year

It is noticeable that both development costs and other costs are considerably lower in the Software division which must contribute to its profitability, in spite of the fact that sales are also lower. It is the only division where sales are increasing.

RECOMMENDATIONS

The indications are that the Hardware market will continue to decline, particularly in the commercial division. Consideration will have to be given to whether it is a viable long-term prospect. It may be advisable to close down this division and to concentrate resources in the Software Services division. The Hardware - Govt division provides a base for further expansion of associated services, but costs should be reduced wherever possible.

To improve above, incorporate more statistics

## SECTION 2

**You are advised to spend approximately 1 hour 15 minutes on this section.**

### Data

You work as an Accounting Technician for a railway company, East Inland Railway, that is owned by the government but is about to be privatised by being offered for sale to private investors.

East Inland Railway runs three lines:

- one is a busy commuter line linking the main urban areas within the district
- the second is a coastal line linking the main coastal resorts, which is busy during the holiday season
- the third line links the rural areas within the district served

The company receives a subsidy from the government as well as passenger revenue from ticket sales. The government has now requested a certain amount of information from East Inland Railway and it has sent a number of pre-prepared returns to be completed.

The financial data for 19X5 for your company has been released to you.

| | *Commuter line* | *Coastal line* | *Rural line* | *Total* |
|---|---|---|---|---|
| Government subsidy | £213,000 | £753,000 | £1,337,000 | £2,303,000 |
| Passenger revenue | £12,256,000 | £7,367,000 | £2,217,000 | £21,840,000 |
| Total costs | £10,313,000 | £6,175,000 | £3,437,000 | £19,925,000 |
| Number of passengers | 9,380,000 | 7,130,000 | 6,750,000 | 23,260,000 |
| Number of train services | 6,033 | 9,017 | 12,213 | 27,263 |
| Average capacity (seats per train) | 1,600 | 1,400 | 1,500 | |

### Task 1

Complete the following government-requested report for East Inland Railway. You are given the ratios for the commuter line and the coastal line.

| EAST INLAND RAILWAY | | | | |
|---|---|---|---|---|
| | *Commuter line* | *Coastal line* | *Rural line* | *Total* |
| Number of passengers | 9,380,000 | 7,130,000 | 6,750,000 | 23,260,000 |
| Revenue per passenger | £1.31 | £1.03 | £0.33 | £0.94 |
| Government subsidy per passenger | £0.02 | £0.11 | £0.19 | £0.10 |
| Costs per passenger | £1.10 | £0.87 | £0.51 | £0.86 |
| Passengers per train service | 1,555 | 791 | 553 | 853 |
| % of seats filled per train service | 97% | 56% | 37% | 63% |

### Task 2

Using the report form below prepare a report on 19X5 performance for the Chief Accountant of East Inland Railway analysing the results for each line as in Task 1 and the information above. Once the service has been privatised the subsidy from the government will be withdrawn. Your report should include the consequences of the loss of subsidy for East Inland Railway and consider the various options open to the company, which are:

(a) to do nothing;
(b) to keep the rural line open and increase profitability; or
(c) to close the rural line.

The contents of this report will form the basis of information provided to potential investors in the railway.

**EAST INLAND RAILWAY**
**REPORT ON 19X5 PERFORMANCE**

To: The Chief Accountant
From: AM Jurley
Date: 21-5-95

Statistics have been compiled, comparing results for the three lines operated by East Inland Railway, and results are as follows:

COMMUTER LINE

This is currently the most profitable line, with 97% of seats filled per train service. It runs the fewest services, but has the highest number of passengers. However, it also has the highest costs per passenger at £1.10.
The Govt subsidy on this line is only £0.02 per passenger, therefore the loss of subsidy would have little effect after privatisation.

**Task 3**

**Data**

It has been decided that potential investors in the railway would want further information about the commuter line and its revenue per passenger.

You are told that total passengers per service have remained constant over recent years on the commuter line.

*Required*

(a) Complete the following table.

| *East Inland Railway Commuter line* | | | |
|---|---|---|---|
| | *19X3* | *19X4* | *19X5* |
| Revenue per passenger | £0.91 | £1.09 | £1.31 |
| UK retail price index | 137.7 | 143.2 | 147.3 |
| Revenue per passenger at 19X5 prices | £ 0.97 | £ 1.12 | £ 1.31 |

(b) Present the original revenue per passenger and the adjusted revenue per passenger for the period 19X3 to 19X5 in the form of a clearly labelled compound bar chart on graph paper.

(c) Write a short memo to the Chief Accountant of East Inland Railway analysing your results in (b). Use the memorandum style below for your answer.

**MEMORANDUM**

To:

From:

Date:

Subject:

# UNIT 7 TRIAL RUN CENTRAL ASSESSMENT 4

## INTERMEDIATE STAGE - NVQ/SVQ3

## PREPARING REPORTS AND RETURNS (R & R)

**December 1996**

The Central Assessment is in two sections

You should complete all tasks.

Time allowed - 2 hours.

You are advised to spend approximately 1 hour on each section

The purpose of this Trial Run Central Assessment is to give you an idea of what a Central Assessment looks like. It is not intended as a guide to the topics which are likely to be assessed. The time allocations indicated above will give you an idea of how long you should spend on each task, but you should not expect to be under time pressure.

**DO NOT OPEN THIS PAPER UNTIL YOU ARE READY TO START UNDER TIMED CONDITIONS**

## SECTION 1

**You are advised to spend approximately 1 hour 30 minutes on this section**

### Data

You are an accounting technician working for a company that specialises in consultancy to the coal-mining industry. Your company has been approached by a small coal-mining company that has two mines: an underground deep mine[1] in the north of the country at Thorington, and a surface open-cast[2] mine in the south of the country at Seaforth. The output from the underground coal mine at Thorington is mainly for home consumption, whilst the output from the open-cast coal-mine at Seaforth is primarily for export. The home market for coal is under threat from competition from cheaper overseas coal and home-produced natural gas, whilst the overseas market is more traditional and there is a steady demand.

The coal-mining company wants to develop a third mine and is unsure whether it should be a deep or open-cast mine. The third mine would be in the locality of one of its two existing mines. The coal-mining company has carried out the prospecting and exploration stages near to the location of its current mines and is now ready to proceed to the development and exploitation stages at the chosen site. Work to date has shown that yields and costs for both potential mines would be similar to the yields and costs of the existing mines in the locality as shown below.

The following data relates to the performance of the Thorington underground mine and the Seaforth open-cast mine over the last three years.

*Note*

[1] Underground deep mine = Mining by excavating under the surface
[2] Open-cast mine = Mining by excavating from the surface

| | *1993* | *1994* | *1995* |
|---|---|---|---|
| *Tonnes of coal excavated (000s)* | | | |
| Thorington | 471.6 | 472.2 | 472.9 |
| Seaforth | 293.6 | 315.2 | 341.7 |
| *Number of employees* | | | |
| Thorington | 237 | 244 | 253 |
| Seaforth | 162 | 164 | 170 |
| *Excavation costs (£000s)* | | | |
| Thorington | 13,456 | 13,892 | 13,999 |
| Seaforth | 9,117 | 9,135 | 9,189 |
| *Net profit (£000s)* | | | |
| Thorington | 6,943 | 6,995 | 7,083 |
| Seaforth | 4,437 | 4,839 | 5,173 |

### Task 1.1

**You are given the following table of performance statistics. Complete the table for the Seaforth coal-mine.**

**PERFORMANCE STATISTICS**
**THORINGTON UNDERGROUND DEEP MINE 1993-95**

| | *1993* | *1994* | *1995* |
|---|---|---|---|
| Coal extracted per employee (tonnes) | 1,990 | 1,935 | 1,869 |
| Excavation costs per tonne of coal excavated (£) | 28.54 | 29.42 | 29.60 |
| Net profit per tonne of coal excavated (£) | 14.72 | 14.81 | 14.98 |
| Net profit per employee (£000s) | 29.30 | 28.67 | 28.00 |

**SEAFORTH OPEN CAST MINE**

| | *1993* | *1994* | *1995* |
|---|---|---|---|
| Coal extracted per employee (tonnes) | | | |
| Excavation costs per tonne of coal excavated (£) | | | |
| Net profit per tonne of coal excavated (£) | | | |
| Net profit per employee (£000s) | | | |

***Note.* Show figures to the same number of decimal places as for the Thorington mine.**

**Task 1.2**

**Prepare a well-presented report for your finance director comparing the performance of the Thorington and Seaforth mines. Your report should address the following issues using the performance statistics calculated, and the information given in this section.**

**(a) Profitability**
**(b) Efficiency**
**(c) Future outlook**

**You should advise your finance director which potential mine should be taken forward to the development and exploitation stages by the mining company on the basis of the data available for the two present mines.**

## SECTION 2

**You are advised to spend approximately 30 minutes on this section.**

### Data

The finance director has asked you to review the coal excavated per employee at the Thorington and Seaforth mines against the industry average for 1993-1995.

| | *Coal excavated per employee Industry Average (tonnes)* |
|---|---|
| 1993 | 1,890 |
| 1994 | 1,920 |
| 1995 | 1,940 |

### Task 2.1

(a) **Prepare a clearly labelled graph showing the performance of the Thorington and Seaforth mines against the industry average performance for the period 1993 to 1995.**

(b) **Prepare a memo for the finance director analysing the trends revealed by the graph you have prepared for the period 1993 to 1995.**

# UNIT 7 TRIAL RUN CENTRAL ASSESSMENT 5

## INTERMEDIATE STAGE - NVQ/SVQ3

## PREPARING REPORTS AND RETURNS (R & R)

**June 1997**

The Central Assessment is in two sections

You should complete all tasks.

Time allowed - 2 hours.

You are advised to spend approximately 1 hour on each section

The purpose of this Trial Run Central Assessment is to give you an idea of what a Central Assessment looks like. It is not intended as a guide to the topics which are likely to be assessed. The time allocations indicated above will give you an idea of how long you should spend on each task, but you should not expect to be under time pressure.

**DO NOT OPEN THIS PAPER UNTIL YOU ARE READY TO START UNDER TIMED CONDITIONS**

## SECTION 1

**You are advised to spend approximately 1 hour 20 minutes on this section**

### Data

You are an accounting technician working for City Hotels Limited, which owns three hotels in London.

(a) The Station Hotel is situated near a main railway station and its customers are mainly railway travellers, business people and weekend visitors.

(b) The Airport Hotel is situated near the airport and its customers are virtually all air travellers who stay at the hotel either before or after their flight.

(c) The Central Hotel is situated in the city centre and is used mainly by tourists, business people and weekend visitors.

City Hotels Limited wishes to compare the performances of the three hotels and has asked you to carry out a series of analyses to enable this to be done.

### Basic data

| | *Station Hotel* | *Airport Hotel* | *Central Hotel* |
|---|---|---|---|
| Number of rooms | 140 | 210 | 90 |
| Standard room tariff | £42.00 | £45.00 | £60.00 |

*Notes*

1 Each hotel only has double rooms. The standard room tariff is the price of a double room per night.

2 City Hotels Limited runs a variety of discount schemes and special offers whereby rooms can be obtained at cheaper rates.

### City Hotels Limited

### Performance statistics for the week ended 31 May 1997

| | *Sunday* | *Monday* | *Tuesday* | *Wednesday* | *Thursday* | *Friday* | *Saturday* |
|---|---|---|---|---|---|---|---|
| *Station Hotel:* | | | | | | | |
| Number of rooms let | 80 | 110 | 108 | 106 | 105 | 96 | 121 |
| Total room revenue | £2,856 | £4,316 | £4,312 | £4,324 | £4,221 | £3,614 | £3,460 |
| Room occupancy rate | 57% | 79% | 77% | 76% | 75% | 69% | 86% |
| Average rate per room let | £35.70 | £39.24 | £39.93 | £40.79 | £40.20 | £37.65 | £28.60 |
| *Airport Hotel:* | | | | | | | |
| Number of rooms let | 182 | 192 | 186 | 174 | 195 | 184 | 173 |
| Total room revenue | £8,074 | £8,460 | £8,241 | £7,542 | £8,418 | £7,840 | £7,518 |
| Room occupancy rate | 87% | 91% | 89% | 83% | 93% | 88% | 82% |
| Average rate per room let | £44.36 | £44.06 | £44.31 | £43.34 | £43.17 | £42.61 | £43.46 |
| *Central Hotel:* | | | | | | | |
| Number of rooms let | 64 | 68 | 69 | 46 | 52 | 65 | 82 |
| Total room revenue | £3,440 | £3,652 | £3,541 | £2,416 | £2,867 | £3,216 | £3,962 |
| Room occupancy rate | 71% | 76% | 77% | 51% | 58% | 72% | 91% |
| Average rate per room let | £53.75 | £53.71 | £51.32 | £52.52 | £55.13 | £49.48 | £48.32 |

*Note.* In London, Saturdays and Sundays are the weekend.

## Task 1.1

**Complete the Summary Performance Statistics below for City Hotels Limited.**

### City Hotels Limited

### Summary Performance Statistics for the week ended 31 May 1997

| | *Station Hotel* | *Airport Hotel* | *Central Hotel* |
|---|---|---|---|
| Total rooms let | | | |
| Average room occupancy rate | | | |
| Total room revenue | | | |
| Average rate per room let | | | |

*Note.* Average room occupancy rate is to be shown to the nearest whole percentage. The average rate per room let is to be shown to the nearest penny.

## Task 1.2

**Prepare a report for City Hotels Limited, comparing the performances of the three hotels for the week ending 31 May 1997.**

**Your report should address the following issues.**

(a) **Room occupancy rates.**
(b) **Rates per room let.**
(c) **Possible recommendations for the future, giving evidence for your reasoning.**
(d) **Any limitations in the data provided.**

## SECTION 2

**You are advised to spend approximately 40 minutes on this section.**

The hotel accountant has asked you to compare the performance of the three hotels in terms of the revenue from rooms let, over the last five years.

### Data

**City Hotels Limited**

**Revenue from rooms let 1992-1996**

| | *1992* | *1993* | *1994* | *1995* | *1996* |
|---|---|---|---|---|---|
| Station Hotel | £1,150,000 | £1,250,000 | £1,200,000 | £1,250,000 | £1,300,000 |
| Airport Hotel | £1,250,000 | £1,400,000 | £2,300,000 | £2,600,000 | £2,750,000 |
| Central Hotel | £850,000 | £900,000 | £850,000 | £950,000 | £1,100,000 |

### Task 2.1

**Prepare a clearly labelled line graph showing the performance of the three hotels for the period 1992-1996.**

*Note.* A bar chart will *not* be acceptable.

### Task 2.2

**Prepare a memo for the hotel accountant. The memo should:**

**(a) analyse the trends revealed by the graph prepared in Task 2.1;**
**(b) highlight any limitations in the trends revealed by your analysis.**

# *Solutions to Unit 7 trial run central assessments*

# SOLUTIONS TO UNIT 7 TRIAL RUN CENTRAL ASSESSMENT 1

**DO NOT TURN THIS PAGE UNTIL YOU HAVE COMPLETED TRIAL RUN CENTRAL ASSESSMENT 1**

## SECTION 1

*Tutorial note.* When writing the report, you should use all the information you are given where appropriate, including the product analysis. Where you think further data is needed, say so.

### Task 1

| | *Kidsfair* |
|---|---|
| Average size of store ('000 m$^2$) | 0.42 |
| Turnover per store (£m) | 0.83 |
| Turnover per m$^2$ | £1,976.5 |
| Net profit/turnover | (1.57%) |
| Net profit per m$^2$ | (£31.09) |

### Task 2

| | *19X3* | *19X4* | *Change 19X3-X4* |
|---|---|---|---|
| | £m | £m | £m |
| Total turnover | 1,163.0 | 1,170.7 | +0.66 |
| Total net profit | 18.7 | 14.3 | –23.53 |
| Total net profit/turnover | 1.61% | 1.22% | |

### Task 3

REPORT

To: Management Accountant
From: Assistant Accountant
Date: 17 June 19X5
Subject: Profitability of National Stores Group

*Overall profitability*

The total net profit of the group has fallen by 23.53% between 19X3 and 19X4, from £18.7 million in 19X3 to £14.3 million in 19X4. This is in spite of a modest 0.66% increase in total turnover.

The fall in profitability is reflected in the reduction in the ratio of net profit to turnover from 1.61% to 1.22%. This fall may be due to reductions in selling prices, perhaps in order to clear stocks, or alternatively to price increases of stock lines not being passed on to customers or rises in selling and distribution or administration overheads. Further data would be required to indicate which of these possible explanations applies.

*Profitability of individual stores*

The turnover and profit of Brighter Homes rose, as did turnover per m$^2$, net profit per m$^2$ and the net profit/turnover ratio. The profitability of these stores in 19X4 has thus shown improvement compared to 19X3, a year when Brighter Homes was already reasonably profitable.

Roberts, the men's/women's clothing retailer, still shows a small profit, but performance as measured by net profit per m$^2$ and net profit/turnover has declined. Turnover per m$^2$ has increased, although this may have been the result of cuts in selling prices to stimulate sales. Hopefully, Roberts will be able to improve its profitability as has been done by Brighter Homes, which retails predominantly in the same sectors - men's and women's clothing.

Kidsfair became loss-making during 19X4. The stores has the highest turnover per m$^2$ of all four of the stores chains, and previously had the highest net profit/turnover ratio. The problem with the store's profitability may concern the pricing of children's clothes and baby equipment and toys which make up the bulk of Kidsfair's sales, or alternatively poor control of overheads.

The performance of Happy Life improved slightly, although it is still loss making. Turnover and net profit both fell, reflecting the closure of one of the larger stores during the year. Turnover per $m^2$, total net loss and net loss per $m^2$ all showed some improvement. Although it has the largest average store size in the group, Happy Life has the smallest turnover per $m^2$. Fixed costs are therefore spread over fewer unit sales. There is a need to take action here. Alternatives include improving turnover, for example by better use of selling space, the selling off of in-store space, for example to small 'in-store' specialist retailers, or thirdly the sale of the business.

## SECTION 2

*Tutorial note.* When drawing graphs, it is important to choose the scales of the axes carefully so that the graph can easily be interpreted.

### Task 1

(a) *International Cola Limited*
*Four year performance data*

| | *19X1* | *19X2* | *19X3* | *19X4* |
|---|---|---|---|---|
| | £'000 | £'000 | £'000 | £'000 |
| Sales | 51,980 | 58,524 | 68,137 | 72,904 |
| Trading profit | 5,393 | 6,865 | 8,030 | 8,189 |
| Trading profit/sales | 10.4% | 11.7% | 11.8% | 11.2% |
| *Additional data and calculations* | | | | |
| UK Retail Prices Index (19W7 = 100) | 130.2 | 135.6 | 137.7 | 143.2 |
| Sales (at 19X4 prices) | 57,170 | 61,804 | 70,859 | 72,904 |
| Trading profit (at 19X4 prices) | 5,931 | 7,250 | 8,351 | 8,189 |

(b)

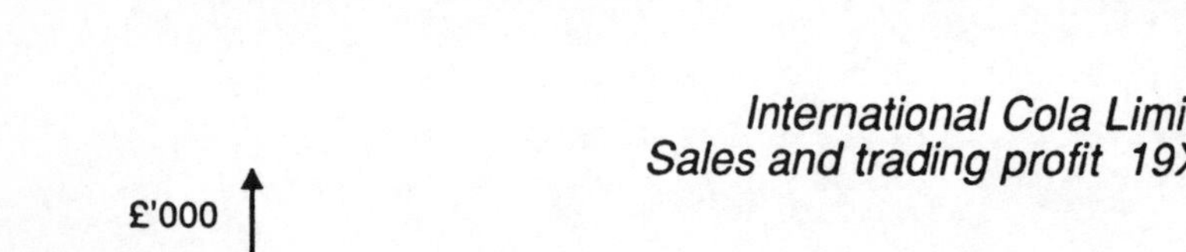

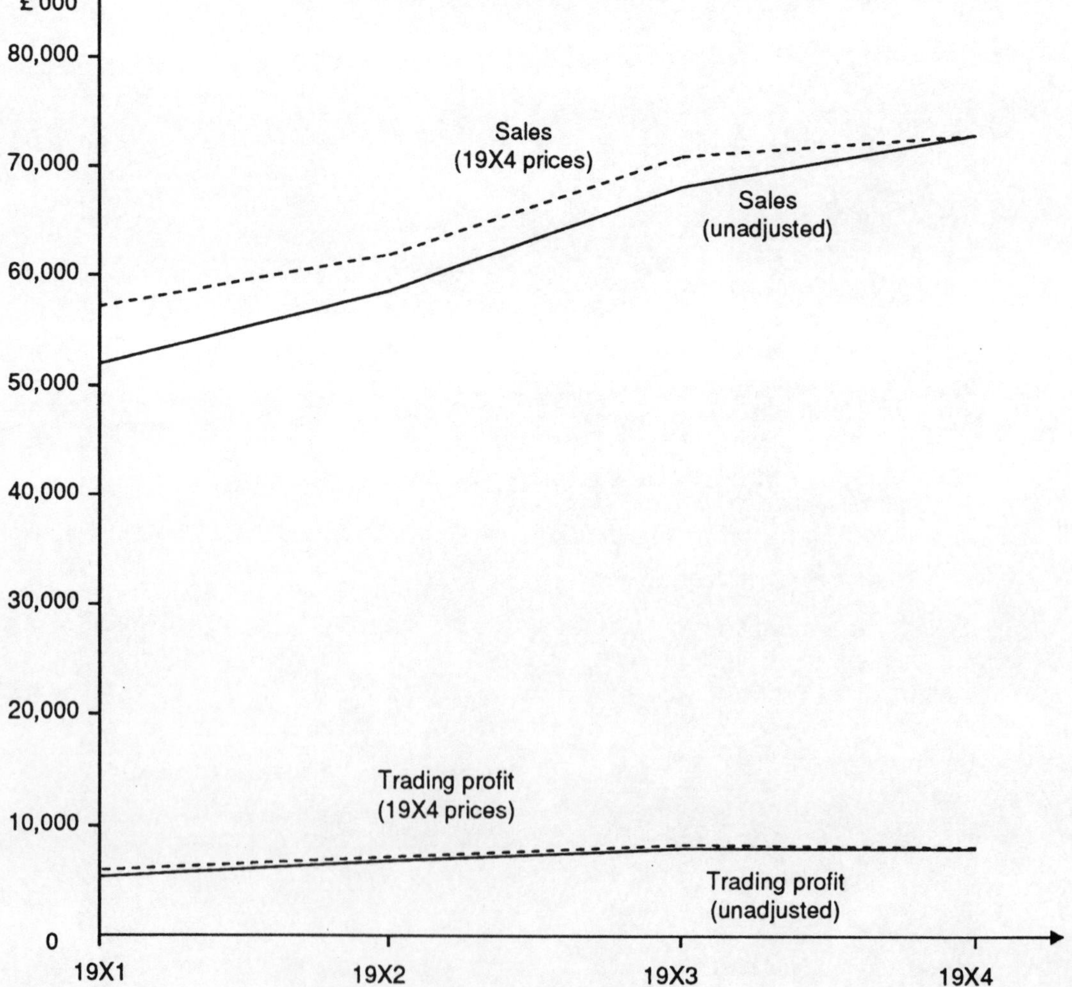

(c)

**MEMORANDUM**

To: Chief Accountant

From: Accounting Technician

Date: 20 June 19X5

Subject: Profitability of International Cola Ltd

In the published accounts for International Cola Ltd, the Managing Director has noted that sales and trading profit rose considerably over the period 19X1 - 19X4.

Although trading profit has indeed risen in money terms over this period, this does not indicate an increase in profitability in real terms in all periods. As you can see from my calculations [attached], trading profit measured in 19X4 prices rose in 19X2 and 19X3, but declined in 19X4.

The trend of sales is positive over the period, in both real terms and money terms (unadjusted for inflation). However, the positive trend of sales is much less pronounced when the figures are adjusted to real terms [ 19X4 prices - see calculations].

**Task 2**

| | *Industrial average* | *International Cola Ltd* |
|---|---|---|
| Gross profit/sales | 49.6% | 46.4% |
| Selling and distribution overheads/sales | 25.4% | 24.8% |
| Administration overheads/sales | 8.6% | 10.3% |
| Trading profit/sales | 15.6% | 11.2% |

REPORT

To: Chief Accountant
From: Accounting Technician
Date: 20 June 19X5
Subject: International Cola Ltd: profitability comparisons and scope for improvements in profitability

The ratio of trading profit to sales for International Cola Ltd (11.2%) is much below the industrial average of 15.6%. The causes of this merit further analysis. Although the ratio of selling and distribution expenses to sales is slightly better than the industrial average, gross profit/sales and administration overheads/sales are worse.

The lower gross profit/sales ratio may result from selling at a lower sales margin than the average for the industry, or alternatively production costs (materials, labour and production overheads) may be higher than average. Further investigation in these areas may involve market research as well as careful scrutiny of the company's costs. If the soft drinks market will not bear higher prices, then costs will need to be reduced.

The ratio of administration overheads to sales is significantly higher than the industrial average. The allocation of overheads between administration and other categories will vary to some extent between companies, and this may partly explain the difference. However, there may well be scope for cost savings on administration to improve profitability.

# SOLUTIONS TO TRIAL RUN CENTRAL ASSESSMENT 2

**DO NOT TURN THIS PAGE UNTIL YOU HAVE COMPLETED TRIAL RUN CENTRAL ASSESSMENT 2**

## SECTION 1

> *Tutorial note.* A formal report with Terms of Reference, Findings and so on was not required. The report should be informal, with conclusions and recommendations. The content of the report is more important than the structure, so do not spend too much time on creating a complex series of headings.

### Task 1

| *Total actual hours:* | *Week 1* | *Week 2* | *Week 3* | *Week 4* |
|---|---|---|---|---|
| South Wales | 16,582 | 18,860 | 20,070 | 19,226 |
| Yorkshire | 14,270 | 15,121 | 16,910 | 15,597 |
| *Ski units completed:* | | | | |
| South Wales | 1,200 | 1,350 | 1,400 | 1,300 |
| Yorkshire | 1,000 | 1,050 | 1,150 | 1,100 |
| *Hours per unit:* | | | | |
| South Wales | 13.8 | 14.0 | 14.3 | 14.8 |
| Yorkshire | 14.3 | 14.4 | 14.7 | 14.2 |

### Task 2

REPORT

To: Mr O'Hagan

From: A Technician

Date: 15 December 19X5

Subject: *Efficiency of the South Wales and Yorkshire factories*

*Introduction*

Performance has been analysed over the period Week 1 to Week 4.

*Hours per unit*

In all weeks except Week 4, the South Wales factory took approximately 3% fewer hours to produce one ski unit (see table of hours per unit). In Week 4, South Wales took 4% *more* time per unit.

The general tendency of South Wales to achieve lower hours per unit than Yorkshire may be due to different machinery being used at the two factories. There may have been some unusual occurrence such as a machine breakdown which would explain the Week 4 result for South Wales, although one should bear in mind that the comparison with Yorkshire is distorted in Week 4 by Yorkshire having a better than usual result. However, data over a longer period is required to make firmer conclusions.

*Variances (hours worked)*

The table of variances compares actual hours worked with the standard time for units produced.

Overall (for all departments), the Yorkshire factory has total adverse variances for all Weeks 1 to 4 while South Wales has a total variance declining from positive in Week 1 to significantly negative in Week 4.

In the Yorkshire factory, the pattern of variances between departments varies, with each department having a zero or positive variance in one week and negative variances in the remaining three weeks.

The declining overall variance in South Wales reflects a significant variance in the Finishing Department in Week 3, followed by large adverse variances in all departments in Week 4 amounting to almost 5% of the standard hours for units produced. The Week 4 performance in South Wales clearly needs some explanation. Apart from machine breakdown, other possible causes might be a change in labour conditions or monthly cyclical factors.

An explanation should also be sought for Yorkshire's generally worse performance relative to budget. There may be reasons for having different budgeted labour hours in the two factories, for example to reflect any differences in machinery. Or it may be that there are special factors behind Yorkshire's poorer performance in these particular weeks, for example power cuts, breakdowns or staff shortages.

*Conclusion*

Further analysis should be carried out over a longer period, and qualitative information should be collected in order to reach firmer conclusions about the overall performance of the two factories.

## SECTION 2

*Tutorial note.* The significance column is a fairly unusual requirement, showing how the Central Assessment may demand that you apply your knowledge to a new situation.

### Task 1

| *Performance return* | | | |
|---|---|---|---|
| | *Eastbridge* | *Westhampton* | *Significance* |
| Number of in-patient days | 126,400 | 112,200 | |
| Bed occupancy rate | 74.5% | 93.2% | |
| *In-patient cost analysis* | | | |
| *Cost per in-patient day:* | | | |
| | £ | £ | |
| Direct patient care | 100.0 | 66.2 | * |
| X-ray | 5.8 | 0.7 | * |
| Pathology | 9.9 | 3.2 | * |
| Pharmacy | 18.4 | 18.1 | |
| Laundry | 1.7 | 1.5 | * |
| Catering | 2.9 | 2.6 | * |
| Administration | 24.9 | 25.5 | |
| *Outpatient cost analysis* | | | |
| *Cost per out-patient attendance:* | | | |
| | £ | £ | |
| Direct patient care | 11.2 | 25.8 | * |
| X-ray | 3.2 | 7.1 | * |
| Pathology | 4.9 | 11.9 | * |
| Pharmacy | 5.1 | 3.6 | * |
| Laundry | 0.1 | 0.8 | * |
| Catering | 0.1 | 0.2 | * |
| Administration | 5.2 | 49.5 | * |

## Task 2

### REPORT

To: Chief Accountant

From: A Technician

Date: 15 December 19X5

Subject: *Efficiency*

*Introduction*

This report concerns performance in the year to 31 March 19X5. In this period, the number of in-patient days was similar at the two hospitals (Eastbridge (E): 126,400; Westhampton (W): 112,200). E had many more out-patient attendances: 126,800, compared with 12,450 at W.

*Bed occupancy rate*

The bed occupancy rate was 74.5% at E and 93.2% at W. A reason for this difference can be found in the fact that W has a much higher average stay, at 132 days, compared with 8 days at E. As a result, E has many more beds becoming empty in a given period, resulting in more non-occupancy. If the average period of non-occupancy per admission could be reduced at E, more revenue could be generated to cover the fixed costs per bed.

*In-patient costs*

The cost per in-patient day are significantly higher at E than at W. The most significant category, direct patient care, is 51% higher per in-patient day at E than at W. This difference can be attributed to the different nature of the work of the two hospitals. W has convalescent wards which are likely to cost less in direct patient care than surgical or medical wards. We are therefore not comparing like with like.

Given the difference in the work of the two hospitals, it is to be expected that other costs will also be lower at W. For example, X-ray and pathology costs are significantly lower at W.

However, the difference in type of work does not explain why laundry and catering per in-patient day should each cost over 10% less at W than at E. There may be scope for cost savings at E in these areas.

*Outpatient costs*

As already mentioned, E had over ten times more out-patient attendances than W. The cost analysis shows that costs per out-patient attendance were significantly lower at E than at W, except for pharmacy, which merits further investigation.

To some extent, the generally lower unit costs at E probably reflect fixed or semi-fixed elements of costs being spread over a much larger number of attendances.

It also needs to be borne in mind that costs may be allocated differently between in-patient and out-patient cost centres at each hospital. This is likely to apply particularly to administration costs, whose allocation is likely to be more arbitrary than for the other cost categories.

*Conclusion*

Many of the differences in unit costs between the two hospitals reflect the different nature of the hospitals' work. Some further information would be required before all cost saving opportunities can be identified.

## Task 3

(a)

| | *19X1* | *19X2* | *19X3* | *19X4* | *19X5* |
|---|---|---|---|---|---|
| | £ | £ | £ | £ | £ |
| Eastbridge (£) | 2,614,900 | 2,862,400 | 3,263,200 | 3,648,000 | 3,994,200 |
| Westhampton (£) | 1,612,300 | 1,982,900 | 2,416,600 | 2,862,700 | 3,479,300 |
| UK Retail Price Index (19W7 = 100) | 130.2 | 135.6 | 137.7 | 143.2 | 146.7 |
| *Administration costs at 19X5 prices* | | | | | |
| Eastbridge (£) | 2,946,281 | 3,096,711 | 3,476,481 | 3,737,162 | 3,994,200 |
| Westhampton (£) | 1,816,624 | 2,145,217 | 2,574,548 | 2,932,668 | 3,479,300 |

(b)

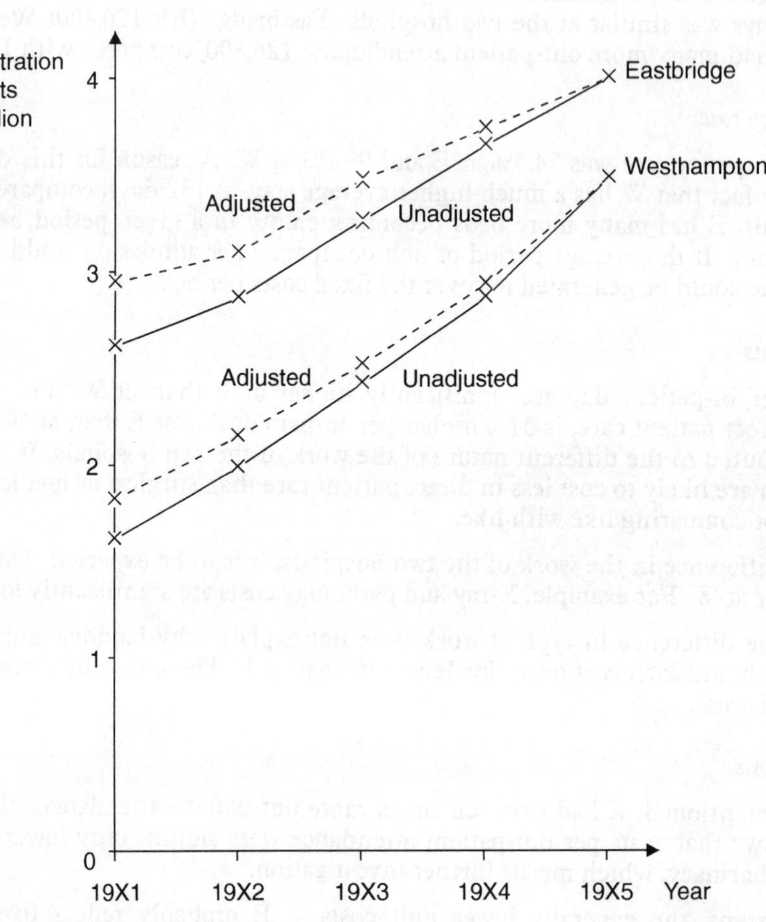


(c)

**MEMORANDUM**

To: Chief Accountant

From: A Technician

Date: 15 December 19X5

Subject: **Trends in administration costs**

Over the period 19X1 to 19X5, administration costs have been rising year by year, both in money terms and in real terms (RPI-adjusted).

The attached graph shows that the rise at Westhampton has been steeper than at Eastbridge. In inflation-adjusted terms, the rise at Westhampton over the four years to 19X5 has been 91%, while at Eastbridge the rise has been 35%.

# SOLUTIONS TO TRIAL RUN CENTRAL ASSESSMENT 3

**DO NOT TURN THIS PAGE UNTIL YOU HAVE COMPLETED TRIAL RUN CENTRAL ASSESSMENT 3**

## SECTION 1

### Task 1

**Business Computers Ltd**
**Table of ratios**

| *Division* | *Ratio* | 19X4 | 19X5 |
|---|---|---|---|
| Hardware-commercial | Net profit/sales | 17.5% | 14.8% |
| | Development costs/sales | 34.7% | 40.0% |
| | Sales per employee | £22,107 | £19,202 |
| Hardware-government | Net profit/sales | 36.6% | 35.5% |
| | Development costs/sales | 30.9% | 31.6% |
| | Sales per employee | £41,200 | £40,804 |
| Software and consultancy | Net profit/sales | 39.4% | 48.5% |
| | Development costs/sales | 21.7% | 18.8% |
| | Sales per employee | £23,614 | £26,875 |

### Task 2

**BUSINESS COMPUTERS LTD**
**REPORT ON DIVISIONAL PERFORMANCE**

To: Financial Accountant

From: Accounting Technician

Date: 18 June 19X6

*Hardware-Commercial Division*

Sales revenue in this division has fallen £1.69 million or 9.5% from 19X4 to 19X5. The net profit/sales ratio has declined from 17.5% to 14.8%, and revenue per employee has fallen 13% from £22,107 to £19,202. At the same time, development costs have risen as a percentage of sales from 34.7% to 40%.

These figures suggest that the Hardware-Commercial Division is not only performing less profitably but also less efficiently. Development costs are rising without generating a proportionate increase in revenue, while the number of staff has not decreased to reflect the down-turn in revenue. It would appear therefore that the division is suffering badly from the effects of increased competition in the commercial computer hardware market.

*Hardware-Government Division*

Sales revenue in this division has also fallen, by £1.21 million or 4.6% from 19X4 to 19X5. The net profit/sales ratio has also declined slightly, from 36.6% to 35.5%, and revenue per employee ha fallen by about 1%. Development costs as a percentage of revenue have risen from 30.9% to 31.6%.

Whilst the results of this division are disappointing, they are not as bad as the Hardware-Commercial Division's and they do contain glimmers of hope. In particular, the fact that sales per employee have not fallen by as much in percentage terms as total sales suggests that the division is operating efficiently and is making the most of its resources. It is impossible to tell how far these figures are affected by general government cutbacks and how much by a lack of competitiveness. However, given that its presence in the market gives our Software and Consultancy Division a 'way in' to government contracts we can conclude that, overall, the Division appears to have performed well.

*Software and Consultancy Division*

Sales revenue in this division has risen by £2.09 million or 22.5% from 19X4 to 19X5. The net profit/sales ratio has risen steeply from 39.4% to 48.5%, and revenue per employee has risen by 13.8%. Development costs as a percentage of sales have fallen from 21.7% to 18.8%.

The Division has clearly had a very good year, and appears to be able to generate increasing amounts of revenue from decreasing amounts of development costs. The only query concerns costs; revenue per employee has not risen by as much in percentage terms as total revenue, possibly suggesting that headcount may have been increased by too much.

*Recommendations for future directions*

Since the Hardware-Commercial Division's performance is declining so badly and its market is becoming more expensive and competitive, it would seem sensible to consider seriously the idea of pulling out entirely. Resources could then be devoted to broadening the customer base of the Software and Consultancy Division and maintaining the strength of the Hardware-Government Division, so that the company is well-placed to exploit the increasing commercialisation of the government sector whilst not being over-dependent on it.

## SECTION 2

### Task 1

| EAST INLAND RAILWAY | | | | |
|---|---|---|---|---|
| | *Commuter line* | *Coastal line* | *Rural line* | *Total* |
| Number of passengers | 9,380,000 | 7,130,000 | 6,750,000 | 23,260,000 |
| Revenue per passenger | £1.31 | £1.03 | £0.33 | £0.94 |
| Government subsidy per passenger | £0.02 | £0.11 | £0.20 | £0.10 |
| Costs per passenger | £1.10 | £0.87 | £0.51 | £0.86 |
| Passengers per train service | 1,555 | 791 | 553 | 853 |
| % of seats filled per train service | 97% | 56% | 37% | |

### Task 2

**EAST INLAND RAILWAY**
**REPORT ON 19X5 PERFORMANCE**

To: Chief Accountant

From: Accounting Technician

Date: 18 June 19X6

The commuter line, operating at 97% capacity per train at high revenue, has obviously performed much better in 19X5 than either the coastal line (56% capacity) or the rural line (37% capacity), and it also receives the lowest government subsidy. The rural line, with low revenue per passenger and low numbers of passengers per train service, only just breaks even at a profit of 2p per passenger when taking into account fare revenue, government subsidy and costs per passenger. The equivalent figures are 23p and 27p for the commuter and coastal lines respectively. Hence the company overall made only 18p per passenger in 19X5.

Ignoring the government subsidy in 19X5 the commuter line made a 21p profit per passenger, the coastal line a 16p profit and the rural line an 18p loss. Overall without a government subsidy the company would only have made 8p per passenger. The commuter and coastal lines are effectively subsidising the rural line, and the full effect of this will be felt once the government subsidy is withdrawn. What, then, should the company do once government subsidy is withdrawn?

OPTION 1: DO NOTHING

All other things being equal, the company would make only 8p per passenger overall. This could have significant impact on the future level of investment the company could afford in order to keep rolling stock etc maintained and renewed, and to respond to changing market forces eg competition from buses.

OPTION 2: RETAIN RURAL LINE AND INCREASE PROFITABILITY

Fare increases on all three lines could be considered. Capacity on the coastal and rural lines - 56% and 37% respectively - could be improved, by more aggressive marketing and better targeting of customer needs, and the number of seats per train on these two lines could be reduced. This would cut costs; currently it appears that they generally have almost the same number of seats as the commuter lines. In addition, the number of services available should be looked at: does the rural line need so many services? Is the coastal line reducing the level of service off-season? Finally, could capacity be increased on the commuter line? Operating so close to full capacity suggests that there may be customers who are choosing not to use the line because of overcrowding.

OPTION 3: CLOSE THE RURAL LINE

Closing the rural line would, on the face of it, remove a loss of £1.22 million from the company's bottom line. However, it would potentially be a costly manoeuvre in terms of redundancy and other closure costs, and the company may suffer backlash from a PR point of view. Undoubtedly there would be social and environmental costs. These would have to be quantified; in addition, it would have to be ensured that the costs attributed to the rural line are not in fact fixed costs which would simply have to be absorbed by the two surviving lines. It is more than likely that, while the rural line is not making a profit, it is at least making a contribution to fixed costs.

CONCLUSION

Option 2 would appear to be the most attractive option for potential investors, but more information about costs, market potential etc needs to be gathered before decisions can be made.

**Task 3**

(a)

| *East Inland Railway Commuter line* | | | |
|---|---|---|---|
| | *19X3* | *19X4* | *19X5* |
| Revenue per passenger | £0.91 | £1.09 | £1.31 |
| UK retail price index | 137.7 | 143.2 | 147.3 |
| Revenue per passenger at 19X5 prices | £0.97 | £1.12 | £1.31 |

(b)

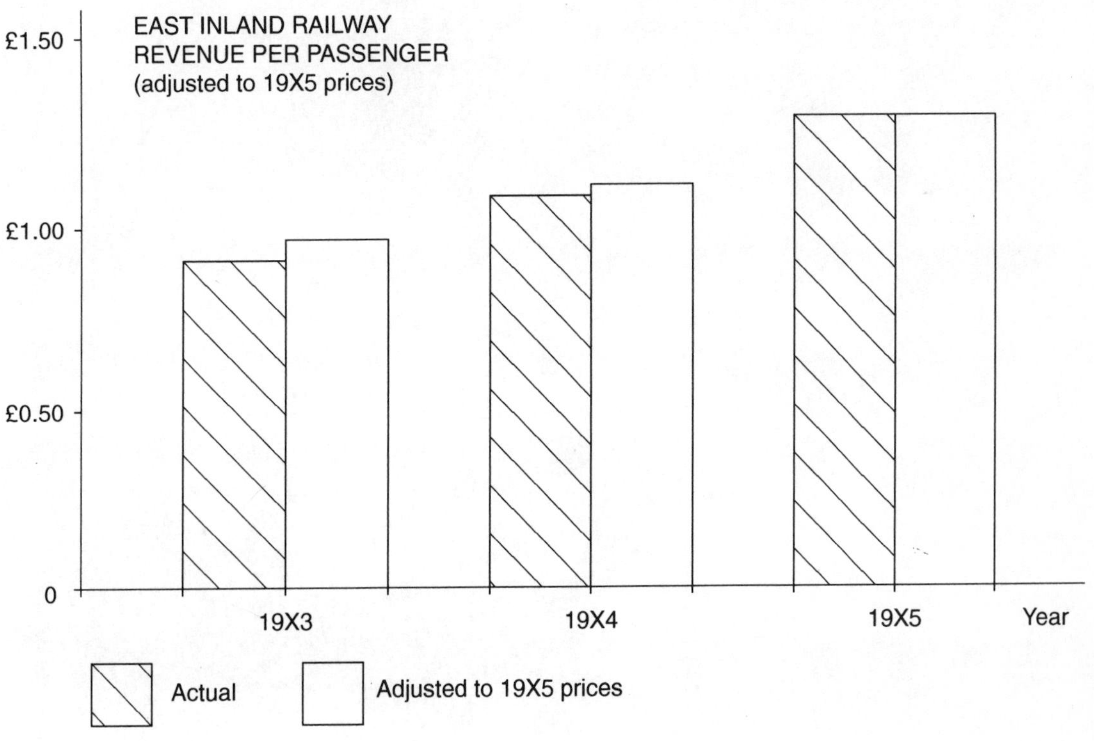

(c) **MEMORANDUM**

To: Chief Accountant

Form: Accounting technician

Date: 18 June 19X6

Subject: **Inflation and fare increases**

The accompanying bar chart shows that, in real terms (that is, after removing the effect of Retail Price Index inflation) the average revenue per passenger has increased from 97p in 19X3 to £1.31 to 19X5. Given that the total passengers per service has remained constant in the period the compound bar chart explains why total revenue has still increased over the period. Whilst this has clearly been of benefit to the company, it is uncertain whether customers will tolerate such large increases in real terms in the future. It maybe goes some way to explaining why the total number of passengers has not increased!

# SOLUTIONS TO TRIAL RUN CENTRAL ASSESSMENT 4

**DO NOT TURN THIS PAGE UNTIL YOU HAVE COMPLETED TRIAL RUN CENTRAL ASSESSMENT 4**

## SECTION 1

### Task 1.1

PERFORMANCE STATISTICS

| | *1993* | *1994* | *1995* |
|---|---|---|---|
| **Thorington underground deep mine** | | | |
| Coal extracted per employee (tonnes) | 1,990 | 1,935 | 1,869 |
| Excavation costs per tonne of coal excavated (£) | 28.54 | 29.42 | 29.60 |
| Net profit per tonne of coal excavated (£) | 14.72 | 14.81 | 14.98 |
| Net profit per employee (£000s) | 29.30 | 28.67 | 28.00 |
| **Seaforth open-cast mine** | | | |
| Coal extracted per employee (tonnes) (W1) | 1,812 | 1,922 | 2,010 |
| Excavation costs per tonne of coal excavated (£) (W2) | 31.05 | 28.98 | 26.89 |
| Net profit per tonne of coal excavated (£) (W3) | 15.11 | 15.35 | 15.14 |
| Net profit per employee (£000s) (W4) | 27.39 | 29.51 | 30.43 |

*Workings*

(W1) Coal extracted per employee (tonnes) $= \dfrac{\text{Tonnes of coal excavated (000s)}}{\text{Number of employees}}$

$$1993 = \frac{293{,}600}{162} = 1{,}812 \text{ tonnes}$$

$$1994 = \frac{315{,}200}{164} = 1{,}922 \text{ tonnes}$$

$$1995 = \frac{341{,}700}{170} = 2{,}010 \text{ tonnes}$$

(W2) Excavation costs per tonne of coal excavated (£) $= \dfrac{\text{Excavation costs (£000s)}}{\text{Tonnes of coal excavated (000s)}}$

$$1993 = \frac{9{,}117}{293.6} = 31.05$$

$$1994 = \frac{9{,}135}{315.2} = 28.98$$

$$1995 = \frac{9{,}189}{341.7} = 26.89$$

(W3) Net profit per tonne of coal excavated (£) $= \dfrac{\text{Net profit (£000s)}}{\text{Tonnes of coal excavated (000s)}}$

$$1993 = \frac{4{,}437}{293.6} = 15.11$$

$$1994 = \frac{4{,}839}{315.2} = 15.35$$

$$1995 = \frac{5{,}173}{341.7} = 15.14$$

(W4) Net profit per employee (£000s) $= \dfrac{\text{Net profit (£000s)}}{\text{Number of employees)}}$

$$1993 = \frac{4{,}437}{162} = 27.39$$

$$1994 \quad = \frac{4{,}839}{164} = 29.51$$

$$1995 \quad = \frac{5{,}173}{170} = 30.43$$

**Task 1.2**

PERFORMANCE REPORT

To: Finance Director
From: A Technician
Date: XX December 1996
Subject: Performance of Thorington and Seaforth mines

*Profitability*

The Thorington mine made a net profit of £6,943,000 in 1993, and in 1994, profitability increased slightly to £6,995,000. Last year, the net profit of Thorington mine had increased further, to £7,083,000. In comparison, the Seaforth mine had a net profit of £4,437,000 in 1993, £4,839,000 in 1994 and a further increase in 1995, saw this mine with a net profit of £5,173,000. The net profit per tonne is also a good indicator of profitability. The Thorington mine showed a gradual increase in net profit per tonne from £14.72 in 1993 to £14.98 in 1995. The Seaforth mine on the other hand showed an increase in net profit per tonne between 1993 and 1994 (£15.11 to £15.35). However, in 1995 profitability fell and net profit per tonne was £15.14.

Another indicator of profitability is net profit per employee. At the Thorington mine, net profit per employee shows a downward trend, from £29,300 in 1993 to £28,000 in 1995. The Seaforth mine, in contrast, shows an upward trend, with a net profit per employee of £27,390 in 1993 which increases to £30,430 in 1995.

The Thorington mine shows the greatest net profit each year, though the Seaforth mine is the most profitable, with greater net profit per tonne of coal excavated, and greater net profit per employee.

*Efficiency*

Efficiency may be measured by calculating the amount of coal excavated per employee, and the excavation costs per tonne of coal extracted.

The Thorington mine results show that the amount of coal extracted per employee has fallen gradually between 1993 and 1995, whereas the excavation costs per tonne of coal excavated has risen. These results indicate that the Thorington mine has become less efficient between the years 1993 and 1995.

The Seaforth mine, on the other hand, has shown that the amount of coal excavated per employee has risen slowly between 1993 and 1995, whilst the excavation costs per tonne of coal excavated have fallen between 1993 and 1995. These results indicate that the Seaforth mine is a more efficient mine than the underground deep mine at Thorington.

*Future outlook*

When comparing the two mines, the Seaforth mine appears to operate more profitably and efficiently, even though the Thorington mine is larger and makes a greater profit.

Whilst the excavations costs per tonne are falling at Seaforth, the profit per tonne does not increase between 1994 and 1995. It is probably advisable to investigate the reasons for this trend.

The Thorington mine is under threat from competition from cheaper overseas coal and home-produced natural gas. In contrast, there is a steady demand for the output from the Seaforth mine.

In conclusion, I feel that it is appropriate to advise the company to consider investing in a new mine in the locality of the Seaforth open-case mine. This is primarily due to the fact that this mine has proved to be both profitable and efficient. In addition, the Seaforth mine is not under threat from imported coal and natural gas, there is a steady demand for its output.

## SECTION 2

### Task 2.1

(a)

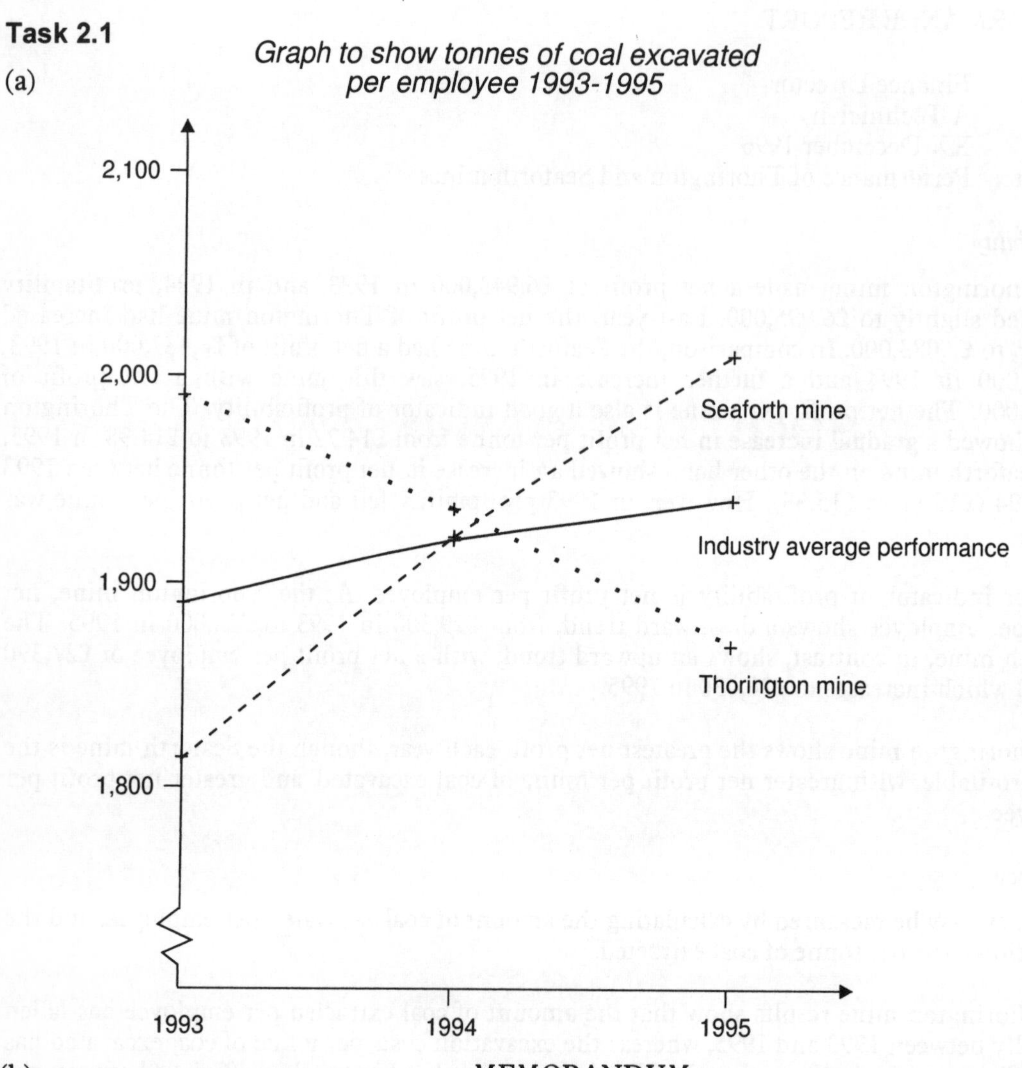


(b) **MEMORANDUM**

To: Finance Director
From A Technician
Date: XX December 1996
Subject: Coal excavated per employee 1993-1995

On analysing the trends in coal excavated per employee during 1993-1995, the following conclusions may be drawn.

The coal excavated per employee at the Thorington mine is on a downward trend during the years 1993-1995. In 1993, it stood at a level above the industry average, and by 1995, it was found to be at a level significantly below the industry average.

In contrast, the Seaforth mine was found to be at a level well below the industry average in 1993. By 1995, it was found to be at a level significantly above the industry average. This mine has shown a marked upward trend during the years under consideration.

The industry average appears to have been on a slight upward trend during 1993-95. The Seaforth mine, however, has shown a greater performance than the industry average, gradually increasing from a tonnage per employee below the industry average in 1993 to a tonnage significantly greater than the industry average in 1995.

# SOLUTIONS TO TRIAL RUN CENTRAL ASSESSMENT 5

**DO NOT TURN THIS PAGE UNTIL YOU HAVE COMPLETED TRIAL RUN CENTRAL ASSESSMENT 5**

## SECTION 1

### Task 1.1

CITY HOTELS LIMITED

Summary performance statistics for the week ending 31 May 1997

| | *Station Hotel* | *Airport Hotel* | *Central Hotel* |
|---|---|---|---|
| Total rooms let | 726 | 1,286 | 446 |
| Average room occupancy rate | 74% | 88% | 71% |
| Total room revenue | £27,103 | £56,093 | £23,094 |
| Average rate per room let | £37.33 | £43.62 | £51.78 |

### Task 1.2

To: City Hotels Limited Management Team
From: A Technician
Date: XX June 1997
Subject: Performance Report

This report has been prepared in order to compare the performances of the three City Hotels which are situated in London.

*Room occupancy rates*

The average room occupancy rate was found to be highest at the Airport Hotel, and lowest at the Central Hotel (88% and 71% respectively). The day which was found to have the highest occupancy rate was Saturday at the Station and Central Hotels and Thursday at the Airport Hotel. Nearly all of the customers at the Airport Hotel are travellers who use the hotel either before or after their flight. The situation of the Airport Hotel is probably the main reason that the room occupancy rate is highest here, because travellers are keen to stay as near to the airport as possible.

The Station Hotel has a steady occupancy rate from Monday to Thursday, probably due to rail travellers and business people. The rate falls sharply on Friday night, only to increase significantly on Saturday night. This increase is due to the weekend visitors, when room occupancy is at a peak of 86%. This peak is followed by the lowest room occupancy rate of 57% on Sunday, which in turn is followed by an increase to 79% on Monday.

The Central Hotel has its lowest room occupancy rate mid-week (51%) and this is followed by a steady rise, until it peaks at 91% on Saturday. Like the Station Hotel, the rate falls significantly on a Sunday night (71%) rising once again until mid-week when it is at its lowest rate.

The peak on Saturday night may be explained by the large number of tourists and weekend visitors in London during the summertime.

*Rates per room let*

The Central Hotel has the highest average rate per room let for the week ending 31 May 1997 (£51.78) whilst the Station Hotel has the lowest average rate for this period (£37.33).

The Station Hotel shows a maximum rate per room let mid-week (£40.79) and a minimum rate on a Saturday night (£28.60). Occupancy is at its highest on Saturday night, showing that the cheaper rates offered on Saturday night are effective in increasing the number of customers.

The Airport Hotel has an almost constant rate per room let on different days of the week. This hotel is conveniently situated close to the airport, and it is this factor which accounts for the room occupancy rate, rather than the rate per room let.

The Central Hotel has a maximum average rate per room let, which corresponds with a very low room occupancy rate (58%). The average rate per room let is at a minimum on Saturday night (£48.32) which corresponds to a maximum room occupancy rate (91%). The cheaper rates offered on Friday and Saturday nights seem to have the desirable effect of increasing the number of customers.

The average rate per room let seems to be below the standard room tariff for all three hotels, although the Airport Hotel does not appear to offer any significant discounts unlike the Station and Central Hotels.

*Recommendations*

Firstly, I would suggest that the standard room tariff is raised at the Airport Hotel. Air travellers are primarily attracted to this hotel because of its location which is extremely convenient for the airport. It is unlikely that a price increase would have any effect on the occupancy rates of the rooms let, as the overriding factor in this situation is convenience.

The Station Hotel offers a variety of discounts. The discount offered for a Saturday night appears to be the greatest, and this is reflected in the occupancy rate. Apart from business people, who tend to use the hotel during the week, the hotel also caters for railway travellers and weekend visitors. The railway travellers are likely to be largely unaffected by any discounts available, whereas the weekend visitors are likely to plan their visits around any discounts available. In order to boost the occupancy rates on Fridays and Sundays (69% and 57% respectively) I would recommend that the Station Hotel extends its weekend discounts to cover a Friday and Sunday also. This may encourage weekend visitors to take a long weekend (three days). Such an extended discount scheme may cause the occupancy rates to increase significantly on Fridays and Sundays.

The Central Hotel is ideally situated for weekend visitors and tourists. In order to increase the occupancy rate mid-week, I would recommend that this hotel considers offering a mid-week break package, when room occupancy rates are as low as 51%. Such a scheme may encourage tourists to visit the city mid-week, and may also encourage more weekend visitors to visit London during the week when the city is less busy and the room tariffs reasonably discounted.

*Limitations in the data provided for preparation of this report*

The exact details of the discount schemes and special offers are not provided. It would be useful to know the details of the schemes, the number of customers using them and the days of the week that they were taking advantage of them.

It would be useful to know the details of the customers at each hotel. The information does not disclose the total number of customers, or their purpose for staying at the hotel. Such information would be useful for deciding on discount schemes and special offers.

The data provided does not indicate whether the rooms are let to one or two people. This type of information could indicate to management that there is a need for single or twin rooms. The double rooms may have a negative effect on the room occupancy rate. Business travellers for example are more likely to be travelling alone, and may favour a hotel where single or twin rooms are available.

The data does not give a breakdown of the average rate per room let. It would be more useful to know the number of rooms let at a particular rate, as this would show just how effective any discounts or special offers were.

## SECTION 2

### Task 2.1

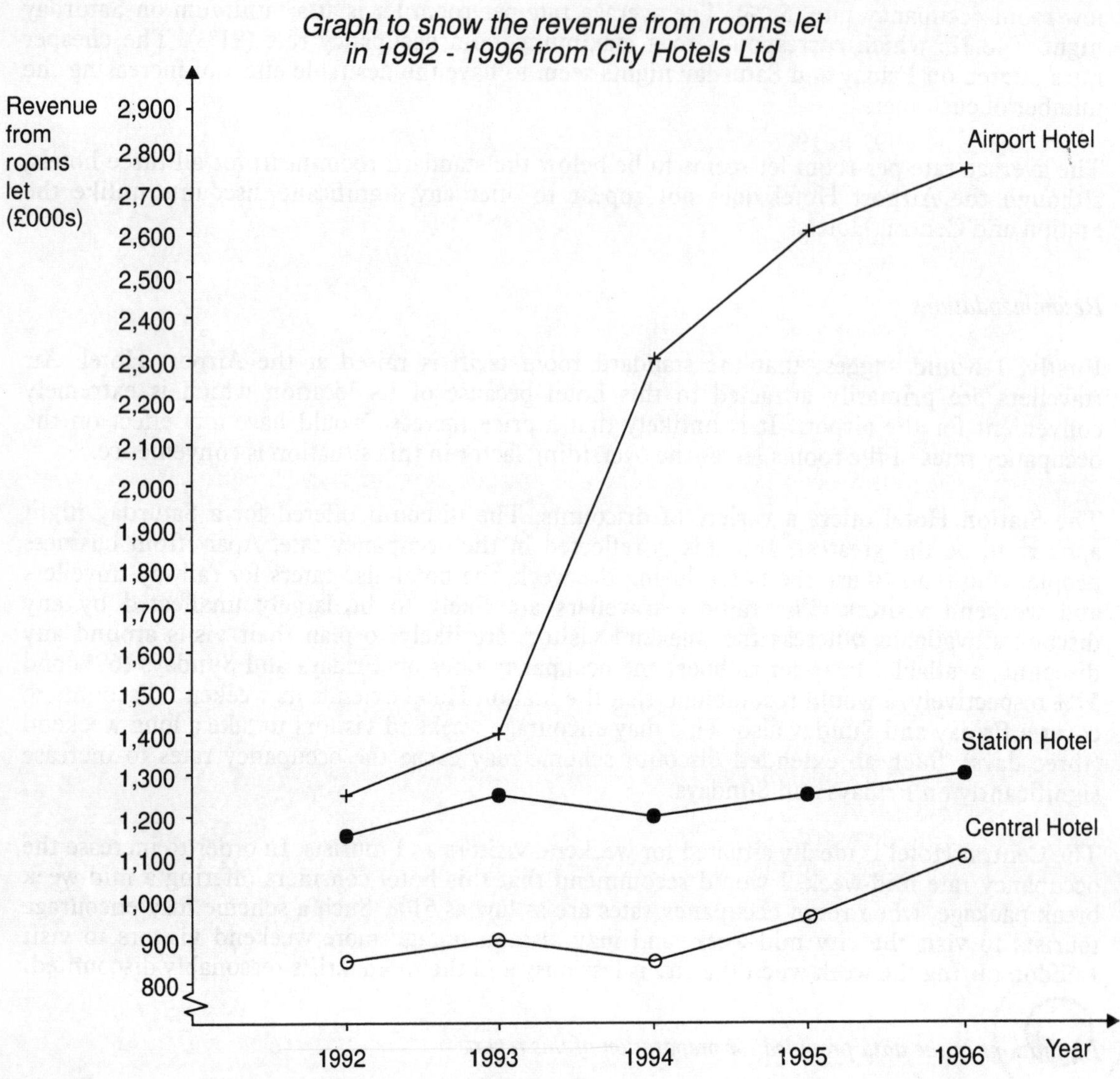

**Task 2.2**

MEMORANDUM

To: Hotel Accountant
From: A Technician
Date: XX June 1997
Subject Revenue from rooms let 1992 - 96

In each year from 1992 to 1996, the Airport Hotel has earned the greatest revenue from rooms let.

The Airport Hotel shows a steep upward trend in the revenue earned from rooms let, with the greatest increase between 1993 and 1994.

The Station Hotel shows a gentle upward trend between 1992 and 1993, followed by a downward trend between 1993 and 1994. From 1994 to 1996, there is an upward trend once again.

The Central Hotel shows a similar trend to that of the Station Hotel of a rise in the first year, followed by a fall in the second year and a marked upward trend in years three and four.

Whilst these trends clearly show the trend in revenue for each hotel in the years 1992-1996, they have the following limitations. They do not give any idea of how profitable each of the hotels are. Whilst the Airport Hotel is earning increasing revenue each year, this trend does not show whether the hotel is operating profitably.

Similarly the trends which are revealed by the graph do not indicate whether the hotels are operating efficiently or not. There is no way of telling whether the increased revenue coincides with increased room occupancy rates, or special discounts or packages which may be on offer.

The upward or downward trends in the revenue earned from rooms let in 1992-96 are therefore limited in the information that they reveal about the hotels.

## ORDER FORM

Any books from our AAT range can be ordered by telephoning 0181-740 2211. Alternatively, send this page to our Freepost address or fax it to us on 0181-740 1184.

**To: BPP Publishing Ltd, FREEPOST, London W12 8BR** **Tel: 0181-740 2211**
**Fax: 0181-740 1184**

Forenames (Mr / Ms): ____________________

Surname: ____________________

Address: ____________________

____________________

Post code: ____________

**Please send me the following books (all editions are 8/97 unless otherwise stated):**

| | | Price Interactive Text | Price Kit | Quantity Interactive Text | Quantity Kit | Total |
|---|---|---|---|---|---|---|
| **Foundation** | | £ | £ | | | £ |
| Unit 1 | Cash Transactions | 9.95 | | ......... | | ......... |
| Unit 2 | Credit Transactions | 9.95 | | ......... | | ......... |
| Unit 1 & 2 | Cash & Credit Transactions Devolved Ass'mt | | 9.95 | | ......... | ......... |
| Unit 1 & 2 | Cash & Credit Transactions Central Ass'mt | | 9.95 | | ......... | ......... |
| Unit 3 | Payroll Transactions (9/97) | 9.95 | | ......... | | ......... |
| Unit 3 | Payroll Transactions Devolved Ass'mt (9/97) | | 9.95 | | ......... | ......... |
| Unit 20 | Data Processing (DOS) (7/95) | 9.95* | | ......... | | ......... |
| Unit 20 | Data Processing (Windows) | 9.95 | | ......... | | ......... |
| Units 24-28 | Business Knowledge | 9.95 | | ......... | | ......... |
| | | Tutorial Text | Workbook | Tutorial Text | Workbook | |
| **Intermediate** | | | | | | |
| Units 4&5 | Financial Accounting | 10.95 | 10.95 | ......... | ......... | ......... |
| Unit 6 | Cost Information | 10.95 | 10.95 | ......... | ......... | ......... |
| Units 7&8 | Reports and Returns | 10.95 | 10.95 | ......... | ......... | ......... |
| Units 21&22 | Information Technology | 10.95* | | ......... | | ......... |
| **Technician** | | | | | | |
| Unit 9 | Cash Management & Credit Control | 10.95 | 8.95 | ......... | ......... | ......... |
| Unit 10 | Managing Accounting Systems | 10.95 | 6.95 | ......... | ......... | ......... |
| Units 11,12&13 | Management Accounting | 16.95 | 10.95 | ......... | ......... | ......... |
| Unit 14 | Financial Statements | 10.95 | 8.95 | ......... | ......... | ......... |
| Unit 18 | Auditing | 10.95 | 6.95 | ......... | ......... | ......... |
| Unit 19 | Taxation (FA 97 Labour) (10/97) | 10.95 | 8.95 | ......... | ......... | ......... |
| Unit 23 | Information Management Systems | 10.95 | 6.95 | ......... | ......... | ......... |
| Units 10,18&23 | Project Guidance | | 6.95 | | ......... | ......... |
| Unit 25 | Health and Safety at Work | 3.95** | | ......... | | ......... |

* Combined Text

**Price includes postage; this booklet is an extract from Units 24-28 Business Knowledge (Interactive Text)

**Postage & packaging:**

| | | | |
|---|---|---|---|
| **UK:** £2.00 for first plus £2.00 for each extra book. | ......... | ......... | ......... |
| **Europe (inc ROI):** £4.00 for first plus £2.00 for each extra book. | ......... | ......... | ......... |
| **Rest of the World:** £6.00 for first plus £4.00 for each extra book. | ......... | ......... | ......... |
| | | Total | |

**I enclose a cheque for £ __________ or charge to Access/Visa/Switch**

**Card number** [ ]

**Start date (Switch only)** __________ **Expiry date** __________ **Issue no. (Switch only)** __________

**Signature** ____________________

## REVIEW FORM & FREE PRIZE DRAW

All original review forms from the entire BPP range, completed with genuine comments, will be entered into one of two draws on 31 January 1998 and 31 July 1998. The names on the first four forms picked out on each occasion will be sent a cheque for £50.

**Name:** ______________________ **Address:** ______________________

______________________

______________________

**How have you used this Workbook?**
*(Tick one box only)*

☐ Home study (book only)

☐ On a course: college ______________

☐ With 'correspondence' package

☐ Other ______________

**Why did you decide to purchase this Workbook?** *(Tick one box only)*

☐ Have used complementary Tutorial Text

☐ Have used BPP Texts in the past

☐ Recommendation by friend/colleague

☐ Recommendation by a lecturer at college

☐ Saw advertising

☐ Other ______________

**During the past six months do you recall seeing/receiving any of the following?**
*(Tick as many boxes as are relevant)*

☐ Our advertisement in *Accounting Technician* Magazine

☐ Our advertisement in *PASS*

☐ Our brochure with a letter through the post

**Which (if any) aspects of our advertising do you find useful?**
*(Tick as many boxes as are relevant)*

☐ Prices and publication dates of new editions

☐ Information on Tutorial Text content

☐ Facility to order books off-the-page

☐ None of the above

**Have you used the companion Tutorial Text for this subject?** ☐ Yes ☐ No

**Your ratings, comments and suggestions would be appreciated on the following areas**

| | *Very useful* | *Useful* | *Not useful* |
|---|---|---|---|
| *Introductory section (How to use this Workbook)* | ☐ | ☐ | ☐ |
| *Coverage of elements of competence* | ☐ | ☐ | ☐ |
| *Practice exercises* | ☐ | ☐ | ☐ |
| *Devolved Assessments* | ☐ | ☐ | ☐ |
| *Central Assessments* | ☐ | ☐ | ☐ |
| *Trial Run Central/Devolved Assessments* | ☐ | ☐ | ☐ |
| *Structure and presentation* | ☐ | ☐ | ☐ |

| | *Excellent* | *Good* | *Adequate* | *Poor* |
|---|---|---|---|---|
| *Overall opinion of this Workbook* | ☐ | ☐ | ☐ | ☐ |

**Do you intend to continue using BPP Tutorial Texts/Workbooks?** ☐ Yes ☐ No

**Please note any further comments and suggestions/errors on the reverse of this page**

**Please return to: Neil Biddlecombe, BPP Publishing Ltd, FREEPOST, London, W12 8BR**

## REVIEW FORM & FREE PRIZE DRAW (continued)

**Please note any further comments and suggestions/errors below**

### FREE PRIZE DRAW RULES

1. Closing date for 31 January 1998 draw is 31 December 1997. Closing date for 31 July 1998 draw is 30 June 1998.
2. Restricted to entries with UK and Eire addresses only. BPP employees, their families and business associates are excluded.
3. No purchase necessary. Entry forms are available upon request from BPP Publishing. No more than one entry per title, per person. Draw restricted to persons aged 16 and over.
4. Winners will be notified by post and receive their cheques not later than 6 weeks after the relevant draw date. Lists of winners will be published in BPP's *focus* newsletter following the relevant draw.
5. The decision of the promoter in all matters is final and binding. No correspondence will be entered into.